MONEY
TO BURN

*What the great American philanthropic foundations
do with their money*

BY

HORACE COON

 BOOKS FOR LIBRARIES PRESS
FREEPORT, NEW YORK

Library of Congress Cataloging in Publication Data

Coon, Horace, 1897–
   Money to burn.

   (Essay index reprint series)
   1. Endowments--U. S. I. Title.
HV97.A3C6 1972   361.7'6'0973   72-1230
ISBN 0-8369-2843-1

PRINTED IN THE UNITED STATES OF AMERICA

To
HELEN A. ROBINSON

A number of individuals kindly consented to read various chapters and to give criticisms and suggestions. For this the author wishes to express his gratitude to W. H. Allen, Elliott V. Bell, E. V. Hollis, Quincy Howe, Gobind Behari Lal, E. C. Lindeman, Ferdinand Lundberg, James Rorty, and T. R. Smith.

CONTENTS

CHAPTER I

PERPETUITIES AND THE PUBLIC

"Contemporary needs are the only needs of which we can be certain," the late Julius Rosenwald told his fellow millionaires in 1929. He gave away more than seventy million dollars during his lifetime, and he instructed the fund which he established to distribute the principal as well as the interest, totaling more than thirty-five million dollars, within twenty-five years of his death. "The dead hand," he said, "has been proved a hindrance if not indeed a menace to mankind," and he advised those who planned large endowments to follow his lead.

A trust in perpetuity, he pointed out, cannot endure perpetuity without sound and conservative business management. It must have the help of investment counselors and financiers gifted with a perspicacity possessed almost exclusively by bankers, lawyers, and brokers on the "inside." Each generation, Mr Rosenwald insisted, should provide for its own problems, and there is no reason to suppose that future generations will be any less intelligent or benevolent than our own.

The best perpetuities, it has been frequently pointed out, are ideas. Hôtel Dieu in Paris is a thousand years old, and St Bartholomew's Hospital in London is eight hundred years old, and they have existed, not because of endowments, but because they met a genuine human need. Harvard College was founded with almost £700 and Yale with £600. One critic of foundations, Hanford Henderson, declared : "An institution which cannot furnish what the public wants at a price it can afford to pay deserves to go under." Mr Rosenwald, in the boom years before his death, argued eloquently with millionaires to give the trustees of the foundations they established the power to spend the entire sum.   He admitted, however, that it is not the donor but the trustees who are timid.

A perpetuity implies a lack of confidence in the future, the Chicago philanthropist wrote, and today's millionaires have no right to inject their fortunes into the affairs of the nation five hundred to a thousand years hence.   Spending seventy-five millions on a project which seems commendable today may be vicious tomorrow.   A half century ago wealthy men were particularly distressed by the plight of orphans and innumerable institutions were endowed with millions of dollars to care for orphan boys and girls, usually boys.   Today the supply of orphans is diminishing and it is regarded as good social practice to place them in individual homes rather than to keep them in institutions.

In spite of that Mr Milton S. Hershey has given his chocolate business to the Hershey Industrial School for Orphans in perpetuity.   Since he has no children, he said, he wanted to make "the orphan boys of the nation my heirs."   Five hundred thousand shares out of a total of seven hundred and twenty-nine thousand shares of the common stock of the Hershey chocolate company will provide an income for the school as long as the public likes five-cent almond bars.   In 1933 at the bottom of the depression the dividends amounted to $1,675,000, because the school not only owns practically everything in the vicinity of Hershey, Pennsylvania, but it also owns, indirectly, a $30,-000,000 sugar plantation in Hershey, Cuba.

Only one parent need be dead for a boy to be eligible.   The cost per boy in the school is $1027.49 a year, yet a boy can be kept in a private home in New York City for $300 a year.   If a boy does not get along in the school and shows that he is not a proper influence on other boys, he is dismissed.   Thus, it has been pointed out, the school "is taking out of the home precisely the children who should be there and excluding those an institution might help." The school cannot begin to spend its income and in order to keep it full, orphans must be imported from other states.

Recently Harvey G. Woodward of Alabama left seven million five hundred thousand dollars for a school to be established not within fifteen miles of a town, and he specified that no ministers could be on the faculty, no religious buildings on the grounds, no foreign languages should be taught, and there must not be any interscholastic athletics, fraternities or examinations. Furthermore, pupils must be native born Americans of British ancestry so far as possible, and the teachers must come from the North. Wills as idiotic as this are not unusual and provide a feast for lawyers. Yet under American law a last will and testament cannot be changed unless it can be proved that the testator was of an unsound mind at the time he wrote it.

In the valley of the Loire at Brissac, France, peasants may be seen tilling the fields dressed as Spanish matadors or decked out in grass skirts, because a Connecticut millionaire became so disgusted with the French that he said that there was no degradation they would not stoop to for money. So he left one hundred and eighty thousand francs to the eighteen employees of his estate on the condition that they wear the outlandish costumes which he had spent a lifetime in collecting. Similar and less amusing examples of galloping futility have marked the history of eccentric bequests.

In 1849 Thomas Grover of Philadelphia left a fund for respectable white widows, housekeepers or rooming-house keepers whose husbands had died in the region of Southwark. It has been some years since widows answering this description have been found.

Another man left a fund to relieve the poor suffering from yellow fever, so they would not have to go to a hospital.

A Boston hospital has a fund to provide wooden legs for Civil War veterans.

A trust was established by a philanthropist for the education of Negroes in Liberia under the misapprehension that American negroes would eventually go there.

An orphan asylum in Baltimore never had an inmate and two well known orphanages founded in 1907 and 1908 with combined assets of eight million dollars were, in 1919, taking care of only 114 beneficiaries.

John Edgar Thompson, one time president of the Pennsylvania Railroad, left a fund of two million dollars to care for the daughters of railroad workers whose fathers had been killed in service on the Pennsylvania. Improved railway engineering and modern safety devices made it impossible for the Pennsylvania to kill enough of its employees to make this fund useful. After considerable advertising twelve girls were found eligible to be helped.

In 1850 Bryan Mullanphy established a fund in St Louis for worthy and distressed travelers and emigrants "passing through St Louis to settle a home in the West." The sight of those stranded in covered wagons, unable either to go on or to return East moved him to this noble bequest, but since that time few homesteaders have been left helpless in Missouri in covered wagons. The income piled up to more than a million dollars, and might now be applied, perhaps, to owners of modern automobile trailers who have gone broke in St Louis, were it not that nearly three quarters of it was spent in administrative charges in the course of litigation fighting those who wished to change the will.* Now, the courts have decided, the remainder may be used to aid travelers of all kinds in St Louis.

Benjamin Franklin believed it would always be difficult for mechanics' apprentices in Boston and Philadelphia to get a start, so he left two loan funds for young married "artificers" not over twenty-five years of age who had served as apprentices. Each might be loaned three hundred dollars at five per cent. When this loan fund had accumulated for a hundred years the Boston money was then to be spent on fortifications,

* *Washington Star*, July 2, 1933.

aqueducts, public buildings, baths, pavements or "whatever may make living in town more convenient for its people and render it more agreeable for strangers." In Philadelphia the money was to be spent to pipe the waters of Wisshicken Creek into the city. The class of men Franklin wanted to help became extinct and the cities of Boston and Philadelphia provided, long before a hundred years elapsed, the improvements he dreamed would then be necessary.

In citing some of these examples of how impossible it is even for those who have accumulated large fortunes to foresee how to spend them wisely, Mr Rosenwald hoped to arouse his colleagues of great wealth to be more enlightened in their public giving. The late Senator James Couzens and several others agreed with him.

The trustees of the Rockefeller foundations may, upon two-thirds vote, authorize the spending of the principal as well as the interest of their funds.

Paul M. Warburg has said that he does not believe in endowments. "Every generation," he said, "should spend the funds it can spare."

The real difficulty, however, is a legal one. In this country there is no supervision whatever of the spending of the two and a half billion dollars in charitable and educational trusts and foundations except that exercised by the trustees and administrators of the endowments. American courts refuse absolutely to change a will. Charters granted to our largest foundations cannot be altered, because to do so would be an abridgement of contract, a constitutional obligation prohibited by the Supreme Court since the celebrated Dartmouth College case argued by Daniel Webster.

We must, therefore, rely on the high purposes, the good will, and the philanthropic motives of the millionaires of today to establish foundations consistent with the public welfare and to provide for the redistribution of their fortunes in ways that will contribute to progress. The common law for persons does

not apply to trusts.   Adam Smith warned that "the effect of
endowment on those entrusted with any cause is necessarily
soporific."   Untold millions are now tied up in perfunctory
services which actually retard progress.   In extreme cases the
legal doctrine of *cy pres* — "as near as"—may be invoked in our
courts, but only when the situation has become fantastic, and
it is long and expensive.   American legal history is full of examples of the refusal of the courts to deviate from the letter of
the law.   Trust officers, bankers, and lawyers can cite many
examples of fortunes tied up because American courts cannot
step in and direct how funds can be spent. Indeed, such litigation is juicy business for the legal profession.   Nothing prevents American millionaires from instituting, through foundations, even more idiotic spectacles than the Canadian "stork
derby," or leaving endowments whose purposes may be at complete variance to the common good.

A fortune left for medical research must be used for that
purpose even though thousands of lives might be saved if the
principal could be used in times of epidemic. A well-intentioned
millionaire may leave a hundred thousand dollars for research,
which provides an income of five thousand dollars a year. It
may take thirty years to discover whether that particular field
of research is worth investigating, but no portion of the principal may be applied at the beginning to see if the work is valuable. Not long ago a Massachusetts court declared that the
McKay bequest for the Lawrence Scientific School, which
went out of existence, could not be given to Massachusetts Institute of Technology but must be kept separate "even though
at variance with our views of policy or expediency."

More than a hundred years ago Moses Brown, John Norris
and William Bartlett laid down their religious credo and made
gifts to the Andover Theological Seminary to teach their doctrines.   Each professor and member of the board of visitors
must recite in full the lengthy statutes embodying their creed

at his inauguration and repeat it publicly every five years thereafter. This is its nature :

"I believe . . . that by nature every man is personally depraved . . . that . . . every man is justly exposed to eternal damnation . . . that God, of his mere good pleasure, from all eternity elected some to everlasting life . . . so that our salvation is wholly of grace ; that no means whatever can change the heart of a sinner, and make it holy . . . that the wicked will . . . with devils be plunged into the lake that burneth with fire and brimstone forever and ever. I moreover believe that God . . . for His own Glory foreordained whatsoever comes to pass . . . that all the evil which has existed, and which will forever exist in the moral system . . . will eventually be made to promote a most important purpose . . . and thus fulfill His pleasure. And furthermore, I do solemnly promise . . . that I will maintain and inculcate the . . . Creed by me now repeated . . . in opposition not only to Atheists and Infidels but to Jews, Papists, Mahometans, Arians, Polagians, Antinomians, Arminians, Socinians, Sabellians, Unitarians and Universalists ; and to all other heresies and errors, ancient or modern. . ."

Every article of the creed "shall forever remain entirely and identically the same, without the least alteration or any addition or diminution." Unless altered by the founders in the first seven years it shall continue "as the Sun and Moon, forever." After a century of controversy and litigation the Seminary found itself unable to attract adequate funds, faculty or students. It moved to Cambridge where a plan of affiliation was negotiated with Harvard. However, the Supreme Court of Massachusetts ruled in 1925 that affiliation was forbidden by the creed of 1807. "The Court has no concern with the degree of public advantage likely to flow from the proposed affiliation. The founders' views are immutable." And any concerns of "expediency or general utility are of no consequence."

Even lawyers cannot always draw up their own wills in such a way that their purposes might not be frustrated by the courts.

Samuel J. Tilden projected a charitable trust in his will that was held invalid by the courts.

Judge Samuel Hitchcock of New Haven left a fund for "the support of pious young men, preparing for the ministry in New Haven," but the Connecticut Supreme Court of Errors found that this was void for "uncertainty."

Robert W. de Forest, an authority on the descent of property, bequeathed a large sum of money to the Adirondack Mountain Reserve "to preserve the forests, lakes, and mountains of the Upper Ausable Valley." But the Adirondack Mountain Reserve proved to be unqualified to receive a charitable trust.

In a little town in New Jersey a lady wished to leave a small fund to purchase books for a church library, and she stated in her will that it was for the library in the belltower of a certain church. The investment was in the common stock of the New Jersey Zinc Company which at the time of her death paid small dividends. But this corporation became a "war baby." In 1915 the dividends rose 50% and paid a 50% stock dividend. The following year there was another stock dividend of 250% and other dividends increased the fund so that the books filled the tower so full that no further purchases could be made. Yet the New Jersey courts held that the books must be kept in that tower and the funds could not be used for any other purpose, not even to build a library.

Two early Americans who made their fortunes in the legitimate business of privateering endowed two of the most discussed foundations.

Stephen Girard in 1831 left two million dollars and the residue of his estate to "the Mayor, Aldermen and Citizens of Philadelphia" for an orphan asylum now known as Girard College. Here 300 fatherless "white legitimate boys" between six and ten years of age, who can produce a marriage certificate of their parents and their own birth certificates, may be admitted to be fed, clothed, and educated until they reach the age of fourteen to eighteen. Preference is given to boys from Philadelphia, then Pennsylvania, then New York City and then New Orleans. His will gave specific instructions on the construction of the buildings, even to the dimensions of the rooms, so that the architects had difficulty in following his directions and yet make the buildings habitable. Furthermore, he specified that a wall 14 inches thick and ten feet high with two gates was to surround the property.

Even Daniel Webster could not break this will. What occasioned the controversy and the lawsuits was the admonition that "no Ecclesiastic, Missionary, or minister of any sect whatsoever shall ever hold or exercise any station or duty whatever in said College; nor shall any such person ever be admitted for any purpose, or as a visitor, within the premises of the said College. . . I desire," he explained, "to keep the tender minds of the orphans free from the excitement clashing doctrines and sectarian controversy are so apt to produce." The heirs attacked this immediately as invalidating the whole bequest as "hostile to the Christian religion." After lengthy litigation, Justice Story upheld the will.

The residue of the Girard estate consisted of real estate which was later found to include a part of the richest anthracite coal fields in Pennsylvania, from which more than 98 million tons of coal have been mined. Mr Girard directed that "if the income is more than sufficient it shall be invested in good securities." This has been done, so that the Girard College endowment is now worth more than seventy-seven million dollars. This, added to the Hershey funds, makes ample provision for the orphans of Pennsylvania.

In 1801 Captain Robert Richard Randall of New York "being weak in body but of sound and disposing mind and memory" drew up a will, probably with the help of Alexander Hamilton, leaving $25,000 in securities and a tract of land on Manhattan Island the income from which was to establish and support a home for "aged, decrepit, and worn out sailors" to the number of fifty and upwards in an "institution that shall be perpetual." The trustees were to be the Mayor and Recorder of the City of New York, the President of the Chamber of

Commerce, the President and Vice-President of the Marine Society, the senior minister of the Episcopal Church and the senior minister of the Presbyterian Church, and the Chancellor of the State of New York. An act to incorporate "The Sailors' Snug Harbor" was passed by the legislature in 1806, and it was amended in 1814 so that the ministers mentioned shall be the Rector of Trinity Church and the minister of the Presbyterian Church of Wall Street. The land was then described as "21 acres, one rood, thirty four perches and 132 feet in the Fifteenth Ward, and four lots in the First Ward." It was here that Captain Randall expected his home for sailors would be built, for he said that it should be erected on "part of the land on which I now reside."

In 1824 the trustees decided that this land was too valuable for such a purpose and purchased in 1831 on Staten Island 100 acres for the sailors' home, where it was opened the following year. The disbursements the first year were $8,357 and the income from the funds invested was $84,782 while the income from the real estate was $24,885. This real estate includes the land from Washington Square North, east of Fifth Avenue, to East Tenth Street, and with a few exceptions all the lots east to Fourth Avenue, including the land on which Wanamaker's now stands. In 1835, $227.55 was spent in the home for medicine, $83.66 for pass tickets on the steamship *Cinderella*, and $271.60 for refreshments "for the Honorable Senate and the Trustees." The rents then brought in $30,587 and the total amount of the funds amounted to $114,105.

With the growth of the city the land became more valuable and in 1922 the ground rents were $1,076,001 and the total income $1,112,524. But the expenses of administration were $893,222 including taxes and the expenses of the institution, which were $499,564. Since then the financial reports have not been published but a financial statement is sent each year to the Board of Aldermen of New York City and to the state legislature. The latest available figures are for 1935, showing a ground rent of $1,022,530, the interest on securities $38,189, and other income $31,741. The expenses of the institution amounted to $423,695 to provide for about eight hundred old sailors, who now include men from the engine-room crew and Gloucester fishermen. The taxes and the costs of maintenance of the Manhattan property were $530,014, and the "general" expenses are $127,219. On this financial statement $90,000 is deducted for depreciation and improvements so that a bookkeeping loss is shown of $81,468.

The total assessed valuation of the property on which taxes are paid is $9,917,000 but this does not include all of the original tract because Wanamaker's and several others who pay ground rents to The Sailors' Snug Harbor pay their own taxes. About $240,000 is paid in taxes, leaving maintenance charges of $293,014, not counting the "general" expenses of $127,219. A part of the property is leased outright, a part is managed and operated, and the cost of maintaining an office for rental and management purposes is considerable. Loft and apartment buildings have been erected and renovated from time to time, so that the institution must retain a staff to carry on the details of a fairly large real estate business, which is, of course, responsible to the board of trustees.

No criterion exists for judging the efficiency of our large endowments. In a sense it may be said that they are run socialistically since no profit motive is involved except the salaries of the administrators. Nobody outside the work of the foundations can judge with any accuracy how well, how honestly, or how business-like they are run. Since there is no supervision of any kind by the state or federal governments it can only be assumed from the financial and other published reports that all these institutions are conducted in accordance with the high purposes of the founders. Some foundations, however, publish no reports and give no information to the public.

The Rockefeller and Carnegie foundations regard themselves as semi-public institutions and it has been generally assumed that they are conducted efficiently and in the lofty spirit with which they were conceived.

Some criticism has been made of the Carnegie Endowment for International Peace, consisting of twelve million dollars. This is used apparently to send Dr Nicholas Murray Butler abroad every year and to publish occasional pamphlets.* It has never made any attempt to come to grips with the modern, accepted theories on the cause of wars or to study how capitalism, fascism, or sovietism may lead to war. Such criticism may be unjustified, however, since no investigation has been made of the Endowment.

A similar legal situation existed in England over a century ago. On August 28, 1818, a Royal Commission was appointed by Parliament "to examine into all breaches of trust, irregularities, frauds, abuses or misconduct of estates and funds." This did not include in its survey the educational endowments of Oxford or Cambridge or schools or endowments of which Universities were the trustees, nor to the colleges of Westminster and Eton, or to any college that had special visitors, governors or overseers appointed by the founders or to funds applicable to the education or for the benefit of Jews or Quakers. At that time in England there were more than forty thousand trusts with a total annual income of £1,200,000. Many eccentric trusts were discovered, such as one to provide ransom for Englishmen captured by Barbary pirates, one to establish a lectureship on coal gas as the cause of malarial fever, and others for like odd purposes. In 1727 Dr Woodward directed that a fund he left should establish a lectureship at Cambridge for all time on his theory of the Natural History of the Earth and to defend it against the theories of a certain Dr Camerarus. Since then both theories have been exploded and the chair abolished. One man left money for the illumination of his wife's tombstone, and another to pay somebody to dance on his grave each year on the anniversary of his death.

* See Chapter VII, "An Endowment for War."

After fourteen years of investigation the Commission of twenty-nine members, including among its members Sir Robert Peel, Lord John Russell, Lord Granville Somerset, Sir Robert Inglis, and Lord Francis Egerton made a report which sounds astonishingly relevant today :

"With funds amounting to more than one million pounds a year, it is obvious that their proper management and right application are matters of national concern as the objects embrace the education and comfort of the people. It is reasoned that the superintendence and administration of all property devoted to charitable uses should be entrusted to a permanent board of three Commissioners who have the duty of superintendence and control of all property devoted to charitable uses, with an accounting and power to summon all parties concerned in management of charitable institutions or funds, to appoint and remove trustees and to take care that no sale, mortgage, or exchange of charity property be effected without concurrence, and that all funds applicable be invested upon real or government security, and to preserve all documents relating to charity estates, to give acquittances of all payments where no competent party can be found, to audit from time to time annual accounts, to have power of removing masters and ushers, to sanction salaries paid, retirement allowances, to authorize such arrangements as shall appear calculated to promote the object of the founder and to suggest such other appropriations as may appear desirable."

By a series of Parliamentary enactments these recommendations have since been carried out. The Commission reported several public schools as typical of what it discovered. The Berkhampstead Free Grammar School, for example, was incorporated by Henry VIII to teach 144 children free. It was discovered that only four children were being taught, and that the Master got two thirds of the rather large income.

In another school no pupils were found and the funds were used in litigation. The Commission remarked, "the parishioners are much dissatisfied with the present state of the charity." This illustrates what can happen, it was noted, to a valuable institution with large funds. Considerable stipends were paid, the schoolhouse was dilapidated, no boys were receiving instruction, and the surplus was exhausted in fighting litigation.

The primary object of the Commission was to examine the nature of the foundations, the management of the property and the mode of income.　Misapplication of funds and inattention were discovered.　In a school in Coventry a master was found 82 years of age and an undermaster not much younger, both of them obviously incompetent even for the one lonely pupil in attendance.　It was almost impossible to remove either master, however, except through long, involved, and expensive proceedings in the Court of Chancery.

In 1915 the Walsh Congressional Commission investigating industrial relations and social conditions in the United States made a survey of the subject of large endowments.　Frank P. Walsh at that time characterized foundations as "a menace to democratic institutions" * . . . and suggested that the government might take them over, "to take back for the people the vast fortunes embezzled from the people."　At that time the Colorado Fuel and Iron Company was under fire, and Mr Walsh was particularly bitter about the two and half million dollars appropriated by the Rockefeller Foundation for migratory birds, $250,000 of it derived from the Rockefeller subsidiary then being criticised.　One worker told Mr Walsh that he wanted first of all a safe retreat for his baby and his wife and inquired : "Is there any person who will not challenge a hundred million dollar foundation exempt from taxation ?"

Samuel Untermeyer, testifying before this committee, was asked concerning the potential control over labor conditions in the hands of large corporations. He answered that large foundations were "not limited by state lines but were international in scope."　A small group of men, he agreed, might exercise through corporations and foundations a widespread control over labor conditions.　The Rockefellers, he pointed out, sought a Federal charter, but were not satisfied with the terms

* The *New York Times*, January 18, 1915.

of the Peters Bill of 1910, so they obtained what they wanted from the New York State Legislature.   The Russell Sage and the Carnegie Foundations did the same.

Mr Untermeyer recommended that foundations should be organized under a Federal law instead of under state charters. Secondly, he said, no perpetual charter should be given because one generation has no right to bind another.   "We may have an entirely different social structure and different conceptions of education in fifty years," he declared.   Third, there should be a limit on the size ; fourth, foundations should not be allowed to accumulate income ; * and fifth, there should be governmental representation in replacing present trustees, because the present control is in the hands of financiers.

Louis D. Brandeis, at that time not yet appointed to the Supreme Court, was another witness.   He was asked concerning the possibility of the power of the great foundations not being applied for the welfare of the people.   He answered that he believed that the highest motives prompted the establishment of foundations, but he had "grave apprehension at the ultimate effect when control has passed out of hands at present administering them to those who may not be governed by such excellent intent."   When it was suggested to him that the power of endowments might be used not always for good, he said : "It is creating power and we do not know into whose hands it may get or how used," and, he added, that he thought large foundations are "inconsistent with democratic conceptions."

Amos Pinchot testified that there is "nothing more powerful, or subtle than the influence of large donations in institutions depending on endowments."   He told of the Audubon Society refusing $25,000 from the Remington Arms Company. "A few days ago," Mr Pinchot went on, "Professor Ross of Wisconsin speaking of our great foundations said : 'Thousands of experiences have shown the tendency of boards to administer

* The Duke Foundation must set aside one-fifth of its income "to snowball" until the original capital of $40,000,000 has been doubled.

a charitable foundation in a narrow or class spirit according to obsolete ideas or exploded theories. To make these foundations safe the whole basis of control should be changed.' It seems to me that if these foundations are allowed to exist one of the problems of this Commission is to suggest a means of control which will to some extent insure their being used in the interest of public opinion and in accordance with democratic principles."

In its majority report, written by Basil M. Manly, the Commission expressed alarm at the "powers of a small group extended through funds for indefinite purposes." The investigation was centered on more sensational matters, and soon afterward the crusade to make the world safe for democracy occupied the whole attention of Congress and the public. There was slight public interest in foundations until Julius Rosenwald provoked discussion by his proposals, and since then little has been published about them until 1936 when Dr Eduard C. Lindeman focussed attention to them by his book on *Wealth and Culture*. Yet since 1915 more than one hundred large foundations have been established and more are now projected.

In 1928 alone ninety-two million dollars additional funds were received by the foundations. Only seven foundations have lasted from the nineteenth century into the twentieth, but now there are more than a hundred well-known foundations operating and many more about which the public hears little until a millionaire transfers the shares of a holding company of a railroad empire to his charitable foundation in order to escape taxes he would have to pay on the sale of his holding company.

We may expect that the number of foundations will increase rapidly, since this is one of the most convenient methods by which millionaires may escape income and inheritance taxes and dispose of their wealth in such a way that the government will get no large part of it. The increase in the size of university endowments has been particularly phenomenal. Harvard, founded with a capital of about seven hundred pounds,

has increased its endowments to $129,000,000. Yale, begun
with a bequest of six hundred pounds, accumulated in its first
two centuries only $4,942,000 ; now has a $95,838,568 endowment. In 1915 only Harvard's endowment exceeded twenty
million, now there are sixteen universities with endowments of
over twenty million dollars. The combined endowments of
Chicago, Columbia, Harvard and Yale have risen from twenty
to more than three hundred and fifty nine million in the last
twenty-five years.

Only one Community Trust existed in 1915, now there are
seventy-eight with forty-five million dollars in funds.

Great Britain in the meanwhile has provided for complete
supervision of charitable and educational foundations. The
first are under the jurisdiction of the Charity Commissioners
and the second are supervised by the Board of Education.
The Colebrooke Commission in Scotland in 1872 recommended
the altering of the provisions of endowments, and providing the
Commissioners with powers for amalgamating, combining or
dividing them, and for establishing new governing bodies. The
British law abhors perpetuities. When it can be shown that
the purposes of the foundation are not adequately-attained, the
Colebrooke Commission declared, society rightly exercises a
power of modifying conditions which obstruct the beneficial
operation of endowments.

By an act of Parliament of 1928 it is the duty of the Commissioners to determine if the endowment is for the best public
interest and whether the funds should be applied to alternative
purposes. The Commissioners have the power to alter the
purposes, to apply the funds to applications they think fit, and
for the grouping, combining, or dividing endowments, as well
as altering the powers of investment. This was done in the
case of Donaldson's Hospital in Edinburgh.

Mrs Margaret Gibson Spier of Beith, Scotland, laid down a
plan in her will for a school for 24 boys of poor working class,
children of parents who had not been on the roll of paupers,

and excluding "children of shopkeepers or tradesmen who live principally on their capital or the employment of others." The Commissioners built the school and opened it to all children of good health and character, subject to examination, and were justified in doing so under the act of 1928.

To do such a thing, it was said by British critics in 1826, would be to dry up the wells of benevolence, for wealthy people would not provide endowments which might be changed so radically from their expressed wishes. But it was discovered by the Oxford Commission of 1882 that bequests were made with greater confidence as to their utility and the wise benefactors were more strongly induced to bestow their wealth for public benefit knowing that they had the assurance that their foundations would be so regulated by the wisdom of the State that they would contribute to their highest purposes forever. History, it was remarked, has justified the confidence of the Commissioners, for more than three million pounds has since been donated in Scotland alone, not counting the Carnegie gifts to Scottish universities.*

It may be interesting to note here that among the trustees of the Carnegie Trust in Scotland are four ex-officio members : the Secretary of State of Scotland, the Lord Provost of Glasgow, the Lord Provost of Edinburgh and the Provost of Dunfermline. In establishing the fund Mr Carnegie gave ten million dollars' worth of bonds in the U. S. Steel Corporation at the market value at that time. It was not thought proper by the Scotch to have funds invested in such an enterprise and so, in accordance with the practice of British foundations, these bonds were sold during the war at their peak price and the proceeds invested in British government securities when they were at their lowest level. In doing this with the Dunfermline Trust the canny Scotch doubled their endowment.

American legislators have not yet begun to follow the road

---

* *Fifth Report of the Commissioners under the Educational Endowments of Scotland, Act of* 1928. Published in 1934.

of investigation and legislation in regard to foundations which the British started in 1818. A. E. Ikin, an English commentator on American foundations remarked that our legislation "has been entirely in the direction of providing endowments rather than in safeguarding them." No inquiry commissions have made a study of foundations in the United States, he notes, and public indifference may lead to public neglect. This might lead to improvement, though it cannot undo previous neglect. Since the fundamental difference is a legal one, inherent in the peculiar nature of the Constitution of the United States and the protection it gives to property rights, the difficulties are considerable. It may be that some lawyers will say that they are insuperable. But if the public should make up its mind that our large foundations should be regulated or placed under governmental supervision, a way will certainly be found to do it.

CHAPTER II

THE FOUNDATION IDEA

On the tablets of Nineveh it is recorded that Sardanapalus was a patron of literature, so it is possible that the idea of the modern philanthropic foundation occurred to him sometime before his death in 823 B.C. The earliest perpetuity was probably the Delphic Oracle in the Fifth Century, B.C. The next perpetual trust was the famous Alexandrian library of the Ptolemies in the Fourth Century B.C., which lasted until it was burned by the Christians five hundred years later. Even longer in existence was the Academy at Athens, founded in 387 B.C. for the systematic study of philosophy, endowed by Plato, and lasting until the Emperor Justinian closed the schools of Greece in A.D. 529. Perhaps the germ of the foundation idea was in Caesar's plan for presenting a library to Rome, and in Augustus' mind when he did it. Pliny used the endowment principle to give life to a school in his native Como, and the support Maecenas gave to Virgil and Horace might be likened to the present activities of the John Simon Guggenheim Memorial Fund.

It was not possible for any of them, however, to establish anything like the present day foundation. The Christian Church came nearest to it, in introducing the principle of large scale organized charity in its monopoly of the philanthropies of Europe from the Fourth Century A.D. to the Reformation. With the breaking up of the monasteries and the Church lands, private charity in the modern sense really began, and a few "perpetual" institutions were established. The property of Sir Thomas Bodley started the Oxonian library in 1602, the French Academy was inaugurated in 1635 under the protection of Cardinal Richelieu, and George III endowed the Royal Academy in London with £5000. A hint of the great foundations that were to come was given in the establishment of the great public schools of England by the tradesmen's companies. The bequest of Dr Gilchrist of a few shares of bank stock "for the Benefit, Advancement, and Propagation of Education in every part of the world," was a forerunner that was almost frustrated by his heirs, for they spent the proceeds of the securities in disputing the will. Only when the case was won and the funds exhausted was it discovered that he had purchased land in Sydney, Australia, for £17.10s, worth, in 1841, £70,000. With this the Gilchrist Fund began anew.

America furnished a number of heralds. When Benjamin Sims of Massachusetts left "200 acres of land and the milk and increase of 8 cows for the maintenance of an earnest and honest man to keep a school" he could have had no conception that this was a humble beginning of the tremendous American educational endowments. Earliest of American endowments to last to the present was that of White-Williams to the Magdalen Society of Philadelphia "for the benefit of unhappy females who have been seduced from virtue desiring of returning to a life of rectitude." Soon after this Captain Robert Richard Randall provided for Sailors' Snug Harbor in New York and Stephen Girard for his orphan home in Philadelphia. The first endowment of any size was that of James Smithson in 1846 : $508,000 for the Smithsonian Institute for the "increase and diffusion of knowledge among men." Other beginnings were made by the Peabody Fund of Boston in 1867 and the John F. Slater Fund in 1882.

Only then did the problem which faces the modern millionaires begin to appear. Whenever any man amasses a fortune greater than he can spend, and greater than any imaginable spending by his heirs, the idea of a foundation occurs to him. The early endowments were usually made by men who had no children. As the industrial revolution has tended toward monopoly and huge profits, however, the fortunes have been much larger than any number of direct heirs can use. "Combination in producing a new crop of fortunes so monstrous,"

wrote Bernard Shaw in *Socialism for Millionaires* in 1896, "as
to make their possessors ridiculous." Since the United States
has produced in a short time the largest crop of millionaires ever
known, it is inevitable that they should discover what Professor Lindeman calls "the unique American answer" to the millionaire's biggest problem.

Others faced it and came to the same conclusions. The
Nobel Prize foundation began in 1890 and the Cecil Rhodes
trust in 1902. But it remained for Andrew Carnegie to see the
problem clearly from the beginning of his career, to state it eloquently, to give it a philosophy, and to show other millionaires
how he thought it should be solved. In 1889 in his essay on
Wealth he wrote : "A great corporation must earn money or
go bankrupt. To stand still is impossible. Hence men must
soon be in receipt of more revenue than can be judiciously expended by themselves." Socialists and Anarchists attack the
foundations on which civilization itself rests, he said, and the answer to Communism is : "The race has tried that." The rich
man, therefore, has three alternatives : He can give his money
to his family or relatives, he can bequeath it to public purposes,
or he can administer it during his lifetime.

The first, Carnegie declared, was the most injudicious, for it
was misguided affection. The second was satisfactory "provided
a man can wait until he is dead before he can be much good in
the world." His bequests are then likely to be monuments to
his folly, and "no man can be extolled for doing what he cannot
help doing." The ideal state, he thought, was one in which the
surplus wealth of the few was administered for the common
good. He believed, however, that the rich men or their appointed trustees should do the administering. The only question in his mind was not how much millionaires should give
away, but "how much dare we retain for our own gratifica-
tion."

"Your position in the history of social development," Abram
S. Hewitt of New York wrote to Mr Carnegie, "will be that of

the man who first compelled wealth to recognize its duties, not merely as a matter of moral obligation but of decent self respect on the part of men who control large fortunes." The little Scotchman recognized this when he was thirty-three years old and making fifty thousand dollars a year. It was then that this man, who J. K. Winkler calls "the greediest little gentleman who ever lived," this perfecter of the bonus and piece-work systems, wrote : "Amassing wealth is one of the worst species of idolatry. No idol is more debasing than the worship of money. To continue much longer must degrade me beyond permanent hope of recovery." Yet for another thirty-three years he continued until, in 1901, the profits of the Carnegie Steel Company were $40,000,000, a world record at that time for any legitimate competitive industry. At sixty-six, charged with the obsession that he must spend his $400,000,000 before he died, he set about the toughest job of his life, the task of distributing it intelligently.

"Out of every $1000 spent in so-called charity today," he wrote in *The Gospel of Wealth*, "it is probable that $900 is unwisely spent." Allen Thorndike Rice, editor of the *North American Review*, suggested : "Make it $950," and he did so. In 1887 he told Gladstone : "It is disgraceful to die a rich man." Hopefully and rather naïvely, with the help of one secretary, he tried to find worthy causes. He was looking for causes upon which he could spend millions. Impatiently, to a man who asked for $5000, he snapped : "I'm not in the retail business !" He gave four millions for a relief and pension fund for his workmen, and he wrote to twelve men asking them their advice on the best purpose for ten million dollars. Each one promptly pleaded on behalf of his own pet institution or philanthropy ; Dr Nicholas Murray Butler asked for the whole ten million for Columbia, and Elihu Root suggested Latin-American scholarships similar to those of Cecil Rhodes. Even he added a postscript : "And $100,000 to Hamilton."

Mr Carnegie was discouraged. It was not as easy as he had

thought. At that moment John S. Billings of the New York Public Library came to him with the suggestion that he build branch libraries in New York. This was an inspiration. The little Scotchman recalled his days as a student, he remembered his love for books, he thought of himself both as an ambitious young man eager for knowledge and as a great teacher whose influence would spread throughout the earth. Happily he built 2811 libraries throughout the English speaking world. Exultantly, he told his friends that he was giving away libraries at the rate of two or three a day. Worthy as this purpose was, after twenty years he was able to spend only a little more than sixty million.

As if this vast wealth were a horrible thing, burning in his pocket and his conscience, the little Scotchman scurried about the world, anxiously looking for ways to spend it. The ferocious energy, so long devoted to the mania of accumulation, became a frenzy in his search for meritorious objects for his benefactions. He gave $2,500,000 to "the toiling masses of Dunfermline to bring into their monotonous lives sweetness and light."

When he asked Arthur J. Balfour for advice about an endowment for the Scottish universities, the latter wrote : "For sheer want of money, our provision in the department of teaching and that of research is deplorably deficient." That made a profound impression on Carnegie. He had been thinking about establishing a university in Washington D. C. Burton J. Hendrick declares : * "An institution that would inevitably come under the jurisdiction of Congress, subject to the fluctuation of politics, did not recommend itself to Carnegie's good sense." So instead of a national university, he gave $22,300,000 to the Carnegie Institution at Washington, incorporated by special act of Congress in 1904, for scientific research. And later, still thinking of Mr Balfour's words, he gave $29,250,000 to the

* From *The Life of Andrew Carnegie* by Burton J. Hendrick, copyright 1932. Reprinted by permission from Doubleday, Doran and Co., Inc.

Carnegie Foundation for the Advancement of Teaching. Then he really struck his stride in public giving : $26,718,000 to the Carnegie Institute and the Institute of Technology in Pittsburgh, $10,000,000 for the establishment of the Hero Fund, $10,000,000 for the Scottish universities, $6,248,000 for church organs, $1,500,000 for the peace palace at The Hague, $420,000 to the Franklin Institute of Philadelphia, $28,000, upon Brander Matthews' suggestion, for simplified spelling. More driblets were disbursed here and there. Frantically he toiled to get rid of his millions.

After ten of the busiest years of his life, working as he had never worked before, he found himself seventy-six years old with more than one hundred and fifty million left. The task seemed hopeless. Unless he hurried, he was in danger of dying rich. Only a few more years remained. "The way of a philanthropist," he complained to John D. Rockefeller, "is hard." Despairing, he talked it over with his lawyer, Elihu Root. With him he discussed his will, establishing a foundation to provide funds for his philanthropies. Doubtfully Mr Root shook his head over the trust clause. It might be attacked. "Why not organize your foundation now, in your lifetime, and transfer to it the bulk of your fortune ?" The tired philanthropist jumped at the suggestion. Declaring his purposes he wrote : "My chief happiness as I write these lines lies in the thot that even after I pass away the welth that came to me to administer as a sacred trust for the good of my fellow men is to continue to benefit humanity for generations untold." The $125,000,-000 in bonds of the U.S. Steel Corporation maturing in 1951 that he transferred to the Carnegie Corporation in 1911 was the largest sum ever dedicated up to that time for human betterment. Afterwards he wanted to transfer ten million of it to the United Kingdom Trust, but he could not legally do it, for the bonds had passed out of his possession, so he gave ten million to his British foundation out of what remained of his fortune.

"I do not wish to be remembered for what I gave but for

what I persuaded others to give," he declared. "Such huge liquid capital placed in perpetuity," wrote Burton J. Hendrick in his biography of Mr Carnegie, "in the hands of trustees for public distribution was something previously unknown. His purpose was of showing men of vast wealth that wealth is largely a creation of the community itself, to which it has a moral if not a legal claim, and to show how to fulfil a useful purpose and to help balance the necessary inequalities of the existing economic system. This may be regarded as achieved. Millionaires who die possessed of great surpluses undedicated to public ends die 'disgraced' indeed." John D. Rockefeller Sr told Mr Carnegie in 1889 : "I am pleased with the sentiments you give expression to. I would that more men of wealth were doing as you are doing with your money, but be assured your example will bear fruits and the time will come when men of wealth will more generally be willing to use it for the good of others." With the zeal of a crusader Carnegie campaigned among his colleagues of great wealth. "You should begin giving," he warned John Wanamaker, "instead of using the whole of your exceptional talents in grabbing for more dollars."

Many millionaires winced at the Scotchman's assertion that rich men were merely the custodians of wealth and men who did not devote their surplus to public purposes were to be execrated. Carnegie had only one child, a daughter. If he had had a son he might not have said : "I would as soon bequeath my son a curse as the almighty dollar." By the time of his death in 1919 he had given away 90% of his wealth, as he had said he would do forty years before. Yet one of his early biographers declared : "The truth stands out that all the work of the philanthropies has hardly squared the debt." And Carnegie himself said : "Few millionaires are clear of the sin of having made beggars."

John D. Rockefeller Sr did not have to learn from anybody the blessedness of giving, for he began at sixteen his Ledger A in which he kept a record of every penny he gave away, and he taught his children to save 10% and give to charity 10%. By establishing the modern foundation Carnegie showed how to give away on a large scale ; Carnegie paved the way and set the pace. Baptist preacher Frederic Taylor Gates of Minneapolis persuaded Mr Rockefeller to make his first large gift : $600,000 to the University of Chicago. Reverend Gates had gone into the money-raising business when George A. Pillsbury gave $50,000 to a college on condition that another $50,000 be raised. Gates did it, and soon he was passing the hat for Chicago. He learned the trick of the "provisional gift" and taught it to Rockefeller. John D. Sr's seventy million placed him on the Baptist sucker list in 1889. Early one morning in May, Dr Gates called at the old Rockefeller home at 4 West 54th Street and talked the oil magnate into what John D. called later "The best investment I ever made."

Thereafter Reverend Gates advised Mr Rockefeller in all his philanthropies and in 1893 he was given a permanent job. One evening Dr Gates noticed a man on a ferryboat reading *The Principles and Practice of Medicine* by William Osler. It gave him an idea. For the next several days he read the book with mounting excitement. Here was an inspiration, a solution of the problem of what Mr Rockefeller could do with his money. Medical research ! They started planning. Instead of giving vast sums outright to medical schools, Dr Simon Flexner was hired to study the needs of medicine. In 1901 the Rockefeller Institute was founded to promote the standards of medicine, health, and research, and up to his death Mr. Rockefeller gave it $59,931,891.

Through Starr J. Murphy the Rockefellers in 1910 applied to Congress for a bill for Federal incorporation of a foundation. After two years of discussion the bill was rewritten so that it provided that if a public institution should be set up by Congress embodying the same purpose as the foundation, the assets should be turned over to that institution. Congress could limit the activities of the foundation ; it should not begin with more than one hundred million dollars, which must be spent and never added to. The property of the foundation was to be exempt from Federal taxes only, and there was provision for public participation in the board of trustees. The bill never reached the President. On May 14, 1913 the New York State Legislature granted the foundation a charter authorizing it to operate "for the well-being of mankind throughout the world." Mr Rockefeller turned over to it securities which included seventy-two varieties of bonds, batches of stock from thirty-three Standard Oil companies, and stock in forty other corporations.

The Rockefellers have given away more than $750,000,000, yet the principal remains intact. When John D. Sr retired on account of ill health in 1896 he had only about $200,000,000, but when he died his public relations counselors announced gifts of $530,000,000. John D. Jr has given away $167,000,-000 on his own account. Such is the geometrical progression of compound interest and the rapidity with which money breeds money that it is probable that the Rockefeller fortune is now nearly a billion dollars. Although John D. Sr's estate was a mere $25,000,000, it is known that he began transferring the bulk of his fortune to his son at least thirty years ago. Only one man reported an income of more than $5,000,000 in 1934, and he had over a hundred million in non-taxable securities. That was probably John D. Jr. In spite of their colossal benefactions the increment of the Rockefeller fortune has grown faster than they could give it away.

Since the establishment of the Carnegie and Rockefeller foundations the number has increased rapidly. Russell Sage began in 1907, two more in 1908, three in 1909, and at least one important foundation every year up to 1919 when five were established. The Juilliard started in 1920, four began in 1921, three in 1922, four in 1923. The Duke and Kresge foundations incorporated in 1924, the Guggenheim in 1925, three more in 1926, four in 1927, and five in 1928. In 1934 one hundred and twenty-three foundations made financial reports to the Twentieth Century Fund and there were at least as many more which did not report.

It is difficult to say how large a part vanity plays in the motives of those who establish foundations. Certainly it is one way by which a rich man may purchase immortality ; certainly emotion plays a very large part. One of the favorite tricks of the professional money-raisers is to show wealthy men an architect's drawing of a building inscribed : "The John Doe Memorial," and it is easy to understand the impulse to perpetuate in perishable masonry the memory of a father, son, wife, brother, sister, or daughter. Mother love and the memory of recent bereavement has helped to endow many colleges. Frequently it is the most fitting and proper way to help others. Like Andrew Carnegie, many rich men find the foundation idea a comforting solace against approaching death.

No one can read the reports of the large foundations without realizing how sincerely they have tried to adapt themselves to the rapidly changing world and to make themselves useful in the midst of economic changes affecting all classes. Unquestionably an attempt is made to conduct them in the spirit of that stewardship of great wealth enunciated by Mr Carnegie. But nobody studying foundations today can overlook the fact that by forming such trusts, as Carnegie did on the advice of Elihu Root, millionaires may thereby escape the payment of huge inheritance taxes. Those who are not disturbed by such taxes do not realize the perturbations suffered by men of great wealth at the prospect that the government will take, at their deaths, a very large share of the fortunes they have spent their lives in accumulating. The sentiment of Plato when he said : "Oh ye gods, how monstrous if I am not allowed to give or not to give my own to whom I will !" is shared by nearly all modern millionaires. Since they have made their money, they assert, they should be privileged to spend it as they wish, to leave it to such friends and relatives as they please, and to endow such charitable institutions as they see fit. Yet Federal and state inheritance taxes are taking away a constantly increasing share. Federal estate taxes alone on estates of more than $50,000,-000 eat up 70% of the net, if they are paid, and state and other taxes may increase this percentage.

It has been remarked that the government will not be able to collect this on Henry Ford's estate when he dies without taking over the Ford Motor Company, because his fortune is entirely in that corporation. Edsel Ford, however, has established a foundation, and it may be that Henry Ford has already transferred a large part of his holdings to his son, who, in turn, may leave them to the foundation. A similar situation confronts Vincent Astor, as was pointed out in a *New Yorker* profile : *

"When the fortune passes out of Vincent's hands, it will have seen its best days and possibly will go out of existence. If he were to distribute it among individuals during his lifetime, it would be subject to 52½%. If he were to hold onto it and die while the present inheritance schedules are in effect, the fortune would be subject to a 70% levy and might conceivably go wholly to the government and still fall short of satisfying the tax. This causes Astor to remark in gloomy moments that he will be the first Astor to die insolvent. The weakness of the fortune from a tax standpoint is the real estate. Such holdings always rank low as liquid assets and the sudden offering for fairly quick sale of a large fraction of Astor's property would have a seriously depressing effect. If Astor should die during a slump, his most dismal dreams might come true. Of course, the fortune could be preserved intact as a memorial to the Astor name if left to charity or education. Disposition in this way would seem a possibility, since Astor has no children, and his sister and half brother are comfortably fixed."

Before the enactment of the 1932 revenue act only about

* By Jack Alexander, March 19, 1938.

15% was paid on estates of $5,000,000 ; now more than 50% is paid. Albert W. Atwood has pointed out that the fortune of a man who leaves $50,000,000 to his widow, who dies in six years, leaving the estate to her son, who, in turn, is killed in an accident, may be reduced to $5,000,000 within a few years by successive inheritance taxes. At that rate no modern large fortune could outlast three generations. At one time a millionaire could avoid some of these provisions by giving large sums to friends or relatives. But since 1932 ever-increasing gift taxes have made this impractical, if not impossible. Furthermore, if a man gives money to his friends or relatives the State, if it can prove that these gifts were made in contemplation of death, may inflict additional penalties for such an evasion of the death dues. It is becoming more and more difficult to outwit the government on income and estate taxes. The establishment of a charitable foundation is therefore the ideal method for providing that philanthropic purposes are carried out. If a millionaire delays, he is not only waiting, as Mr Carnegie declared, to be dead before he can be of use to the world, but the possibility that his will might become involved in litigation imperils his whole scheme.

The foundation, once it is incorporated, is free from taxation. If a man gives 15% of his income to charity, that 15% may be deducted from his taxable income. While the government doesn't get it, as the professional money-raisers are quick to point out, a worthy charity is benefited. If a man with an income of $500,000 gives to charity, or a charitable foundation, $250,000 in four instalments annually of $62,500 each, the cost to him is not really $250,000 but only $129,000, because the difference would go to the government in taxes. A million dollars might thus be given to a foundation in four instalments of $250,000, meaning a possible saving of $400,000 in taxes. If a New Yorker leaves $10,000,000 to his family, it gets less than $4,800,000, but if he leaves $6,000,000 to charity his family gets $2,500,000. The charitable bequest does not cost the family $6,000,000 but only $2,300,000. It is possible that organized charity may have had a small hand in framing those laws.

The late George Eastman, it is said, was so intelligently advised by his lawyers that he was able to make his gifts without paying any taxes whatever. A few years ago millionaires were aghast to learn that fourteen cents out of every dollar of Henry C. Frick's estate went to taxes or administrative charges. Today the government would take 70%. On an estate of $80,000,000 the Federal tax would amount to $53,000,000. On an estate of $30,000,000 the tax would be $18,500,000.

Recently George A. Ball, the Muncie fruit-jar maker, bought for $3,121,000 control of the three billion dollar Van Sweringen railroad and real estate empire. After forming the Midamerica holding company, he transferred his common stock in it to a philanthropic trust, the George and Frances Ball Foundation. A few weeks later this Foundation found buyers for this stock, which paid no dividends, and on April 27, 1937, it was announced that a group of financiers headed by Young, Kolbe, and Kirby, had purchased it for $6,375,000. If Mr Ball had kept the Midamerica stock and sold it himself, he would have made a profit of about three million dollars, which he would have had to include in his capital gains column as a part of his year's income. If he had died with this profit unspent, the inheritance tax on his estate would have been considerable, depending upon how many millions he had. By transferring the stock, he avoided most of these taxes. Probably he planned to give his Foundation a large sum, and this seemed to him the best way to do it. The Foundation got it, and it remains to be seen how much the government will get. Whether you condemn Mr Ball or applaud him for conserving his wealth for charitable purposes, you must admit that he has not only dramatized the dilemma of the millionaire today, he has also illustrated one way a wealthy man may escape taxation.

If the foundations are to be used for such purposes, the whole foundation idea is jeopardized, for the government might retaliate, if not by taxing them, then possibly by taxing their income. Resentment against taxation is an American tradition, and taking from men who believe fanatically in rugged individualism such a large part of their income and their capital intensifies their resentment a hundredfold. In some quarters it is considered legitimate to "gyp" the government if possible. In fact, it has been more or less the practice of many wealthy men to take every possible advantage of income and inheritance laws, going to such extremes as "wash sales" to show capital losses. J. P. Morgan and John J. Raskob, it may be remembered, paid no income taxes in 1930.

There is nothing Mr Carnegie would have condemned with greater passion. "The growing disposition to tax more and more heavily large estates left at death," he declared, "is the cheering indication of the growth of a salutary change in public opinion." Speaking of the British death dues, he said : "Of all forms of taxation this seems the wisest. Men who continue hoarding great sums should be made to feel that the country, in the form of the State, cannot thus be deprived of its proper share. . . By taxing estates heavily the State marks its condemnation on the selfish millionaire's unworthy life." With approval he quotes Shylock : "The other half comes to the privy coffer of the state." Perhaps he would not have been so enthusiastic about 70%. "This policy," he wrote, "would induce the rich man to administer wealth during his lifetime, as being the most fruitful for the people. Nor need it be feared that this policy would sap the root of enterprise and render men less anxious to accumulate. 'So distribution should undo excess, and each man have enough.' "

Such, however, is not the sentiment of today's millionaires seeking to avoid payment of the bills of the New Deal. Made jittery by Mr Roosevelt's gold policy, many are reluctant to part with capital sums. Their estates will not have enough liquid capital to pay the inheritance taxes, they complain. Yet if they do part with capital sums for charitable purposes, their capital is lessened, no tax is placed on the gift, and small taxes need be paid on the smaller income, — and on the remaining capital. It seems probable that they would prefer to establish foundations than to have their millions contribute toward meeting the national indebtedness caused by what they consider Mr Roosevelt's reckless spending. They appear to be caught in a rather unpleasant dilemma from which death will not excuse them. Those who say that soak-the-rich taxes make the establishment of new foundations unlikely because such a large share of wealth is taken by the government overlook the fact that the foundation is one of the few remaining refuges for large sums. While several large fortunes are breaking up, new ones are now being made. In the process of creating immense fortunes a time comes when it is no longer sensible to plough under profits, to set up additional reserves, to reinvest for more profits. Even Andrew W. Mellon, who did this for most of his life, left his estate to a charitable trust.

Human needs are not decreasing. The human race is capable of still further improvement. Professional money-raisers can show you a long list of worthy causes, and many critics have pointed out a number of flaws in our present economic system. Since educational bequests are tax-free, and Americans have an almost mystical belief in education, our colleges have tremendous endowments. Yet university presidents still cry for more. We are only just beginning to realize what large sums are needed to fight disease ; the nation is only now becoming aware of the necessity for the launching of a new and greater war for public health, for what Paul de Kruif calls "the fight for life." Only the national government itself can muster such resources. Meanwhile more foundations might be established. The most pressing, immediate, insistent human needs — food and shelter for the unemployed — are those to which the government is responding. In a sense the Roosevelt relief program has been a gigantic philanthropic foundation. Those who object that it may not be perpetual may be wrong. This is not the place to discuss the practical, political, or economic difficulties of stopping a social service once the State has started it. What alarms the millionaires is that they are being made to pay the expenses of a foundation they do not themselves manage. Mr Roosevelt has added to their difficulties one more painful choice : pay for these social services through taxation or through foundations.

Mr Carnegie endowed at his birthplace the Dunfermline trust to engage in whatever useful charities the city does not perform. Charitable work, "made" work, sociological surveys, public buildings, hospitals, laboratories, improvements, parks, etc., which the WPA and similar public agencies have engaged in are precisely the sort of projects formerly carried on by charitable foundations. Benjamin Franklin thought that in a hundred years Boston and Philadelphia would need civic improvements and he provided for them in his will. But in less than a century those improvements were built by the city. The State now cares for the sick, infirm, aged, and unemployed. These tasks are far greater than any private fortune or combination of fortunes can shoulder. Relief needs far outdistanced, in the early days of the depression, the resources of the private charities. It is unlikely the time will come when philanthropic trusts may once more assume these burdens.

The tendency at present is clearly in the opposite direction. The large foundations have refrained from direct charitable relief. Their function, as they see it, is to supplement and to assist, by objective research, agencies directly concerned with social services. The Rockefeller Foundation has done this in a number of fields. The Carnegie Corporation gave $1,-193,000 to New York City Unemployment Relief, but the city spent more than twice that in one month. The Russell Sage Foundation has cooperated by its technical resources with the New York City Home Relief Bureau. But all these efforts are comparatively slight in the face of the tremendous problem presented. Millionaires who contemplate setting up charitable trusts to take over governmental social services should remember that Mr Roosevelt spent in one year more than the total capital assets of all the foundations and college endowments in the country. They would all have to be wiped out to pay the relief bills for a single year.

Foundations have weathered the depression with their capital funds intact. With these they can continue their researches, the importance of which cannot be overestimated. Because of their dependence upon the profitable operation of the economic system of which they are a part, their activities must be necessarily restricted. As soon as they enter the social and economic fields their efforts must be palliative or they risk the temptation, or the criticism, of using their funds for political ends. The foundation idea in its larger sense has outgrown the private philanthropic trust and has been taken over by the government. Many thinkers within the foundations have admitted that since the problem of wise spending is so great it might be better to have large sums raised by taxation and spent by the people through the government. If millionaires use the foundation idea as a means for their own protection, to conserve their fortunes into perpetuity, to maintain through trustees who are relatives or business associates a financial or industrial oligarchy, to glorify their names while avoiding taxes, to guard their group interests by influencing education and public opinion, they may set in motion forces which will eventually take over for the government the foundations themselves. The State may declare : "If you are giving money away, you should actually give it away, not merely go through the motions while in fact keeping control of it."

CHAPTER III

PHILANTHROPY WITH A PURPOSE

It is no coincidence that it was in 1915 the Rockefeller name began a rapid transformation. In December 1915, thin-skinned John D. Jr, already in charge both of the business and the philanthropies, stunned by the Ludlow massacres in 1913, stung by public condemnation, and faced with a Congressional investigation, acted upon the advice of the late Arthur Brisbane and borrowed from the Pennsylvania Railroad Mr Ivy Ledbetter Lee. A month later this advisor to corporations became a director of the Colorado Fuel and Iron Company, upon which he turned his "social X-ray" by mailing from Denver information about Colorado industrial conditions written in his office in Philadelphia. At once he began to change the public's picture of the Rockefeller family. Never again was there an audible outcry against them.

For twenty-five years John D. Rockefeller Sr had been the great American ogre and whipping-boy. From the time he organized the Standard Oil monopoly, buying refineries, pipe lines, and wells, raiding the industry for brains, squeezing out competitors ruthlessly, undercutting prices and obtaining secret rebates ; through the days when he was excoriated and exposed by the muck-rakers, trust-busted by Theodore Roosevelt, and fined $29,240,000 by Judge Kenesaw Mountain Landis, the elder Rockefeller had withstood every variety of vituperation. From the day when the *Atlantic Monthly* published Henry Demarest Lloyd's "The Story of a Great Monopoly" to the years when *McClure's* serialized Ida M. Tarbell's "History of the Standard Oil," no criticism of John D. seemed too harsh. In 1907 he was blamed for the panic and in 1911 he postponed his

birthday reception in fear of assassination.   He was the most
hated man in America, yet he "sawed wood and said nothing,"
confident of eventual vindication.

"Sometimes things are said about me that are cruel and they
hurt," he said.   "But I am never a pessimist.   I never despair.
I believe in man and the brotherhood of man and am confident
that everything will come out for the good of all in the end."
Already he had established the philanthropies which made him
the world's greatest giver.   The Rockefeller Institute for Medical Research was founded in 1901 and the General Education
Board a year later.   In 1913 the Rockefeller Foundation got
its charter from the State of New York and a hundred million
dollars from Mr Rockefeller.   For twenty years he had been
giving money to universities and to medical research.   Hookworm, yellow fever, and malaria had been fought throughout
the world with his money.   In spite of all that, public opinion
considered him the personification of greed.

Vindication did not come of its own accord.   It came with
favorable publicity.   Mr Lee was no ordinary press agent,
however.   "I try to translate dollars and cents and stocks and
dividends into terms of humanity," he declared.   To the newspapers he said that he would send them information guaranteed
to be accurate, that he would welcome inquiry and answer questions ; to the millionaires he suggested policies which, "when
placed before the public, will be approved."   He always denied that the idea of giving away dimes was his, yet to him goes
the credit for the spontaneous epitaph of thousands : "He
wanted to live to be 100 and I'm sorry he didn't do it."   The
pleasant old gentleman toward whom there was general good
will was a creation of Ivy Lee.   After his investigation of the
troubles in Colorado, he advised John D. Jr to stop being the
goat.   W. L. Mackenzie King was hired to study labor relations for the Rockefellers, but his studies were cut short by his
political career in Canada.   Rapid-fire talker Dr George E.
Vincent, one of the most persuasive public speakers in the coun-

try, was placed in charge of the Rockefeller Foundation. Inde-
fatigably he toured the country, telling the public about its
work.

Soon the newspaper readers began to hear about the war
work of the Rockefeller Foundation. Between 1914 and 1919
$22,444,815 was contributed. In 1917 nearly five millions was
given, of which $3,544,372 was to the Red Cross, for which Mr
Lee, incidentally, was handling the publicity. Dr Vincent in
1918 reported that in addition to the contributions to war work,
the Foundation was engaged in a Prevention of Tuberculosis
campaign in France, in malaria control in Arkansas and Mississippi, in yellow fever work in Guatemala and Ecuador, in hookworm and sanitation programs in twenty-one foreign countries,
in public health work in Brazil and Australia, and was making
contributions to the School of Hygiene at Johns Hopkins, a
medical center in Peking, medical schools in China, and many
studies in mental hygiene. Gradually the picture changed :
the greatest capitalist of his age became known as the greatest
philanthropist and patron of higher education, scientific research and public health in the history of the world.

Today the projects of the Rockefeller Foundation are bewildering in their variety and complexity. Its functions, however, are clear. Grants are made to yellow fever studies for
field research in Cuba, Puerto Rico, Albania, Bulgaria, Greece,
Italy, Portugal, Spain, and India. Local currency amounting
to $34,600 was appropriated for work in animal husbandry in
the National Central University in Nanking, China. Studies
are being carried on in Egypt in soil pollution. Gramophone
records of the Hausa and Efik languages are being made in connection with Professor Lloyd James' study in African linguis-
tics. An investigation is being carried out demonstrating how
Hippelates flies can carry yaws infection from men to rabbits.
Yale University has $30,000 to support excavations at Dura-
Europos in Syria. Dr de Jong in Amsterdam is producing cata-
tonia, one of the signs of dementia praecox, in cats. In the

mandated territory of New Guinea natives are being studied with the idea of helping the rulers understand the local social organization. The opossum and marmot are being used in studies of endocrinology in the University of Virginia. A grant has been made to the John Casimir University in Lvov, Poland, toward studies in constitutional and international law. Emergency grants for public health have been given to the State Hygienic Institute in Budapest, to the School of Public Health in Zagreb, Yugoslavia, and for native medical students in Suva, Fiji.

Lest the diverse activities of the other foundations become too institutionalized, the Laura Spelman Rockefeller Memorial was established in 1918 to carry on philanthropies in which she had been interested. Aware of the functions of a foundation in modern society, this promptly developed a "policy," and in 1929 it was merged with the Rockefeller Foundation when Dr Vincent retired and Max Mason became president. A further merger, which makes the general design of the philanthropies less confusing, was made in 1936 when Raymond B. Fosdick took charge, not only of the Foundation, but also the quite separate General Education Board. The latter's activities, chiefly the granting of university endowments, have now been brought within the Foundation orbit. Already a model of corporation precision, the Foundation may thus work even more efficiently as a smoothly geared, impersonal business organization whose stock-in-trade is philanthropy.

To understand its functions, let us look at the appropriations for 1936. For public health $2,460,000 was appropriated, for the medical sciences $1,623,750, which includes $400,000 to the China Medical Board, Inc. For the natural sciences, chiefly experimental biology research in fourteen colleges, $1,370,350. For the social sciences, $1,581,550, and for the "humanities" $3,073,416. To the program in China went $342,540; administration ($815,517) and miscellaneous ($65,000) appropriations brought the total to $11,332,123 for 1936.

Mr Fosdick gives "the advance of knowledge with research as its chief tool" as the definite object of the Foundation. Although 700 fellowships were given, forty-one local and national governments aided, forty-four educational institutions helped, and work in fifty-three countries, from Scandinavia to Java included, the resources of the Foundation were not scattered. A carefully thought-out policy had been carried out from the beginning. From the time when John D. Sr was sent by his father to buy a cord of wood, to the present day, the Rockefellers, in all their activities, have always got full measure. The Foundation concentrates now upon experimental biology ; in the social sciences the emphasis is upon social security, international relations, and public administration ; in medicine it is upon psychiatry ; and in what it calls the "humanities" it studies the "techniques by which cultural levels are affected." By that it means the radio, non-professional drama, museums, libraries, and language problems.

In all the reports of the Foundation it is clear that those in charge have given many anxious moments to the difficult choices before them : What should a Foundation do, and what should it refrain from doing ? Mr Fosdick asks rhetorically : "What special branches of knowledge should be enlarged ? Is all knowledge equally important ? Is anybody wise enough to determine the relative significance of different types of knowledge to a social order struggling for equilibrium ?" No one is more perplexed by the problems of the modern world than the heads of foundations. Sir Josiah Stamp is quoted as saying : "We are producing progressively more problems for society than we are solving." The foundations exist in a democratic country, subject to the laws of a representative government. How far can they be paternalistic ? To what degree must their policies be determined by public opinion ? With an economic system in a precarious condition and their income dependent upon the smooth workings of that economic system, should the foundations attempt to bolster up the system ? Can they in fact, however much they desire to be in theory, be objective ?

Mr Fosdick does not attempt to answer these questions, nor even to ask them, but they seem to be the ever-present ghost at the appropriation banquet. With these difficulties in mind, a policy must be found, and this is the way it is done : One half of the money spent on research in Great Britain and the United States, it is discovered, goes for industrial research or for pure research in physics and chemistry. Of the remaining half, 50% is spent in research on military matters, 25% in agriculture and the branches of biology in connection with it, and the amounts spent on medicine, health, and the social sciences complete, by infinitesimal fractions, the whole. Almost nothing goes into research in the "humanities." So, finding this field unoccupied, the Foundation marches in.

Mr Fosdick has his own conception of what constitutes the social sciences and he states it : "Obviously the problem of man in relation to his fellow men which, in special fields, is being subject to scrutiny . . . the underlying interest is in the general problem of individual and social living, with the aim of progress through understanding. . . An endeavor is being made to shape the program toward what has been called the science of man." With this in mind money is given to the Canadian Institute of International Affairs, the Council of Foreign Relations in New York City, the Foreign Policy Association, the Geneva Research Center, Switzerland, the International Studies Conference in Paris, the Institute of Economics and History in Copenhagen, the Library of International Relations in Chicago, and the Royal Institute of International Affairs, London.

In order to justify such expenditures it is necessary to be optimistic. "The difficulties of transferring the results of this research into everyday life are staggering," observes Mr Fosdick, "but unless we are to adopt a defeatist attitude and take the position that human intelligence is powerless to plan a more rational life for mankind, we are bound to support the attempt, faulty though it may be in many of its approaches, to make knowledge available for social purposes." For these reasons social security is being studied under Rockefeller auspices in the Dutch Economic Institute in Rotterdam, by the Industrial Relations Counselors, Inc., in New York, by the Social Research Council in New York, and at the University of Louvain, Belgium. Public administration is being studied at Dalhousie University at Halifax, Canada, the University of Minnesota, and the University of Virginia. Previous programs are being supported in Harvard, McGill, the University of Oslo, Norway, the University of Stockholm, Sweden, and the Welfare Council of New York City.

The Laura Spelman Rockefeller Memorial spent a total of twenty-one million dollars in the field of the social sciences and the Foundation has appropriated twenty-eight million dollars. "There is something fundamentally wrong with a society," philosophizes Mr Fosdick, "in which raw materials exist in plenty, workers are more than ready to apply their productive capacities, adequate industrial plants and equipment are at hand, and yet enterprise is periodically halted and millions find themselves out of employment and unable to command the necessities of life." Something must be done, but it must be done within the limits of foundation policy. "The entire situation is so unmistakably one of maladjustment that the possibilities of ultimate remedy, or at least of some substantial degree of amelioration, seem promising." However, whatever is done must be "objective." "Certainly," adds Mr Fosdick, "the opportunities for scientific attack on the problem are clear." He does not say what they are, but "There are obvious restrictions upon what a foundation can wisely do."

Agencies must therefore be selected of recognized standing for "detachment" and "objectivity." Only by selecting carefully such institutions as those listed above may the Foundation stimulate with confidence the development of the factual bases for the adaptations which social ideas and institutions

must make in a changing world. After all, the heads of the
foundations are aware that ideas and even facts may sometimes
contain highly explosive material. If the right point of view is
taken, however, it is safe to make researches into the description and measurement of cyclical and structural change, and
even into the analysis of the causes of instability, such as an inquiry into the question of protection against the main hazards
that confront the individual, such as sickness, accident, old age
dependency, and unemployment. Social conditions may thus
be translated into words and removed from reality into the anti-
septic realms of sociology. Not that the Foundation does not
look into the future. Public administrators will be needed who
are "well trained." So the Foundation in 1935 decided to make
this a definite field of concentration by offering advance training not only to "promising recruits for public service" but also
to "outstanding men and women" already established in governmental positions. Thus the idea of "internship" originated,
and it is now being tried out in Washington with the cooperation of the government and the colleges.

Looking even further into the future, Mr Fosdick reflects :
"When some future archaeologist digs down through the crust
of our civilization, it would be a sad reflection on our sense of
balance and proportion if he had to report that ours was a day
of steel and speed . . . but with only faint traces of aesthetic
appreciation." In order to help earn the good opinion of those
far-off generations, as well as to aid the well-being of present-
day mankind, the Foundation has contributed $40,000 to the
World Wide Broadcasting Foundation for trial work in the
development of programs of "cultural and educational value."
After all, Mr Fosdick says : "In the long run a civilization or a
community is judged, not by its factories but by its libraries
and museums ; not by the physical and material basis of its life,
but by its architecture, its schools, its music, its drama, and its
general aesthetic resources." Hence the Foundation is attempting to give the "humanities" a better position in the race

with science. Although there is value for a dictionary of Indo-European synonyms and in the exegetical commentary on the fourth book of Virgil's Aeneid, such as the Rockefellers have, in the past, supported, it is now felt that something more is needed. Hence experiments are being made to determine whether radio audiences are not prepared for better programs. Efforts are being made to bring the radio industry and the universities into closer cooperation. The Museum of Modern Art in New York City was given $120,000 for a library of films ; and a card index of all films of interest since 1889 has been compiled.

It is important to bear in mind the considerations which influence the selection of a project. The best expression of what these considerations are was voiced by John D. Sr himself. The first disease to be attacked by the Rockefeller philanthropy was hookworm. Why this should be chosen is explained by Dr Victor Heiser in *An American Doctor's Odyssey* * : "Mr Rockefeller invited a small group of leaders of the medical profession to meet him. 'I want to ask you gentlemen a question,' he said. 'Is there a disease affecting large numbers of people of which you can say . . . "I know all about this and I can cure it, not in fifty or even in eighty per cent of the cases, but in one hundred per cent ? . . . Furthermore, it should be possible to prevent by simple means. It should be a disease of which the cause can be clearly seen — nothing so vague as microscopic bacteria, but something visible to the naked eye. If you could name me such a disease you would not have to discourse in vague generalities about public health, but would have something concrete which the masses could understand, and concerning which they could be convinced by large scale demonstrations.' "

Dr Charles W. Stiles of the U. S. Public Health Service had the answer. Hookworm was made to order for Mr Rockefeller. Spending money on its eradication would show tangi-

* W. W. Norton and Co., 1936.

ble results and not a cent would be wasted.   Dr Wickliffe Rose
was lifted from the chair of philosophy at the University of
Tennessee to head the Rockefeller Sanitary Commission.   In
spite of Southern pride and the indignant denial that any Southerners had hookworm, the Commission did pioneering work in
1910 to 1914, laying down the organization to be carried on by
the national and local health services.   Dr Rose administered
the work in such a way that the Commission showed what could
be done, what had to be done, and thus made it imperative that
local and state authorities take over the burden.   This is the
policy which the Foundation has followed with yellow fever
and malaria.   When the Southern states were won over to take
up the battle, Mr Rockefeller declared : "I know now what I
want to do with my money.   I made it all over the world and
will spend it there.   Get the people interested in their diseases."

So the Foundation went to work, but always with the Rockefeller slogan : "Philanthropy must pay dividends."   Nowhere
has it paid bigger dividends than in the hookworm campaign.
More than half a million cases were treated before 1914 when
the International Health Board took over the work and spread
it throughout the world.   The publicity resulting was tremendous.   It put people in the frame of mind to combat other
diseases, and it stimulated the states into public health and
sanitation work.   It would be invidious and hardly fair to
point out how closely the Rockefeller name has been associated with these great movements.   Mankind has been helped,
and incidentally and quite deservedly, some of the glory has
been reflected upon the name of the man who supplied the millions.

When Major Walter Reed in 1900 proved that the yellow
fever scourge was being spread in Cuba by a certain type of
mosquito, this was considered the definite cause of the disease.
For a time it was thought that yellow fever had been eliminated.
In 1925 only three cases were reported in the entire Western
Hemisphere.   Then, without warning, the jungle struck back,

and the whole line of battle against the disease had to be completely altered. The original idea that the yellow fever was an urban disease transmitted by the mosquito found in Cuba, so that the cycle of the disease was man — mosquito — man, had to be abandoned. The notion that there were only a few key centers, where the disease was rampant, was found to be only partly true. In Ecuador the International Health Board stamped out yellow fever by cleaning up the breeding places. But then it was discovered that the disease occurred in districts where no *Aedes Aegypti* mosquitoes existed.

This, General Gorgas had said, was impossible. Even Noguchi had been led astray by the difficulties of accurate diagnosis. Instead of discovering the germ of yellow fever, he isolated the germ of infectious jaundice. The mosquito was not the only villain : there could be other hosts than man. At the invitation of the Brazilian government the Rockefeller Health Division swept into infected areas like vanguards of an army, and by 1931 the last epidemic had been halted. One million dollars had been spent : the Brazilian government contributing 70% and the Rockefeller Foundation 30%. Then, in 1932, in the Valley of Chanaen it broke out where the carrier mosquito did not exist, and in 1934 there was a frightful scourge. Vast areas of South America and Africa, it was discovered, were endemic centers of the disease. Where did it come from ? How did it get into the human blood ? This is the riddle upon which the International Health Board is now concentrating. Cooperation with the National Health Board of Brazil, with the National Department of Health of Colombia, with other controls and surveys in South America, helped by the research laboratories in New York and a special study in East Africa, indicates an eventual solution. A method of vaccination has been discovered and in six years the staff has had no
· cases of yellow fever while prior to 1931 five scientists died of it in the Division.

Even more complicated so far as control work is concerned

is the problem of malaria, a disease which circles the globe. Not one, but many different varieties of mosquitoes carry it. In any complete program of world-wide health service, malaria must be considered among the first jobs to be tackled, and so the Foundation tackled it. Although it has been known for centuries that malaria comes from swamps and that quinine prevents serious consequences, much more than that must be known to wipe out the sources of the disease. Not all the Rockefeller money spent on this alone would eliminate malaria altogether. The policy of the Foundation is adhered to : this problem is something which can only be solved by the united efforts of communities and governments. What the Foundation can do is to start the job, to show how it can be solved, and to stimulate activity so that the state or the aroused community will carry it to conclusion.

In three states of the United States, in four countries in Central America, eight in Europe, three in South America, in one country in Asia, and in Puerto Rico, Jamaica, and the Philippines the authorities are being aided. Italy offers the best example of how this work is done, for there the Foundation has been active for ten years, where the problem has always been serious, and warfare on the disease has been carried on since Roman times. Drainage alone does not eradicate it. The *Anopheles maculipennis* is at home in the cold waters of England as well as the canals of Sicily. In 1925 the Public Health Department of Italy, aided by the International Health Board, established an experimental station in Rome. As a result of its work the *Gambusia*, a small minnow-like fish, which eats the mosquito larvae and multiplies rapidly, was introduced into Italian waters. No horizontal vegetation, however thick, can protect the larvae from these fishes which constantly patrol every square inch of water surface. In an area of eight square miles under observation in Istria, malaria has been practically abolished by the use of these fishes alone. With properly built drainage canals, and the cooperation of the *Gambusia*, no mosquitoes can breed in the area surrounding Ostia and the Tiber delta. If the peasants can be persuaded not to catch and eat the fish, this may be a solution of the malaria problem in other parts of Italy.

The river-breeding *Anopheles,* however, are too much for fish, so Paris green mixed with road dust is spread on the water by a blowing apparatus or from an airplane. Even a few specks of this dust are enough to kill the eggs. The Fascist government has made *Anopheline* breeding a nuisance under the law, and insisted on the wide use of screens in houses, teaching children in the schools the necessity for mosquito-proof screens. Mussolini, by his laws, has cooperated with the Foundation so that a constant united front is maintained against malaria. Research in Italy has disclosed that the malaria mosquito may include 150 varieties, each presenting problems of its own. Selected areas have been treated also in Albania and Portugal. In the United States the *Anopheles* usually breeds in quiet waters, but in the Philippines it prefers rapidly flowing streams.

The Foundation has looked for opportunities where it can be of the greatest and most useful "service," hence medical science has been its chief interest since its inception. The General Education Board has contributed $84,000,000 to medical schools in the United States, while the Foundation has given its attention to the outside world, spending $64,000,000 up to 1936. Beginning in 1929 a change of emphasis was made, shifting attention more than ever upon research, particularly in mental hygiene. This was done because it was the most backward, the most needed, and potentially the most fruitful field for progress. A tragic lack of knowledge in psychobiology led to the appropriation of $1,073,150 for work in many diverse approaches in the medical institutes of America, the Netherlands, and England.

The first entry young John D. Sr made in his famous "Ledger A" as a boy was "10 cents for the missionary cause." The Baptist Rockefellers have never lost their interest in foreign missions, and it is probably a natural development of this interest that much attention has been given by the Foundation to China and its problems.   At the University of Chicago a five year program is being supported for historical research and for the investigation of the methods of teaching Chinese to Western students.   Aid was given Princeton for instruction in Far Eastern subjects, and for the purchase of the Gest Chinese Research Library ; seminars at Harvard and Columbia were financed, and advanced students, who have had two years' residence in the Orient, are helped in individual programs of study.   At Yale the mastery of the modern colloquial Chinese language is attempted, while in China efforts are being made to teach English by means of a series of books prepared in Basic English, using a vocabulary of 850 words.

A study was made in 1913 of the medical needs of China, which resulted in the China Medical Board, Inc., to which $14,-500,000 has been given.   The Peiping Union Medical College has received $18,000,000 more.   In 1934 a million dollars was appropriated for a three year program of rural reconstruction and health work.   While the Standard Oil sold oil for the lamps of China, the Foundation made appropriations to the Chinese Mass Educational Movement, to Yenching University, and Nankai University for training men and women for administrative posts.   Aware that the per capita income in rural China is only $10 a year, a program was drawn up designed so that it could be supported by meager existing resources.   Not even in China were the Rockefellers to be left assuming the whole burden.   It was thought to be a disservice to China to create an organization beyond the financial means of the local population.   The emphasis in all its work in China has been to train promising young men and women for leadership.   Nobody knows where China is headed, but whatever the fate of the country, this American Foundation is of the opinion that education can do no harm.   "The gifts of our industrial life," remarks Mr Fosdick, "if indiscriminately accepted, may do incalculable damage. . . With the knowledge of the mistakes which our industrial civilization has made, China may avoid some of the distressing difficulties which have come to us."

Those in charge of the Rockefeller benefactions have always felt that a large portion of the funds spent might be considered as an investment in brains. The Laura Spelman Memorial made a $19,000,000 investment in fifty-five hundred individuals, and the Foundation is continuing this policy. Although officials of the Foundation admit that it is a gamble with talent, it is felt that it is underwriting a portion of future scientific thinking. Whether the influence penetrates beyond scientific support into the social and economic ideas of the recipients is open to question. Usually the fellowships are limited to those who have finished their graduate work, have had several years of practical experience, and are certain of jobs when the fellowship ends. The initial application does not come from the candidate, but from his superior who knows his work. This shifts most of the responsibility for the selection to academic departments of the universities. Mr Fosdick uses a significant word in speaking of those who have held such fellowships : "Today," he notes with pride, "they hold important *strategic* * positions in research laboratories and government." In 1936 seven hundred fellowships were granted, costing $1,210,000. Here, certainly, the influence of the Foundation is by no means negligible.

Of course, it has had to refuse many who asked for its help. "The man will be most successful who confers the greatest service on the world," wrote John D. Sr, but, he added : "It is easy to do harm in giving money." Many people do not understand the functions of a foundation and think that any plea made to it would be legitimate. Hence the necessity for a policy. In 1936 nine hundred and twenty applications were declined because "the type of assistance requested did not fall within the scope of the activities of the organization determined

* Not italicised in report.

by its present policies." Two hundred and seventy research projects were rejected, two hundred and twenty-nine local institutions refused aid, one hundred and thirty educational institutions, seventy-five publications, twenty-four public health projects, seventy-four cures, remedies, investigations of theories and one hundred and eighteen miscellaneous requests were turned down. Only those who have been turned away know the specific suggestions refused. It is explained that the Foundation does not make gifts or loans to individuals, or finance patents or altruistic movements involving private profit, or contribute to the building or maintenance of churches, hospitals, or other local institutions, or support campaigns to influence public opinion on any social or political questions, no matter how disinterested these questions may be.

The Laura Spelman Memorial was supposed to be a catch-all, to take care of causes not within the scope of the other organizations. But it soon developed a policy. This is unavoidable, it is inherent in the conception that not a penny shall be spent unwisely. Every dollar must have a purpose. Once Mr Rockefeller Sr found himself without any cash and borrowed a nickel from a secretary, who urged it upon him as a gift. "Oh, no, Rogers," he admonished him. "A nickel is a year's interest on a dollar."

Dr Heiser tells how when insulin was first discovered appeals almost beyond belief in number and poignancy were made to the Foundation and to the Rockefellers personally. John D. Jr felt that something should be done, and on Dr Heiser's suggestions gave several big hospitals $50,000 for free instruction in administering insulin, and to supply the drug free to those who needed it. Many of the gifts of "Mr Junior" have been to causes which appealed to him and which did not fall within the scope of the Foundation. By thus supplementing the institution, the Rockefeller name in giving was saved from a hard-and-fast, one-track attention to a comparatively few objectives.

It is not without significance that there has been almost no public criticism of the Foundation since its inception. Only one book has been published, *Rockefeller, Giant, Dwarf, and Symbol* by William H. Allen, which has undertaken to criticize the activities of the Rockefeller philanthropies. Mr. Allen's thesis is that Carnegie gave himself with his money, but Rockefeller kept close control of his Foundations. They should be considered, he says, "quasi-public utilities." His most telling point is that no independent, outside audit has ever been made of the Rockefeller Foundation such as Professor W. Z. Ripley suggested for big corporations. In an age when everything has been exposed, criticized, and investigated, it is amazing that the Foundation has escaped attention. One answer is that there is no basis for any hostile criticism. Beyond occasional remarks about the Foundation serving as a means of avoiding inheritance and income taxes and the observation that such organizations would be superfluous in a socialist society, not even the radicals have attacked the Foundation. Little has been said of the possible influence of the Foundation in maintaining the economic *status quo*, and it has never even been hinted that the prestige of the Foundation helps the business of the Standard Oil. The dual Rockefeller role in China, as in the rest of the world, is probably completely separate and completely unconscious. It is a beautiful example of the typical American split personality : never even being aware that the left hand is alleviating the mistakes, or helping unconsciously, in the work of the right hand. At one moment we grasp greedily for profits and the next we give generously for the benefit of mankind.

It is often suggested in private conversation that nobody dares to criticize the Rockefellers. Mr Allen declared that several publishers refused his book on the ground that they were afraid to antagonize the money-power of the Rockefellers as exerted through the banks. Occasionally it is whispered that the Foundation is too insistent upon publicity and immediate results so that the scientists in the Rockefeller laboratories are urged on by the unspoken but pervasive pressure to make discoveries, not only for the sake of science, but to enhance the glory of the Rockefeller name.   This is very doubtful.

From this examination of its activities it is easily seen what the Foundation officials consider its functions.   It does, in this modern world, some of the things that the state, the government, or the community cannot, or does not do.   Whatever is imperative, in the light of human betterment, what should be done, it tries to do through projects so planned that they will not be dependent for support on the Foundation alone.   Needs are met temporarily until a public or private agency can take on the burden.   Solutions are demonstrated rather than provided. That policy is implicit in all that it does, a demand early insisted upon by John D. Sr himself when he began by making his gifts conditional.   If it was known that the Rockefellers were contributing to anything, others would step out, leaving them with the burden.   That is not the Rockefeller idea.   No Rockefeller is ever left holding the bag for anybody, not even in philanthropy.

In a democracy many things are not done until the public is aroused to their need for being done.   Thus hookworm was attacked by a representative government when pressure was exerted upon the representatives to do it.   That is an important function of any foundation, for in this way it can do things which have not been done because the public is uninformed or unaroused to the need.   The significant thing, so far as the Rockefeller gifts are concerned, is to note the type of projects selected.   Hookworm is the best example, and Mr Rockefeller's words to the doctors are full of significance.   He demanded results, and the Foundation today demands results. Projects are selected with that in mind.   We, the public, must see something tangible.   The dividends must be declared on time and be unmistakably dividends and not liabilities.

The Foundation can do what no other agencies at present

can do. Since the world is split into nations and races, and antagonistic governments, only an international foundation can carry on related researches under unified auspices into such diseases as hookworm, yellow fever and malaria in all parts of the world and make the results available in all countries. The Foundation has taught governmental departments ways in which they can practice international cooperation. Often it supplements governmental activities, and provides information or research facilities for which there are no state appropriations. When the State steps in, the Foundation steps out. Thus this huge, smooth-running, carefully planned, thoroughly thought-out organization adapts its functions so that they mesh with what is actually being done in the world and its gears are adjusted to social change without committing the Foundation to political or economic ideas. That the business is not carried on for money profit does not make it any less necessary that it be efficient and well-managed ; all the more reason why each penny should be carefully scrutinized before it is spent.

It has never been among the functions of the Foundation to bring John D. Sr absolution for his sins. It might, however, be used as an example for those who wish to justify the capitalist system, although one scientist has observed that the things the Foundation did were being done in Russia by the Soviet government. It must not be forgotten that it is only simple, enlightened intelligence which induces a rich man to use his money for benevolent purposes rather than for personal aggrandizement. In fact philanthropy may be his best investment, a protection against criticism, as well as a means of preventing violent social change, particularly if it establishes his name forever as among the world's greatest givers. It is for this that Mr Rockefeller will be remembered, and the universal tribute paid him at his death is a magnificent monument not only to him but to the public relations counselor who erected his character in the public mind. Long before May 23, 1937 the work of Ivy Lee was complete : the embodiment of ruthless capitalist privateering died as "one of the greatest benefactors the human race has ever known."   His philanthropy, however, always had a purpose and this was unquestionably among the purposes.   Looked at from this point of view it must be admitted that the half a billion dollars given to "philanthropy" during the course of seventy-nine years were well worth the investment.

Note : All figures in this book concerning the Rockefeller philanthropies are taken from the published reports of their foundations or from the *New York Times*. These figures are subject to possible contradiction, however, by Rockefeller agents since the figures they give are frequently contradictory. The way in which announcements are made may confuse the public : announcements usually state that a gift is to be made, that it is made, and that it has been made.   Appropriations must not be confused with disbursements. Appropriations may be made, or announced, and the payments spaced over a period of years, or, for some reason, never paid in full.   The public is likely to read of "appropriations" and believe that the sum has actually been paid.   Another source of confusion is the categories into which the Rockefeller foundations divide their gifts.   Such resounding terms as the "humanities," for example, may mean almost anything you want it to mean.

CHAPTER IV

THE SCIENCE OF GIVING – AND GETTING

Amidst the spirit of buoyancy and good cheer with which the foundations established by Andrew Carnegie celebrated his Centenary in 1935, the Principal and Vice Chancellor of the University of St Andrews, Sir James Colquhoun Irvine, paid tribute to his memory in these words : "He was indeed the father of giving on the grand scale and more than any other man of his time he transformed giving from an ill-developed art into a well-organized science ; above all, and for the reason that he regarded benevolence as a duty, there was no savour of charity to make bitter the acceptance of his gifts."

That he gave on a grand scale no one can question. Before creating the Carnegie Corporation of New York, Mr Carnegie endowed five great agencies : The Carnegie Institute of Pittsburgh in 1896, the Carnegie Institution of Washington in 1902, the Carnegie Hero Fund in 1904, the Carnegie Foundation for the Advancement of Teaching in 1905, and the Carnegie Endowment for International Peace in 1910. When the "father of giving" first started to get rid of his fortune the art of getting was more fully developed and practised than the art of giving. Just as Mr Carnegie demonstrated the most artistic methods in getting huge profits through combination of companies and speed-up industrial techniques, so he demonstrated and preached in the last twenty-five years of his life the fundamental principles of the art of giving. It remained for the Carnegie Corporation to try to elevate it to a science.

Mr Rockefeller's gifts were coldly calculated after long deliberation ; they were intellectual in origin and shrewdly purposeful. Mr Carnegie tried to be selective ; he searched

for good causes, but there was always an emotional impulse
prompting him in every one of his benefactions.   With all his
other Scotch qualities, he had a passionate idealism which could
be successfully appealed to, and it was from that most of his
philanthropic impulses sprang.   Incidentally, the same quality
of idealism may be detected in the writings and speeches of
those he selected to carry on his philanthropies.   Pittsburgh
was such a filthy city he could not bear to stay there ; he wanted
to make a cultural contribution to the region from which he
gained most of his wealth.   Hence the Carnegie Institute, with
its museum of fine arts, music hall, museum of natural history,
and public library in Pittsburgh.   It hurt him to think that
scientists and teachers were underpaid ; he feared and hated
war.   After a mine disaster in 1904 the thought of the widows
and orphans stirred him to establish the Hero Fund.

So this little parent of large giving was the first to put an emphasis on the humanities and he insisted that his funds be perpetual.   Those in charge can spend only the interest and cannot touch the capital except for reinvestment purposes.   This
responsibility has compelled them to concentrate not only on
the science of giving but also on the science of getting, for they
are not only faced with the tremendous problem of how to
spend the income, but the even more staggering problem, in
these times, of conserving the principal in such a way that there
will be an income to spend.

Mr Rockefeller in his business life kept a close personal touch
on every detail of his business so long as he was active in it.
Carnegie, although he served for the first eight years as president of his philanthropic corporation, always looked for the
right man for the particular job, and then gave him that job
with the minimum of supervision.   The elder Rockefeller kept
a watchful scrutiny on his philanthropies until he was certain
he could trust the judgment of his son, and John D. Jr has maintained his father's vigilance.   Carnegie picked the men who
were to administer his trusts as carefully as he picked the super-

intendents of his steel plants. But he had no son to carry on
his work, so he created the Carnegie Corporation to be his immortal embodiment.

After more than ten years of strenuous giving, when he discovered, to his dismay, that he still had the bulk of his fortune
in his hands, he established, when he was 76 years of age, the
Carnegie Corporation as a sort of holding company * for all his
benefactions, so that out of its reservoir of capital those causes
and institutions in which he was interested would be amply provided with funds. It is not in any sense a supervisory body,
and the other trusts are referred to in its annual reports as "sister institutions." Always the biggest sister of the lot, she has
been well able to grant large funds to her elder but somewhat
smaller sisters. Beginning with an initial endowment of $25,-
000,000, the Corporation received on January 16, 1912 $75,-
000,000, and the following October another $25,000,000. As
a legacy under Mr Carnegie's will in 1923 came an additional
$10,300,000.

Out of this original endowment of $135,000,000 the Trus-
tees up to 1936 have been able to appropriate $167,000,000. Of
this nearly $70,000,000 has gone to the "sister" institutions.
As stated in the charter, the Corporation was established "for
the purpose of receiving and maintaining a fund or funds and
applying the income thereof to promote the advancement and
diffusion of knowledge and understanding among the people of
the United States and the British Dominions and Colonies, by
aiding technical schools, institutions of higher learning, libraries, scientific research, hero funds, useful publications, and
by such other agencies and means as shall from time to time be
found appropriate therefor." In this legal language the principles of the science of giving were laid down. All of the fund
was applicable to the United States except $10,000,000, the in-

* Not a holding company in the ordinary, accepted sense as in utilities.
Mr Carnegie called it a "reservoir." E. V. Hollis dubs it "Andrew Carnegie
Inc."

come of which was to be spent in the British Dominions and Colonies. The original charter, received from the State of New York June 8, 1911, had to be amended April 23, 1917, so that the proceeds from the British fund could be spent in the Dominions and Colonies. Since then the constitution has been amended several times to increase the number of trustees from eight to ten and then to fifteen. Six of the trustees are ex-officio, heads of the Carnegie institutions, the other nine have five-year overlapping terms.

The Corporation has unquestionably done its best, limited by the vision and wisdom of those in charge, to carry on the transformation of the art of giving into a well-regulated science. Gifts to the Carnegie institutions have been for additional endowment, for real estate and buildings, for support, research, and general capitalization purposes. Started by the gift of $26,718,000 from Mr Carnegie, the Carnegie Institute of Pittsburgh got $25,510,354 from the Corporation, most of it for endowment. The Carnegie Foundation for the Advancement of Teaching, originating with a $15,000,000 endowment, received $16,663,608 since 1911, of which a million and a quarter was for the Division of Educational Inquiry and $12,017,382 for professors' pensions. The Teachers Insurance and Annuity Association was put on its feet by the gift of $9,364,000, of which $6,700,000 was for capitalization purposes. $4,000,000 of that came from a reserve fund created out of income, and the remainder is being paid in installments.

This insurance company was organized by the Carnegie Foundation for the Advancement of Teaching and by the Corporation to cooperate with the colleges and universities to put reserve-supported and contributory pension systems into operation and to act as the agency to administer these systems. It has also written life insurance for several thousand teachers and by this final gift for capitalization purposes it became an autonomous company not dependent upon the Corporation for further funds. Participation in this enterprise makes certain that the professors will get their pensions and hence is considered by the Trustees a substantial contribution to the "advancement and diffusion of knowledge and understanding." In addition to this, since 1911 $5,400,000 has been set aside and is being spent on the purchase of professors' annuities, supplementing the pensions.

The original endowment of the Carnegie Institution of Washington was $10,000,000. This was subsequently raised to $22,000,000. Between 1911 and 1936 it got $7,032,690, of which $5,000,000 was for endowment and $682,409 for specific research. The Carnegie Endowment for International Peace, which the little father of giving started with $10,000,000, got $2,453,000 from the Corporation for research, publications, and support. The Church Peace Union, established with $2,000,000, paid by the Corporation, got $382,000 for support. The Hero Fund Commission got $5,000,000 in the original endowment and $100,000 from the Corporation to supplement it. Of course, each of these institutions receives incomes from the securities in which its endowment funds are invested, and these funds are each separately administered. It was to carry out Mr Carnegie's expressed wishes that the trustees have made these contributions as they deemed advisable.

Certainly there has been no "savour of charity" about any of these gifts, nor have the fifty-two institutions of learning which have received grants of two hundred and fifty thousand dollars or more shown any trace of bitterness about the acceptance of funds. The duty of benevolence has prompted the appropriation of $38,784,038 for universities, colleges, and schools up to 1936, of which $6,342,678 was for institutions in the British Dominions and Colonies and $615,700 for secondary schools. In 1935 the Corporation tried to call attention to the relative neglect of women's colleges by gifts to Bryn Mawr, Smith, Vassar, Sweet Briar and Scripps colleges totaling $754,000.

It has been said that college presidents, compelled to be professional large-scale panhandlers by the positions they hold, have approached the big foundations hat in hand, with one eye on their economics departments. Lately, however, the Corporation reports, there has been an encouraging increase in interest in the problems of education on the part of college presidents. Now, Dr Frederick P. Keppel remarks : "Although the public still retains something of the fretfulness of its attitude toward education and its costs which developed during the depression, and although teachers' oaths in twenty-six states and the District of Columbia still furnish pathological manifestations of ignorance as to what education really is and the spirit in which it must be conducted, there are nevertheless encouraging signs of a resumption of a sane and capable educational leadership in the country." It is possible that we may even find out what education really is and where it is going, for Dr Keppel notes, "the number of clarifying public statements upon the problems of general education."

Continuing its duty of benevolence, the Corporation granted to twenty-three "general agencies" $26,205,347, chiefly for research, up to 1936. It admits responsibility for the establishment of the Institute of Economics, now included in the Brookings Institution, and the American Law Institute. To the National Academy of Sciences, National Research Council, it gave funds for building and endowment. It contributed substantially to agencies engaged in war service during the World War, and in the early days of the depression, before the government assumed the burden, it gave $3,810,000 to national welfare agencies. Although Mr Carnegie never went to church, he loved organ music, and he thought church-goers would appreciate good organs, so he and the Corporation gave $6,220,-646 for church organs, a practice discontinued in 1917. $13,-067,592 was spent by the Corporation to carry on Mr Carnegie's most famous benefaction, free public library buildings, a practice also discontinued in 1917.

Instead of giving money for library buildings, the Corporation, in developing its policy of scientific giving, has preferred to contribute to library "interests."   Up to 1936 the American Library Association got $3,227,750.   Support was given to library schools in the University of Chicago, the University of Michigan, the University of Denver and Hampton Institute. As a part of its program for the improvement of library service, it was the intention to help the junior colleges, but this has been found difficult because it seems that such colleges have not been very sure where they are going.   In the last year, however, $300,000 has been appropriated to junior colleges for the purchase of books.

Library development in the British Dominions was aided, gifts having been made to the University of Stellenbosch in South Africa, and for the purchase of books by Otago University and Aukland College in New Zealand, as well as the University of Western Australia.   The total appropriated for library interests was $642,050.

Mr Carnegie thought of libraries as a means of education. After careful investigation the Corporation has made large gifts for the endowment of institutions of higher learning.   The adult education movement did not begin until 1926, seven years after Mr Carnegie's death.   It is precisely the sort of project which would have aroused his enthusiastic idealism, and it was logical, therefore, that the Corporation should take a lead in its promotion.   So it gave $1,404,830 to the youngest of national educational organizations : the American Association for Adult Education.   Founded by a group of liberals imbued with the persistent notion that intelligence and education will somehow save the world from destruction, this society proposes to educate "the whole man" in art, politics, economics, to keep minds open so that judgments may be based on facts, to keep abreast of knowledge, to prepare adults for new occupations, to improve teachers and teaching, to help adults to achieve true security ; all by means of schools, forums, library service, extension courses in universities, lectures, and radio programs. By helping this cause, the Corporation not only demonstrates what it means by "well-regulated scientific giving," it also serves the democratic ideal.   Under state socialism such services would be provided by the government, but in a capitalist democracy a foundation exercises its function by using the profits set aside by its founder for services much needed which the state does not or cannot perform.

At the nadir of the depression, however, the state stepped in and took up the work inaugurated by the American Association of Adult Education, expanded it, and spent sums upon it that made the foundations look like pikers.   In 1934 the Federal government spent $2,000,000 a month on adult education, giving jobs to 50,000 teachers and instruction to two million adults. Although Federal spending is now diminishing, the government is definitely committed to a program of adult education. Meanwhile the Corporation has pioneered in radio education, supporting the National Advisory Council on Radio Education to the extent of $308,500.   While frankly recognizing that radio broadcasting in this country is primarily a business operated for profit, the Corporation, with characteristic idealism, became interested in the long-range problems and implications of broadcasting.   What these are, the Sixth Annual Institute for Education by Radio meeting with the Fifth Annual Assembly of the National Advisory Council on Radio Education at Ohio State University in 1935 revealed in its proceedings. Most of the speakers were worried about the possibilities of the radio in America being used for such purposes as Hitler and Mussolini have used it abroad, and they raised significant questions concerning the function of radio in a democracy, particularly as it involves problems of free speech.   Anxious about the influence of radio upon American culture, the Advisory Council has investigated problems of educational broadcasting, demonstrating through sustaining programs how it can be done, and helping to organize educational broadcasts.   Levering Tyson, in charge of this work, admits : "The educational world has no more presumptive right to the air than business,"

yet he points out that sixty radio stations in the United States
are now owned by educational institutions.   More people have
radios than telephones.   We are only just beginning to realize
its advertising possibilities and its power to influence public
opinion.   Since the easiest effort in modern science is moving
the dial on a receiving set, the Advisory Council has tried to
persuade the radio audience to move dials to educational broadcasts and to persuade broadcasters to give interesting educational programs.

As a part of its efforts to make giving a well-regulated science, the Corporation has contributed steadily to the arts.   In
1936, $857,750 was contributed, chiefly for arts teaching equip-
ment in educational institutions, for specific projects at universities, museums, and for activities in music.   "While colleges and schools understand that to get good music they must
pay for it," the 1936 report remarks, "they still attempt to get
their exhibitions for nothing if possible."   Several traveling art
exhibitions are aided, but the Corporation feels that the missionary stage has passed and a more critical attitude toward
standards should now be encouraged.   Efforts are being made
to place the burden of art activities upon independent organizations.   Here again, the government has stepped in and done on
a big scale what the Corporation has inaugurated on a comparatively modest scale, so that the inclusion of art projects in
the PWA and WPA has taken much of this burden.   Dr Keppel comments : "Much, perhaps most, of the great art of the
past was created under conditions in which subject, medium,
dimensions, and general manner of treatment were determined,
not by the artist himself, but by the requirements of the job
upon which he was put, and this is precisely the situation in
which the worker on a PWA project finds himself."   However, looking toward the time when Federal spending may
cease, it is noted : "The spread of new opportunities for art appreciation must depend in large measure upon the assurance of
a reasonable profit to the manufacturer and distributor."

Contrary to popular impression, the Corporation does not administer a fund from which pensions are provided for ex-Presidents of the United States and their widows. The origin of that impression is in the request of Mr Carnegie in 1912 to provide such pensions. When the idea met with public disapproval the Trustees voted against it. Instead, Mr Carnegie left a number of people life annuities in his will, including Mrs Grover Cleveland, Mrs Theodore Roosevelt, and William Howard Taft.

"A foundation executive lies in a cultural no man's land," *School and Society* observed August 1, 1936. "He has neither the time to be a scholar nor the opportunity to be a teacher, assuming he is qualified to be either." Dr Frederick P. Keppel, President of the Carnegie Corporation, has no enviable job in steering a safe course for the largest foundation in the world. "Our exemption from taxation," he declares, "rests upon public confidence." Mr Carnegie provided a chart, and the Trustees have obviously endeavored to do as they imagine Mr Carnegie would have wished. In trying to create a well-regulated science they have contributed out of the income of the Corporation to the Carnegie institutions as seemed wise and necessary. Public opinion has approved of this, as well as of the vast contributions to higher education. Gifts for general endowment purposes have diminished, however, and grants are now limited to those more or less identified with the program of the Corporation. A few selective projects have been financed, the support dependent upon what they accomplish.

"The chief trouble with voluntary organizations for worthy purposes," Dr Keppel declares, "is that there are too many of them. . . A foundation grant has frequently proved a very doubtful blessing to an organization of this character since it has been followed by a reduction in support from other sources. Ambitious projects carefully planned in advance should, in principle, be particularly attractive to foundations. The world is full of big questions today and if the funds were made available, the right men and women should be able to organize themselves to study and answer them.   Many such projects were financed during the years 1922–1930.   In certain cases the results were impressive.   In others, there was a tendency to bog down after a year or so of rather feverish activity, or run into a number of relatively trivial channels.   On the whole it may be questioned whether these enterprises have not proved unduly expensive for the results obtained. . . Even with the greatest care in selection, grants to individuals are bound to include a substantial number of unprofitable investments ; but, if such care be exercised, some few brilliant successes should far more than counterbalance the losses."

These are some of the difficulties in transforming the art of giving into a well-regulated science.   Critics occasionally question whether it can be called a science at all, and much has been said in the past about Mr Carnegie's "tainted money."   That was not the question which faced the little Scot or the big foundation.   The question was what to do with the money, and the answers found by Carnegie and his Corporation may or may not be satisfactory to public opinion.   C. Hartley Grattan in the *American Mercury*, August, 1928, wrote of "Saint Andy" : "He preferred to help what he called 'the swimming tenth.'   It was impossible for him to imagine that men could be defeated by forces beyond their control.   His libraries were designed to help those already on the upgrade.   Most of his funds and foundations were planned so they assisted those already freed from the effects of grinding poverty.   His most spectacular endowments — those connected with the peace movement — have chiefly been of use to established and respectable scholars."

Interesting as it is to try to discover by what activities the operations of the Carnegie Corporation can claim to be called a "well regulated science," even more fascinating is it to take a look into the means by which it provides for its own perpetuity. Mr Carnegie intended that it should be immortal, and he evidently had high hopes for the indefinite continuance of the capitalist system. Most of his gifts were in the form of bonds in the United States Steel Corporation. With these as a safe income-producing capital, the Corporation began in 1911 with an endowment of $125,000,000, augmented later by other gifts, lifting it to $135,600,000. So well regulated has the science of getting been practiced by the administrators, however, that the Corporation in 1936, after giving away more than $160,000,-000, reported assets of $156,801,000. By shrewd investment they have steadily increased the capital assets of the Corporation. But only the income can be spent.

In theory this income is supposed to be a liquid asset for each generation so that if the Trustees should spend unwisely in one generation, the next generation would still have the principal and could spend the income while it was in its charge upon other, and perhaps worthier, objects. Appropriations made by one generation, however, may in practice not be paid until the next. Obligations may thus be incurred that the next generation in charge of the Corporation may have to pay. Appropriations made in one year are frequently paid over a number of years. For example, in 1920 a grant of $21,800,000 was made to the Carnegie Institute of Pittsburgh and the Carnegie Institute of Technology, an obligation not yet completely paid off. When Dr Keppel became president in 1923 there was a total of $40,000,000 of such obligations, which have since been reduced to $8,700,000.

Before 1928 the Corporation's investment problem was not very complicated because not much more was required than to clip the coupons of the Steel bonds, and one man was sufficient to do that. All except $25,000,000 was in the steel bonds. These other investments were chiefly in railroad bonds given by Mr Carnegie and the financial committee saw no reason for selling them and purchasing other securities. In 1926 the appropriations of the Corporation were limited to $2,000,000 annually so that charges against future income might be reduced.

In that year the Corporation began buying bonds of public utilities. $1,871,517 worth of securities was redeemed, sold or transferred. Thus began a fairly respectable investment business.

When the United States Steel Corporation refinanced in 1928, it retired the bonds held by the Carnegie Corporation, paying 115 for them, so that the bulk of the assets of the Corporation, amounting to $90,000,000, were sold at a profit of nearly $16,000,000. Other high grade bonds were then purchased : Canadian : $7,247,000, foreign : $5,180,000, industrial : $13,040,000, public utility : $25,138,000, railroad, $66,-480,000, and U.S. government : $8,000,000. This last item, it was explained, was merely for temporary purposes, for the government bonds were sold and replaced by other purchases.

So scientifically did the investment officers do their work that the income of the Corporation jumped nearly a million dollars and the assets rose from $142,000,000 to $157,000,000, reaching a peak in 1932 of $161,000,000. Since then the interest on high grade bonds and the value of such securities have decreased, yet the total is still $13,000,000 more than it was when the investment counselors began their work, and $21,-000,000 more than the original endowment. Mr Carnegie intended that the Corporation, as well as his other foundations, should be perpetual but it is not his money which makes them perpetual, it is the well-regulated administration of it. The foundations will endure only so long as high grade bonds and other investments continue to pay interest, only so long as the investment officers administer wisely and profitably. As the 1936 report remarks : "Philanthropic objectives can be reached only if money is made by somebody." This "somebody" is the American industrial system and those who compose it.

Let us examine a little further the financial record. The profit on securities sold in 1930 was $703,188. In that year the U. S. government bonds were sold at no profit. The following year, when the depression was deepening, the assets of the

Corporation rose nearly $2,000,000, while the appropriations remained the same, or nearly half what they had been in 1929. The 1931 report remarked : "The relations between the foundations and the grant-consuming public are improving." That year the profit on $6,828,733 worth of securities redeemed, sold or exchanged was only $18,700, but the income was more than $7,000,000. The following year the depression caught up with the investment officers and the Corporation portfolio showed a loss of $680,685 on transactions of $3,971,782.

As long as the investment department shows a profit its operations are not likely to be questioned. But these officers are only human, and even with the best advice available, they are liable to error, particularly in times of rapid economic change. Theirs is the responsibility of keeping the foundation perpetual, and if their judgment should not be accurate, their selection of investments may be criticised. The total loss on securities redeemed, sold, or exchanged amounts to nearly $8,000,000. Fortunately the profit on the steel bonds more than offsets that, showing a total profit of more than $7,000,000. It is possible, if another financial crisis should destroy the value of the investments, some critics may rise to say that while the income of the Corporation only may be spent, and not the principal, the investment officers have been gambling with that principal. Yet, in a sense, what else can they do under circumstances which make all investments a gamble?

At the bottom of the depression, in 1933, an effort was made to improve the quantity and quality of the investments, and for the first time common stocks in American industrial corporations were purchased at a time when they were at their lowest level. The loss on securities traded in that year was reduced to $173,720. The next year, however, was the worst in the history of the Corporation. $1,615,590 was lost on bonds, $709,-415 on preferred stocks while a profit of $19,346 was realized on common stocks, chiefly by selling American Tobacco "B,"

Chesapeake and Ohio, Borden, National Biscuit, and U. S. Gypsum.   The total loss was $2,335,120.

It was not quite so bad in 1935.   The total loss was $612,165 on transactions amounting to $47,998,027.   But notice how the size of the transactions has grown since 1926.   Profits on common stocks were $191,215, chiefly Allied Chemical, Consolidated Gas of Baltimore, Dupont, and General Motors.   During 1935–36 the Corporation began to participate in the "Roosevelt recovery."   A profit of $528,929 was made on the trading of securities.   Bonds which had cost $111,806,827 had a market value of $119,856,650 ; preferred stocks showed an appreciation of $397,059 and the portfolio of common stocks rose $11,893,508, thus vindicating the judgment of the investment officers.   Securities costing $48,679,471 were sold for $49,-208,401.   They must have been busier than the disbursing department, for nearly one third of the total assets of the Corporation were involved in active security operations in that one year.

Such are the problems of a modern philanthropic foundation in these days of rapid change.   In order to continue the science of giving, the science of getting must be practiced.   Assets are increasing, the income diminishing, administrative costs increasing.   When the number of trustees was increased in 1921 the $5000 fees paid them were abolished.   In 1912 when the Corporation was administered chiefly by Mr Carnegie himself and there was no rent to pay, the administrative costs were only $55,000.   When the reorganization was effected in 1921, new quarters rented and equipped the administrative costs were $218,000.   When Mr Keppel became president they were $113,000 ; in 1935–36 they were $315,000.   Much of the recent increase has been due to the cost of the investment service. We are indeed living, as Mr Keppel observes, in an unbalanced world.   "Is it inertia or cowardice," he asks, "which continues today the support of enterprises in such fields as adult education, bibliographic research, the appreciation of art or music, or is it, rather, a sound instinct ?"

No more than anybody else does Mr Keppel know the answers. "If the way were clear for foundation trustees to make telling contributions toward balance in the world itself, the answer would be easy, but the way is not clear. It is indeed none too clear how far we can contribute toward balancing individual lives, but surely it is only by applying the very best we have in imagination and in intellect to our processes of education that we can hope to be of service. In the light of what has actually been accomplished, we can at least tackle the problem with courage, if not with complete confidence, and in the hope that the balanced men and women in the world will, before too long, find a way to balance the world itself once again."

Fortified by such idealism, by the good intentions of the trustees, and the realistic determination of the investment officers, the Carnegie Corporation is doing its best to remain perpetual as long as possible.

CHAPTER V

CREATING A PROFESSION

THE RUSSELL SAGE FOUNDATION

For nearly ninety years tough old money-lender Russell Sage was the embodiment of the Yankee skinflint. His cold, grim hunger for dollars, dating from his Oneida County boyhood, whetted by a small fortune made in the grocery business in Troy, grew insatiable by profits realized in railroad financing. A term in Congress opened his eyes to the possibilities in railroad consolidation, so he bought from the city of Troy the Schenectady railroad at a bankrupt price and sold it to what was later the New York Central at a profit of $200,000. A chance meeting with Jay Gould led him into stock market speculation, which he insisted was with him a business, not a gamble. By inventing the "put and call" system in 1872, he made it a business, for by this system the small investors with twenty-five to one hundred dollars could be induced to bet against Sage's millions. Although he lost $7,000,000 in the panic of 1884, he learned his lesson and soon afterwards had $27,000,000 loaned out at usurious rates of interest. Shrewdest and most conservative of the great financiers, Sage met all appeals for generosity or mercy with a complete lack of expression, and his stinginess was one of the nation's oldest traditions.

It was said that he deducted ten cents from an office boy's wages because the lad brought him a fifteen, instead of a five cent, sandwich. Often he was seen haggling with the Wall Street apple woman over the number of apples he could have for a penny, or arguing with an Italian candy vendor over the price of a chocolate bar. In 1891 when maniac Henry W. Norcross tried to blow him up, he used William R. Laidlaw, his bookkeeper, for a shield, and when this man, crippled for life, sued Mr Sage, the old millionaire fought the case interminably, declaring that whatever gratitude he might have felt was wiped out when the fellow entered suit. Russell Sage's idea of charity was to give the poor children of Poughkeepsie an annual picnic. That was practically his only interest in philanthropy.

His widow, however, made philanthropy her career, and established a foundation designed to associate her husband's name with philanthropic interests into perpetuity. Mrs Margaret Olivia Sage spent her life and her fortune in compensating for a usurer's greediness. As a school chum of the first Mrs Sage, who died in 1867, she had reason to know well the man who was already, when she married him in 1869, on his way to making a large fortune. Born in Syracuse in 1828, she went to the Troy Female Seminary, and taught for a short time at the Ogontz School in Philadelphia. She was the Puritan schoolteacher type who later blossomed, while her husband was busy in Wall Street, into a bustling committee woman of broad philanthropic interests. When she saw horses fall down on the macadam of Fifth Avenue, she phoned a newspaper friend and started a crusade on behalf of horses. Sage had sold rum in Troy, but Mrs Sage was an ardent prohibitionist. She wanted to do good and she was too intelligent to become an old-fashioned Lady Bountiful type of charity worker. Being childless, she had time to investigate social conditions and she concluded that the poor should be made to help themselves. Late in life she picked up a tramp on the road and took him to her country estate where she gave him a job.

The newspapers in 1906, reporting Sage's death, announced in the same story that his widow would distribute his fortune philanthropically. "So far as the next hundred years are concerned," he said just before he died, "we cannot set any limit to the wealth that an individual may own." If he had lived he might have built a fortune rivaling Carnegie's or Rockefeller's. He left not a cent to charity ; the bulk of his $64,000,000 went to his widow. At once she began to get three hundred letters a day telling her how to spend it. But that was a question she had studied for thirty years. The Woman's Hospital, the New York Exchange for Women's Work, the college in Troy, the Y.W.C.A., and many other institutions were to be aided. Something more, however, was on her mind, and it probably was her lawyer who suggested the idea of the Russell Sage Foundation. He was Robert W. de Forest, counsel for the Central Railroad of New Jersey, director in half a dozen banks and insurance companies, and president, for forty years, of the Charity Organization Society. He was the man who organized the Foundation in 1907, set it in operation, and served as its president for twenty-five years.

Apparently the foundation idea does not appeal to women, whose gifts are usually concentrated upon religion and health. Only one other foundation of any size — the Milbank Memorial — was established by a woman's money. In the near future there may be others, for capital is now 70% in women's hands, and \$210,000,000,000 of the nation's wealth is controlled by them, largely because two-thirds of the estates are inherited by women. They give very little to education, recreation, or movements to improve the conditions of the under-privileged. Reform, foreign and domestic relief, health and religion appeal to them. To institutionalize a fortune into perpetuity is a masculine idea, and it is usually the product of a lawyer's advice. When the legal mind is occupied with social welfare there is born such a foundation as the Russell Sage.

By a special act of the New York State Legislature it was created "for the purpose of receiving and maintaining a fund, or funds, and applying the income thereof to the improvement of social and living conditions in the United States of America." To do so "it shall use any means to that end which from time to time shall seem expedient to its members or trustees, including research, publication, education, the establishment and mainte-nance of charitable or benevolent activities, agencies and insti-tutions, and the aid of any such activities, agencies or institu-

tions already established."   In turning over $10,000,000 in
securities, Mrs Sage wrote : "The scope of the Foundation is not
only national, it is broad.   It should, however, preferably not
undertake to do that which is now being done or is likely to be
effectively done by other individuals or other agencies.   It
should be its aim to take up the larger, more difficult problems
and to take them up so far as possible in such a manner as to
secure cooperation and aid on their solution."   She believed
such aims to be broad enough to avoid the pitfalls of perpetuity.
At her death she left $5,600,000 more to the Foundation.

Asking for advice from charity workers, those in charge decided at the outset what the Foundation would not do.   It
would not contribute to higher education or attempt to relieve
individual or family need.   It would not make any grants for
religious purposes.   It would seek out the underlying causes of
poverty chiefly through research and to make "the facts behind
conditions" known to those in a position to further reform.
Although it made grants to the anti-tuberculosis campaign and
joined in the "safe and sane Fourth" agitation, its main attention
was the accumulation of what social workers call "data."   In
the days when the Foundation started there were very few
social workers, and it was not yet a profession.   Such work was
then called "charity" and most of it was voluntary.   In the
thirty years since the Russell Sage Foundation was started charitable activities have grown from a part-time avocation to a full-
time profession, the whole approach to relief and welfare has
been revolutionized, and what was once an "interest" of a few,
has become a lifetime occupation of thousands.   To engage in
charitable work was once very simple ; now we are told it is a
science, and can be done properly only by highly trained
specialists who have graduated from "recognized schools of
social work."

The social workers now in charge of the Russell Sage Foundation are very sensitive to criticism and reluctant to give any
information about its history or its activities.   They would

probably deny that the Foundation has played a leading part in creating the profession to which they belong, but it is obvious that by its research, its publications, its grants to schools for social work, its function as a clearing house for information for social workers and agencies throughout the country, its aid in finding jobs for professional social workers, its publicity and promotion for the idea of bigger and better social work through pubic and private agencies, no other institution has ever had a comparable influence in the creation of a new profession. At the very beginning of its work it hired the best available social workers to study what happens to children in city slums, how sick and aged are cared for, under what conditions women work in sweatshops and factories. These investigations not only helped to cure abuses and initiate reform, they set an example and furnished a method to be followed by hundreds if not by thousands of social workers who have followed them. Miss Mary Van Kleck began in 1910 the department of women's work which later became the Department of Industrial Studies and her influence has been so great that those who know it would not attempt to measure it. About the same time the late Miss Mary E. Richmond organized the Charity Organization Department of the Foundation, and through her teachings and writings indicated what social workers should learn and know to be considered "professional."

It is true, as those in charge of the Foundation will tell you, that its work is chiefly "research." This is a typical understatement of a consistently self-effacing institution. The work done for the Foundation by Miss Van Kleek and Miss Richmond has revolutionized the fields in which they did their "research" and they alone by their influence have been enough to launch a new profession. Compared with some other foundations, the capital assets are not large, and its size gives no hint of its tremendous effect on American life and thought. Not until the depression created a need for people who had ideas of what to do for the millions who were starving, not until the cities became frantic about the problem of the unemployed, not until the government was compelled to support a large portion of the population did it become clear that here was the opportunity for which a new profession had been preparing, that here was a chance to use the "techniques" and the results of the "research" made by the Russell Sage Foundation.

If you inquire :   "What is the relation between the Foundation and the New York School of Social Work ?" you will be told : "No relation at all."   Theoretically that may be correct, yet the Foundation has granted $206,581 to the endowment fund of the New York School of Social Work.   The School occupies five floors of the Foundation building ; * lectures in the School may be heard in auditoriums of Russell Sage ; the libraries are combined ; the staff members lecture at the School ; the Foundation publishes many of the books used by the School and helps to place many of its students in jobs. The School was founded by the Charity Organization Society at a time when Robert W. de Forest was president of both the Society and the Foundation.

In 1898 the Charity Organization Society began a six weeks course in charity work, the first step toward creating a group of trained workers.   In 1903 this was extended to six months, and in 1907, the year the Russell Sage Foundation began, chiefly at the instigation of Mr de Forest, the New York School of Philanthropy was organized.   Three years later there were seven such schools in the United States.   Now there are more than thirty and many colleges are giving courses in social work.   The Foundation has made grants to social work schools in Boston, Chicago, and St Louis as well as to the New York School.

The publishing department of the Foundation in 1936 issued a book, *Social Work As a Profession* by Esther Lucille Brown of the Department of Statistics, giving information about "the rapidly expanding profession of social work and the opportuni-

* The Russell Sage Foundation building at Lexington Avenue and 22nd Street is tax-exempt.

ties for training." She is devoted, like most professional social workers, chiefly to "private" rather than "public" agencies. In the 1930 census, she declares, 31,241 persons admitted that they were social or welfare workers, of which 27% were men. Now she estimates that there are at least 40,000. In 1914 the salary below that of supervisors was $860 a year, and the executives received very little more. Now the salary for executives in cities under 25,000 averages $2100 and in cities of half a million or over it runs from $2400 to $12,500. These, of course, are in the private agencies. During the height of the relief spending under the direction of social workers Harry Hopkins and Aubrey Williams higher salaries were frequently paid, for that was the social worker's great opportunity and the profession expanded almost to proportions of a national industry.

In preparation for that time the Russell Sage Foundation had made statistical investigations, invented forms, printed innumerable pamphlets, developed case work systems, and collected in its library complete files of reports, local, federal, state, and institutional relating to social work. Members of the staff had for years been taking the leading part in "conferences," national and international, and in such societies as the American Association of Social Workers, which has "accepted" about 10,000 members, and the American Association of Schools for Social Work, which has "recognized" thirty-one schools. Ralph G. Hurlin, head of the department of statistics, was requisitioned by the New York City Home Relief Bureau to reorganize and direct the statistical work of the Bureau. Another member was borrowed by the FERA in Washington. Techniques developed by Miss Richmond, formerly director of the Charity Organization department, and presented by her in *Social Diagnosis,* the social workers' bible — (whose fifteen editions have been published by the Foundation) — became the accepted method for approaching the relief problem. Case-work methods, evolved by Miss Richmond, were hastily taught to thousands of investigators and supervisors. To aid them in dealing with people who applied for relief they studied a pamphlet published by the Foundation entitled *Interviewing and Casework Recording.* The nation became aware of the "professional" approach to the problems of charitable relief which have been studied for a quarter of a century by the Foundation's staff.

These problems were approached by the method of the "survey" used for the first time in the famous "Pittsburgh Survey" begun with the establishment of the Foundation and carried on over a period of years. In 1930 Allen Eaton of the department of surveys and exhibits, in collaboration with Shelby M. Harrison, now director of the Foundation, published a *Bibliography of Social Surveys* showing how the movement and practice has spread. Since Pittsburgh was "surveyed," 2,775 surveys had been made in this country by private and public agencies up to 1928. Among the surveys made by the Foundation was one of the Southern Highlands and the handicrafts practiced by the people of that region.

Miss Joanna C. Colcord, now in charge of the charity organization department, which receives monthly reports from 44 case work agencies throughout the country, has made a number of surveys and published her findings through the Foundation. She has studied cash relief, community planning in unemployment emergencies, and the problem of setting up a program of work relief. One of her most popular books is *Broken Homes* which describes the attitude of social case workers toward family "maladjustments," their cure and prevention. Shelby M. Harrison in an article in the 1936 *Americana Annual* declared: "The activities of this department (charity organization) during the depression have focused largely on a study of the social effects of unemployment, and on community programs for its relief. During the past two years the department's emphasis has shifted somewhat from local unemployment relief programs to those of the developing Federal and

State emergency relief administrations. During the year just elapsed, field visits were made to 14 States and a considerable number of cities to gather current material on FERA and WPA developments. Ten monthly bulletins giving somewhat extended accounts of new and interesting relief methods and procedures instituted in different states have been prepared and distributed to the several State emergency relief administrations." A history of relief in previous depressions was also prepared.

It is admitted that the staff of the Foundation played an important part in formulating public relief policies. A digest of social work opinion was assembled called *Looking Toward a Public Welfare Plan* and Dr Hertha Kraus' manuscript on "Aiding the Unemployed in 24 Foreign Countries" was edited by the Foundation at the request of the New York State TERA. The staff also contributed to the *Social Work Year Book* (published annually by the Foundation), to the *Annals of the American Academy of Political and Social Science*, to the *Survey* and the *Family*. Miss Colcord, it is reported by Mr Harrison, "gave an institute on Problems of Public Relief Administration in connection with the State Conference of Social Work in Illinois, spoke before a number of regional conferences of social workers, and was called to Washington, D.C., as a member of a group to advise on social work problems with the President's Commission on Economic Security. She also taught several courses at the Summer School, Graduate Division of Social Work, University of Washington, Seattle. The assistant director gave three courses at the New York School of Social Work on Problems of Unemployment Relief Administration and participated in several conferences, among them the University of Chicago Conference on revision of the poor laws; the Delegates Conference of the American Association of Social Workers in Washington; conferences on Economic Security and Welfare Mobilization in Washington; and the Florida Transient Division Conference in Clearwater, Florida. While on the latter mission, he collaborated with a representative of the National Association of Travelers' Aid and Transient Service in making an informal survey of many of the transient camps and shelters in Florida."

That gives a fairly good idea of what professional social workers do. Meanwhile Miss Mary Van Kleek, one of the most popular as well as one of the most radical of social workers, has been making surveys, speeches, writing books and articles, and directing the department of industrial studies since it outgrew the original studies in women's work. After a fifteen year study of the coal mines, she recommended in 1934 a socialization of the mines as the only solution of a problem which she considers one of the inherent evils of the capitalist system. Since then she has centered her attention on industrial relations "particularly in relation to workers' organization to management." "Field work," declares Mr Harrison, "has been done in the coal, steel, automobile, tire, hosiery, and textile industries with some attention to occupations of longshoremen and seamen on the Pacific Coast." Six books of Miss Van Kleek's have been published by the Foundation ; the most recent, *Miners and Management*, is a record of what happened when the miners' union and the Rocky Mountain Fuel Company of Colorado entered into an agreement which not only provided for collective bargaining but undertook to stabilize employment, production, and markets through cooperative endeavor.

One of the most discussed surveys made by the Foundation is the New York Regional Plan for what has been called "The City Livable." "The Foundation took up this activity," Mr de Forest wrote in the *Survey*, November 1929, "with much hesitation. But it had among its trustees men who were singularly fit to make a regional plan. Hardly had this enterprise been fairly started when all of them were taken away by death." New leaders were found, however, and at the expenditure of a million dollars the plan was completed. It now serves as a basis for discussion in all plans proposed for the city of New York and its future. In 1935 the Foundation published an *Outline of Town and City Planning* by Thomas Adams, a history of the movement and an analysis of the influence, aims, forces and methods of modern city planning. It has a foreword by Franklin D. Roosevelt.

Thus the Foundation is not only active in research but also in publishing and in publicity. The public is not told about the Foundation, but it is told repeatedly through its department of social work interpretation about the importance of social work. Those familiar with social workers might suppose that this department might translate the jargon of social workers into every-day English. Instead, the public is told about the necessity for social work, (and incidentally for more social workers), and efforts are made to teach social workers how to get publicity for themselves and their causes. This department is an outgrowth of a department of exhibits which presented in graphic form, by charts and show window exhibitions, facts about social problems uncovered by the research department. If it is discovered that a certain city is menaced by typhoid, for example, and the authorities seem unwilling to do anything, a show window is prepared which tells the citizens in a vivid demonstration the danger of typhoid infection. Mrs Mary Swain Routzahn, who studied at the New York School of Social Work and who now gives courses there, has written a number of books and pamphlets telling social workers how to get publicity. She is particularly interested in the relation of public understanding to financial support and to what is called "social action." Her department sponsors an organization known as "The Social Work Publicity Council" which encourages volunteers to help promote and "interpret" social work and which issued bulletins on how to write the annual report, and *Social Work at the Microphone*. In collaboration with her husband Mrs Routzahn prepared a book on the *A B C of Exhibit Planning* which tells the what, why, and how of exhibits, including how to arrange for Baby Week and how to plan the budget.

It is ironical that a part of the income of the fortune which Russell Sage accumulated by usury should be spent in a campaign against small loan sharks. This is one of the oldest and most aggressive of the Foundation's activities, and has resulted in the enactment of regulatory legislation. State officers charged with the administration of these laws have been brought together for annual conferences with the director of the Remedial Loan department serving as secretary.

Unlike the Carnegie and the Rockefeller foundations, the Russell Sage publishes no annual reports, so it is not known from what sources or securities its income of about $650,000 a year is derived or how it is spent. In 1934 it reported to the Twentieth Century Fund assets of $15,457,575. It may be that the publishing department could show a profit, for many of its books and pamphlets have gone into several printings.

Although from the beginning it has been a part of its program to urge an elimination of the worst features of tenement house congestion, the suggestions made by many advisors at the beginning that a part of its funds be invested in model tenements were ignored. Instead, 142 acres were purchased at Forest Hills, Long Island, and a model suburban development for the well-to-do was inaugurated where homes costing from $8,000 to $25,000 were built, sold, or rented. "The cost of the land and character of the surroundings preclude provision for the day laborer," Mr de Forest declared at the time. This development, of which William E. Harmon, expert real estate promoter was in charge, was intended to show how such a project should be planned. It was also intended to make money for the Foundation, which it did, and stock in the Sage Foundation Homes Company was finally sold to the residents. It is probable that the Foundation has a financial interest in apartments in Sunnyside, Queens, for in 1931, when evictions were taking place, the residents of Sunnyside Gardens planned to present the Foundation with a coffin as a token of their gratitude for the foreclosures. Lawson Purdy, lawyer and professional social worker, president of the Foundation, was also chairman of the Sunnyside Bondholders Protective Committee.

In order to write a history of the Foundation, John M. Glenn, who was president for a quarter of a century, retired in 1931, although he still remains a trustee both of the Foundation and the New York School of Social Work. Robert W. de Forest died the same year. Their places were taken by Shelby M. Harrison, who teaches at the New York School of Social Work, and Lawson Purdy. The *Survey* magazine summed up the work of Mr Glenn editorially : "Those twenty-five years have been years in which social work as a profession has been coming into stature, when the social survey began and grew, when social research claimed a place alongside research in the physical sciences, when city planning broke over into regional planning, when tenement house reform blossomed into garden cities, when the *Survey* graduated as a house organ and became a magazine. In all these the Sage Foundation has taken a vigorous part. Though the total capital is no more than the annual income of some foundations it has made an affirmative impression on American life."

As we watch the effect and the influence of professional social workers on American government and politics, as their number and their power grows, we can have no doubt about the "affirmative" impression or the part that this relatively small Foundation has played in creating a new and extremely vocal profession.

CHAPTER VI

DOLLARS ADVANCE SCIENCE

THE ROLE OF THE FOUNDATIONS IN SCIENTIFIC PROGRESS

It is curious how little attention has been given to the economic bases of scientific advancement. Much has been spoken and written about the nobility and the self-sacrifice of the men and women who have devoted their lives to science, and no tribute can exaggerate the idealism of thousands of men and women, known and unknown, who have surrendered everything to the conquest of knowledge. Many have starved, many have lost health and limbs ; many have supported themselves at menial and stultifying tasks that they might carry on their research. In the popular mind scientists are fanatics who persist in their experiments against overwhelming odds. In a sense this must be true. Yet, as Julian Huxley has pointed out, scientists must also live. They must eat, and in an economic order such as ours they must earn money. Either they must have gainful employment, or they must be supported so they can do the work that is their mission.

Scientists in the past have lived in all the variety of ways by which men subsist : they have worked at meager salaries, they have held governmental or university positions, they have been supported by relatives, lived on inheritances, begged from friends. A few have been endowed. In the nineteenth century, the century of greatest scientific advancement the world has ever known, they got along in all these ways, and economically their lot was usually far from easy. The microbe hunters and hunger fighters described by Paul de Kruif existed, for the most part, on small university or governmental salaries. Only recently have such men had the good fortune to be supported by foundations and endowments. With the advent of large scale philanthropy, however, and the interest of Mr Rockefeller and Mr Carnegie in scientific research, a new element entered what might be called the economic bases for scientific advancement. Formerly the scientists worked in isolation, but with continued progress, coordination and cooperation were necessary. The early scientists seldom needed large, expensive laboratories and a host of research assistants. With the increase of knowledge, the cost of further and continued research increased. The philanthropists stepped in at a time when they were most needed. Before the foundations began making grants, providing laboratories, building observatories, endowing exploration and research, the leading men of science got along as best they knew how.

Now, however, the recognized scientists, if they have no other source of income, are usually supported by industry, by government, or directly or indirectly by the big philanthropic foundations.* Science supported by industry is applied science, done for the sake of profits, and only incidentally for the advancement of knowledge.† Science supported by government is usually in the interests of war or autarchy, and only incidentally in the interest of humanity.‡ Upon the foundations, therefore, falls the chief responsibility for the promotion of pure research for humanitarian ends. Their contribution is but a fraction of the total amount spent on research, yet this fraction is of tremendous importance. Looking at the matter from another point of view, a revolutionary centralization may be discerned. The support of scientific progress may be traced

* Of course, a certain amount of research is done in the state universities, supported by appropriations by state legislatures, and an undeterminable amount by unknown and unrecognized researchers, supported God knows how.

† Dr Irving Langmuir has, it is said, almost a free hand at the General Electric Laboratories and some of the scientists at the Bell Telephone Laboratories may also be said to be working on "pure science." But even these researches may not be entirely unrelated to "applied" science.

‡ The United States Public Health Service and the U. S. Bureau of Standards are, of course, exceptions.

to a single source : the profits of private industry. Business profits pay for industrial research, taxes on those profits pay for governmental research, and the hoarding of the profits create fortunes which endow, through universities or foundations, pure research.

Considered in that sense, it may be said that in the nineteenth century science was struggling economically, but it was free. It had many diverse sources of support. In the twentieth century it is dependent upon the profits of the economic system. In applied science the ends and purposes are chosen by dictators or business men, and this constitutes the bulk of scientific research today. More is spent on one battleship than any single government spends on scientific research in one year. The Radio Corporation of America spends more on research than all the philanthropic foundations put together. In "pure" science, supported by the foundations, it cannot be shown that those in charge of philanthropic funds have tried to direct or control research, or that they have used the funds for a malignant influence upon scientific work. Frequently philanthropists choose the disease to be attacked : hookworm or yellow fever. But once the problem has been selected, the scientists are provided with the necessary equipment. Today the scientists who are supported by the big foundations are generally free to choose their own objectives. The grants made to them set them free, in most cases, to work unhampered, with all the means at their disposal. Some grants are made for only a brief period, from year to year ; sometimes there may be an unspoken insistence on results. Those are factors inherent in a system of support based upon private philanthropy. Greater achievements might be realized if such agencies as the United States Public Health Service were expanded and large funds appropriated to it for research purposes.*

* It must be conceded at once that there is another side to the picture given here. Science, of course, does not depend entirely upon well-endowed laboratories for its progress. New discoveries are not necessarily restricted to those researchers supported by foundations. The isolated physician, work-

Certainly the army of science might well be larger. More is spent on cosmetics than on scientific research. Herbert Hoover declared : "There is no price the world could not afford to pay these men. Our whole banking community does not do the public service in a year that Faraday's discoveries do for us daily. . . The wealth of this country has multiplied far faster than the funds we have given for pure scientific purposes. And the funds administered in the nation today for it are but a triviality compared to the vast resources a single discovery puts in our hands." The money to pay those working in the pure sciences comes from a comparatively small group of large funds. The income of these funds is derived from investments in large scale American industry. The advancement of science has accumulated an ever-increasing momentum. It is to the interest of the human race that this acceleration be not retarded. In the realm of pure science, and particularly in the field of medical research, it is important that the work go on unhindered. Yet it is seldom noted that this accelerated momentum is tied up with, and dependent upon the profitable operation of the economic system. Splendid as it is that industry should finance the advancement of science, what becomes of the onward march of scientific progress if anything should happen to the system ? It is a responsibility not to be considered lightly.

Foremost among the contributions to the well-being of mankind throughout the world is the work of the Rockefeller International Health division in combating yellow fever. Six million dollars has been spent on this campaign alone since 1915. Dr Hideyo Noguchi and four others died in that war. The Rockefeller scientists are still working at frontiers where the

ing out his own ideas in his spare time may make greater medical discoveries than were ever achieved by the richest modern laboratory. It is a matter of chance, just as it was a pure gamble which led the Carnegie Corporation to make the grant which led to the discovery of insulin. Banting might have done it without the grant. But equipped and supported as they are it is reasonable to suppose that well-endowed institutions have, generally speaking, a better chance to establish and verify important results than have the poor, lone unrecognized experimenter.

danger is greatest. In vast areas in South America and Africa where the disease is endemic they are fighting for a cause worth dying for. When it is finally eradicated mankind will have the Rockefeller Foundation to thank for a major part in completing the work of Dr Walter Reed.

Four hundred thousand people in the United States died in 1918 of influenza and twenty million more were infected. No serum, no vaccine, no specific drug was available. The following year Dr P. K. Olitsky of the Rockefeller Institute for Medical Research succeeded in establishing that the disease is due to a filter-passing virus, that is, an invisible particle so tiny that it can pass through the pores of the finest porcelain filter. In 1935 the virus was isolated in this country from material sent by the Rockefeller International Health Division field force from Puerto Rico. Intensive study of it is now being made in the laboratories of the Institute.

Support given to science by the Rockefeller philanthropies is international in scope. In three places in the United States, in Jamaica, and in Austria tuberculosis work has been aided. Prevalence and distribution of the disease are being studied in Lee County, Alabama. In its effort to develop an effective program for tuberculosis control tuberculin tests are being applied to population groups, studies are made of certain districts in New York, and investigations made of the value of control procedures now in practice. In Eisenstadt, Austria, the International Health Division cooperated with the local health department not only in tuberculosis work but also in the immunization against diphtheria. Research in diphtheria has been supported in Peiping, China. Yaws is being combated in Jamaica, where a method has been found for treating and controlling this disease, which is usually contracted in early childhood and cripples or disfigures its victims for life.

Twelve million people in Egypt are afflicted by a blood disease for which snails are responsible. Rockefeller scientists are at work on this problem as well as upon the hookworm, which the Rockefeller Sanitary Commission fought successfully in the South, the first big job of the Rockefeller fund. Today it is turning its attention to mental diseases, since this is one of the fields about which the medical profession knows least. In 1935 $2,733,050 was appropriated on the medical sciences by the Foundation, of which $1,159,450 was for projects in psychiatry. Training in psychoanalysis and child psychology was supported in several colleges. The National Hospital, London, received a grant of $600,000 for building and endowment for research. Maudsley Hospital, London, was also aided and studies at the Galton Laboratory, University of London, were helped. The list of grants in the medical sciences is pages long in the annual reports of the Foundation.

"Some of the most dramatic developments which have come from experimental biology in the last quarter century," declares Raymond B. Fosdick, president of the Foundation, "are those tending to show the importance in terms of human welfare and behavior, of substances so minute in quantity that only the most exact and delicate techniques of science are able to identify and measure them." These genes, the "cargo ships of heredity," carry the whole load of inheritance from one generation to the next. "Our bodily structure, the color of our eyes, our immunity to disease — all except that which we gain from environment — were potential or inherent in the genes of our two parents. It has recently been estimated that if all the human sperm cells which are to be responsible for the two billion individuals who will constitute the next generation were gathered together they would occupy the space of half an aspirin tablet. If, of the corresponding egg cells, only the nuclei, which carry the stuff of life, be taken, they too would occupy the same space." In other words, "the original and essential substance for the development of two billion individuals could be contained in a capsule no larger than an aspirin tablet."

Dollars from the Foundation are going into universities and medical schools, hospitals and research laboratories engaged in research upon these little things whose importance is out of all proportion to their size. Investigations are also being financed into the hormones, powerful drugs in minute amounts in the ductless glands. In the normal human being there is concentrated in his thyroid gland about as much iodine as could be picked up on the tip of a penknife. Yet that small amount spells the difference between health of mind and cretinism. During 1936 the Foundation made 27 grants to aid studies of the ductless glands. "In this whole area of the infinitesimal, experimental biology is faced with the necessity of doing quantitive analyses of uncommon delicacy and accuracy," Mr Fosdick remarks. "The microscope and ordinary chemical analyses are not enough. Micromanipulators enable operations to be performed within a single cell. Protoplasm is being subjected to the terrific forces of the ultra-centrifuge in order that information may be obtained as to its molecular structure ; the penetrating eye of the spectroscope is being turned from the stars to the blood stream ; even the skill developed in radio engineering is employed when science needs to raise infinitely weak energies to the perceptible level."

In addition to the work of the Foundation, the Rockefeller General Education Board, a separate institution, has appropriated a total of $84,000,000 to medical schools. For the natural sciences the Foundation spent $2,179,938 in 1935. A contribution of $1,000,000 was made to the Woods Hole Oceanographic Institution ; $54,000 was appropriated for the University of Copenhagen ; $12,500 for the researches of Professor H. C. Urey in "heavy hydrogen" at Columbia University ; $75,000 for the National Research Council for its committee's study of the effects of radiation on human organisms. Other important researches aided were those on biological tissues at the University of Leeds by Professor W. T. Astbury, the work of Dr Dorothy Wrinch at the University of Oxford in mathematical physics, and Professor Svedberg's work at the University of Uppsala, Sweden, on the physical-chemical properties of proteins and other heavy molecules.

Nothing illustrates the importance that the foundations play in the advance of science better than the support they give to the National Research Council. In May, 1918, it was established, with the help of the Engineering Foundation, to coordinate the scientific work being carried on in this country. By executive order, Woodrow Wilson had it set up as a part of the National Academy of Sciences for the development of research leadership. The Rockefeller Foundation pledged funds for fellowships, and the Carnegie Corporation appropriated $5,-000,000, partly for a building and the remainder for endowment. It has also made additional annual grants. The General Education Board in 1921 pledged $50,000 a year for fellowships, the Commonwealth Fund gave the Council $2000 a month for six months for running expenses, the Chemical Foundation made a $7500 grant for chemical research, and the American Telephone and Telegraph Company made a contribution for general expenses. Comparatively little came from the government. An important function of the Council is to support post-doctorate fellowships. The outstanding men in science in the United States have held these fellowships, and the funds to finance this work have come chiefly from the Rockefeller and the Carnegie foundations. This is something that the government might do well to support, yet the responsibility for this work, which cannot be underestimated, has fallen on the philanthropic foundations. During 1937, 613 fellows were supported by the Rockefeller Foundation at a total cost of $740,000. The National Research Council was responsible for 76 of these. Such grants may be small in amount but the results accomplished by the recipients are often of far-reaching importance.

In the advance guard of medical research is the Rockefeller Institute, an entirely separate organization, independent of the

Rockefeller Foundation. Up to the time of his death John D. Sr gave it a total of $59,931,891. Founded in 1901 its object was announced to be "to conduct, assist, and encourage investigation in the sciences and arts of hygiene, medicine and surgery, and allied subjects, in the nature and cause of disease and the methods of its prevention and treatment and to make knowledge relating to these various subjects available for the protection of the health of the public and the improved treatment of disease and injury. It shall be within the purposes of said corporation to use any means to those ends which from time to time shall seem to it expedient, including research, publication, education, and the establishment and maintenance of charitable or benevolent activities, agencies, or institutions already established or which may be hereafter established."

It began by making grants to scientifically trained men engaged in medical research. In 1902 it decided to build a research laboratory. A board of scientific directors was established responsible for the appointment of the staff and the general policies of the investigations. Direction was entrusted to a Scientific Director who was himself an investigator. Each researcher was accorded complete freedom. The original staff consisted of Simon Flexner, pathologist and director ; Hideyo Noguchi, Eugene L. Opie, and J. E. Sweet, pathologists ; Samuel J. Meltzer, physiologist and pharmacologist ; and P. A. Levene, biological chemist. Soon after opening the laboratory in 1906, need was seen for a hospital attached to it where disease in man could be investigated under as favorable conditions as possible. This was ready in 1910, next to the laboratory at the East River and 66th Street, New York City.

The number of diseases studied at any one time has to be limited and only patients suffering from one of the diseases under investigation can be accepted. The staff of the hospital divides its time equally between observational and experimental studies. No charge is made to the patients accepted.

Bulletins are issued to the medical profession giving notice of the subjects chosen. During 1936-37 the diseases being investigated were : (1) blood diseases, such as pernicious anemia, (2) nephritis, in initial, acute stages ; arterio-sclerotic nephritis in adults and young children, (3) heart disease, advanced heart failure, (4) rheumatic fever and acute sore throat, (5) chicken-pox, measles, and encephalitis following measles, whooping cough or the common cold, (6) acute respiratory diseases such as acute lobar pneumonia. An oxygen chamber is available and an ambulance will be sent if necessary.

Until 1914 the Institute was located wholly in New York City, but in that year a department in animal pathology was created, with Theobald Smith as director, about three miles from Princeton, N. J., where comparative aspects of the pathology of disease in various animal species, especially in the domestic animals, could be studied. In order to bring to light such processes as are clear in animals but obscure or difficult of access in human beings the work was extended in 1931 to include a laboratory in plant pathology. Meanwhile, in New York, departments of chemistry, experimental surgery, pathology, bacteriology, physiology and biophysics were established.

The pathology and bacteriology laboratory was first to open in 1904, under the direction of Dr Simon Flexner. Studies were made chiefly on problems relating to infectious and epidemic diseases particularly prevalent between 1904 and 1935. Dr Flexner resigned in May, 1935 and Dr Herbert Spencer Gasser, professor of physiology at the Cornell School of Medicine, was appointed. Until then pathology had been the main interest of the Institute and dominated medical research throughout the world. With the appointment of Dr Gasser, a change of policy occurred, so now the emphasis is shifted from what causes diseases to how the body works. Dr Gasser and his associates, in concentrating upon the functions of the body, are investigating with electrophysiological methods the properties of mammalian nerves and the nature of conduction across synapses in the central nervous system.

The Institute absolves its staff from the necessity, as in medical schools, of devoting time and energy to formal teaching or to the consideration of subjects chosen for reasons other than because of their promise for the advancement of science. Thus fundamental problems can be attacked, and research may be continued under favorable conditions and with adequate support for an indefinite period, unhurried, unhindered. Appointments to the scientific staff are made by the board of scientific directors. The following grades have been fixed : Member of the Institute, Associate Member, Associate, Assistant, and Fellow. Appointments of Members are made without limit of time ; others are appointed for a definite term of years. Full time must be given to the work, permitting no gainful occupation outside the organization. A few volunteer workers, usually persons holding fellowships from abroad, are permitted to work in the laboratories under the direction of one of the staff. All discoveries and inventions made by any person while receiving compensation from the Institute or using its facilities, become the property of the Institute to be placed by it at the service of humanity in accordance with its purposes.

Not least in importance among its activities, the Institute disseminates reports of the investigations through the *Journal of Experimental Medicine*, a monthly edited by Simon Flexner, Peyton Rous, and Herbert S. Gasser, the *Journal of General Physiology*, issued bimonthly, founded by Jacques Loeb, edited by W. J. Crozier of Harvard, John H. Northrup and W. J. Osterhout of the Institute. Studies and monographs are published from time to time ; 97 volumes of studies and 23 monographs have so far appeared.

Many tissues of which the body is composed are potentially immortal. Nobel Prize winner Alexis Carrel has found it possible in his laboratory to cultivate in nutritive fluids outside the body small pieces taken from living animals. A piece of connective tissue, taken from a chick before hatching, has been kept alive longer than the full normal life of the hen and, most astonishing, the rate of growth and multiplication of the cells has not decreased. Julian Huxley declares that the unchecked multiplication of any sort of cell, if the right conditions are provided, can continue indefinitely. To further these investigations Charles A. Lindbergh constructed what has been called the "Lindbergh pump" : artificial heart and lungs, which keep tissues and whole organs alive. This invention has since been demonstrated to the leading scientists of Europe at Copenhagen.

Equally as far reaching in its influence and as important in the advancement of science is the work of the Carnegie Institution in Washington. Founded by Andrew Carnegie in 1902 with U.S. Steel bonds worth $10,000,000, it received $10,000,000 more in 1907, $10,000,000 in 1911, and additional amounts have been given it by the Carnegie Corporation of New York. At first it supported a wide range of projects ; now the policy is to concentrate on major projects the solution of which require long periods. It attempts to advance research in fields not normally covered by the work of other agencies. Sometimes it has given aid as an initiating and supervising agent on work done under other auspices. Yearbooks describing its work and other publications issued number more than 665 volumes. Many of these are scientific reports designed to help those actively engaged in research. News releases are sent to newspapers and schools, exhibitions are held illustrating its work, and every year in Washington the Elihu Root Lectures given under its auspices bring leading scientists to discuss the relation of science and research to current thought.

The work is separated into eight divisions : animal biology, historical research, plant biology, geophysical laboratory, seismological research, meridian astrometry, Mount Wilson observatory, and terrestrial magnetism. The first is operated in conjunction with Johns Hopkins in Baltimore. In 1913 a grant was made to Professor Franklin P. Mall for research on the human embryo. Since his death in 1917 George L. Street has been in charge of a permanent staff in the Hunterian Laboratory of the Johns Hopkins Medical School. More than 12,000 human embryos have been collected. Light has been thrown on anatomical variations and racial differences heretofore unknown. Knowledge previously fragmentary is now complete enough to permit scientific study. A colony of macaque monkeys has been installed so that investigations can be pursued in a primate form approximating man as closely as feasible in an experimental animal.

Research in biology was one of the first subjects to get consideration from the Institution. A tract of land of about nine acres at Cold Spring Harbor was leased and a laboratory opened there June 11, 1904. In 1910 Mrs E. H. Harriman established the Eugenics Record Office there, purchased a farm of about eighty acres, and in 1918 transferred it with buildings and endowment of $300,000 to the Carnegie Institution. Investigation of the laws of inheritance in plants, animals, and man comprise the work carried on in genetics, which includes also studies in variation in organisms, of the physiology of reproduction, growth, and development, of the nature of sex in general, and the factors in organic development.

The Eugenics Record Office is directed by H. H. Laughlin who is trying to aid in building a constructive science out of the uncoordinated data on human heredity and those factors which tend to improve or impair the racial qualities of future generations. Field workers are trained to gather data and attempts are made to maintain a scientific staff for interpreting it, developing standards of measurement, and discovering rules by which Nature transmits qualities from one generation to the next. Special studies have been made of the "Hill Folk" of Massachusetts, the "Nam" and "Jukes" families of New York and similar family groups.

Following the researches of Professor W. O. Atwater of

Wesleyan University of Middletown, Connecticut, in nutrition and dietetics, the Nutrition Laboratory was established in Boston in 1908. One of the most famous Laboratories built by the Carnegie Institution is that at Tortugas, Loggerhead Key, Florida, in 1904. Here problems of the tropical ocean and its life are studied under conditions permitting many experiments which could be carried out elsewhere only with great difficulty. Archaeology has been fostered also through grants for excavations in Turkestan, Rome and Yucatan. A number of institutions have collaborated in the work in Mexico where studies in the ancient Maya civilization has led to further excavations in Guatemala.

The Rockefeller Foundation does not support directly any archaeological work, but it does contribute indirectly to excavations in Egypt through grants to the Oriental Institute of the University of Chicago. During the last ten years Rockefeller agencies have contributed $10,000,000 to this institution. Its budget of half a million dollars a year supports as many as a dozen expeditions at a time. One of the most significant is that at Megiddo or Armageddon, in the center of the great fertile crescent running northwards from the Nile across Babylonia to the Persian Gulf. This great mound contains a series of civilizations going back to prehistoric times.

The Carnegie Institution has from the beginning been interested in American historical research and it has prepared many publications, issued reports on source materials, prepared guides to important collections and foreign archives, explored and catalogued important material here and abroad. Forty-three volumes have been published and studies in the post-conquest history of Yucatan have been started. In 1929 a section was founded to facilitate researches upon the history and philosophy of science, under the direction of Dr George Sarton of Harvard.

The process of photosynthesis, by means of which green plants utilize solar energy, is a phenomenon upon which virtu-

ally all life depends.   For years it has been studied by scientists
supported by the Institution.   Three experimental gardens in
California have thrown light on the history of plant life and its
differentiation into its present complexity.   A significant series
of changes in the vegetation of western America during later
geologic time have been indicated by studies in palaeobotany.
Forests of the earliest epochs were characterized by trees whose
modern equivalents live in Mexico and Central America today,
and the climate of western America may be supposed to have
been much warmer and more humid at that time than at
present.   Gradual cooling resulted in the southward restriction of this forest, which was followed by the redwood forest.
Researches show that redwoods once grew on St Lawrence
Island in the Bering Sea, and that a former land connection between North America and Asia made migration of land plants
and animals possible.

The methods and equipment of modern quantitative chemistry and physics can now be brought to bear through the geophysical laboratory upon a study of rocks.   Through grants
to the U. S. Geological Survey and the Institution's laboratory
in Washington studies have been made which have changed
geology from a descriptive to an exact science.   Investigations
have been made of the quantity of heat in mineral reactions.
Active volcanos have been approached and collections made of
their gases.   During the war this laboratory took charge of the
development and manufacture of the optical glass for range-
finders, periscopes, and other instruments of precision.

Under Dr Benjamin Boss the department of meridian astrometry is attempting to determine the positions and motions of
more than twenty-five thousand stars.   This will provide data
for studies on the systematic motions of the stars and a more
accurate determination of the sun's motion in space.   The
work is divided between the Dudley Observatory in Albany,
N. Y., and the southern station at St Luis, Argentina.

Most publicized of the Institution's observatories is that at

Mount Wilson, California, established after careful tests of atmospheric conditions had been made in California, Arizona and Australia.   Here the structure of the universe and the evolution of celestial bodies are observed under the best possible conditions.   Closely related studies, interpreting one another, all directed to a common objective, are pursued.   The constitution of matter is being investigated here in cooperation with the Norman Bridge Physical Laboratory and the Gates Chemical Laboratory of the California Institute of Technology.   Special attention has been given to the invention and use of new instruments, such as Michelson's interferometer, which measures the diameter of stars.   Much new knowledge has been gathered through the use of the giant 100-inch telescope, but with the help of the Rockefeller Foundation a new, 200-inch reflector telescope is being installed, to be ready in 1940.   This is costing $6,000,000 and will permit studies of nebulae twelve hundred million light years away.   It is twenty-two feet in diameter and sixty feet long.

The surface of the earth and the oceans, as well as the atmosphere, has been included in a survey by the department of terrestrial magnetism on the character of the magnetic field and the significance of continuous changes.   Two hundred magnetic exploratory expeditions have been sent out to remote and little explored regions.   Data were obtained from 6000 stations and about 700 were revisited.   The *Carnegie*, specially designed for magnetic work in all oceans, was the third such ship employed.   Observatories were established at Waterloo, Western Australia, and at Huancayo, Peru.   Stations in Alaska, Canada, and Cape Town contributed information, while experimental work in terrestrial electricity was conducted at the main laboratory in Washington.

In addition to all these departments relations are maintained with a large number of research associates, comprising many of the leading scientists of the day, some allied with the Institution temporarily and some working independently under special grants.   Significant among these is the work of T. H. Morgan of the California Institute of Technology in experimental evolution.   Investigations of H. B. Vickery of the Connecticut Agricultural Experiment Station and L. B. Mendel of Yale University on vegetable proteins are yielding important results. Special grants were made to R. A. Millikan and A. A. Noyes for investigations on the constitution of matter in close association with the Mount Wilson Observatory.   The cooperative studies there by the late A. A. Michelson with H. N. Russell of Princeton, Joel Stebbins of Wisconsin, and J. H. Jeans of London, brought results of extraordinary importance relative to the organization of the stellar universe.   The remeasurement of the velocity of light by A. A. Michelson and the work of R. A. Millikan and A. H. Compton on the penetrating radiation of cosmic rays were also of the utmost importance.

It would take many volumes to survey all the work of the Carnegie Institution alone and many more to record the researches supported by the Rockefeller philanthropies.   No attempt can be made here to review all the scientific work done in the world today.   Some of it, of course, is independent of any of these research agencies.   Much more is carried on in the laboratories of universities supported by endowments furnished by American foundations.   As mentioned before, work in applied science is usually supported by governments engaged in war preparations or by corporations interested in profits. Several industrial establishments spend more on research than all the foundations put together.   Julian Huxley estimates that six million pounds are spent in Great Britain annually on all kinds of research and more than $40,000,000 in the United States.   Many corporations are unwilling to reveal the amounts of such expenditures.   It is impossible to discover how many discoveries may have been made and suppressed because their use might injure an established investment.

Even though the contribution of the foundations to scientific research is a fraction of the total spent upon all research, the point remains the same ; scientific advancement is dependent upon the profitable operation of the present economic system, since the bulk of the funds come from investments in that system. Through such institutions as the Rockefeller Institute and the Carnegie Institution, the great army of science is able to advance upon greater and more important objectives. Thus we have a situation in which the advancement of science becomes dependent upon the financial stability of the American economic structure. Tax these foundations out of existence, or ruin them financially through a blundering monetary policy, and the whole edifice, the whole forward movement of science throughout the world would be seriously endangered. The tremendous centralization of economic support effected in this century places upon relatively few hands the decision for the continuance of scientific progress. It is a noble undertaking for American industry to assume, but considering the instability of the capitalist system it is also a hazardous responsibility.

A foundation of a different type is the Smithsonian Institution, whose existence and perpetuity are guaranteed by the United States government. It is an "establishment" created by an act of Congress which owes its origin to the bequest of James Smithson, an English scientific man, who left his entire estate to the United States of America "to found at Washington, under the name of the Smithsonian Institution, an establishment for the increase and diffusion of knowledge among men." After ten years of Congressional debate, turning partly on the question whether the government ought to accept such a bequest at all and thus put itself in the unprecedented position of the guardian of a ward, Congress accepted the trust and created by enactment an "establishment" consisting of the President of the United States, the Vice President, the Chief Justice, and the members of the President's Cabinet. It also has a secretary, the executive officer of the Institution, who is the keeper of the National Museum. Smithson's money, which amounted to more than half a million dollars, and later to three quarters of a million, a great fortune in 1846, was lent to the United States Treasury, and the government agreed to pay perpetually 6% interest on it.

By this act of Congress the Smithsonian is governed by a Board of Regents, composed of the Vice President and Chief Justice of the United States, three regents appointed by the president of the Senate, three by the Speaker of the House, and six selected by Congress, two of whom must be residents of the District of Columbia and the other four from different states, no two from the same state.

The Institution's work consisted in the beginning chiefly of the publication of original memoirs containing actual contributions to knowledge and their free distribution to important libraries throughout the world. It gave popular lectures in Washington, published and distributed them to libraries and individuals. Soon it was stimulating scientific work by providing apparatus and grants of money to worthy investigators cooperating with governmental departments. The present Weather Bureau owes its inception to the Smithsonian ; the beginning of cooperation in library work was at the Institution. Experiments in fog signaling, in the acoustics and ventilation of public buildings were made, and for years it was virtually the only representative of scientific work directly or indirectly connected with the government. Its influence upon the character of scientific work was considerable, since in those days the avenues for publishing were few and the funds for the purpose slender.

After the death of Joseph Henry, the first secretary of the Institution in 1878, Spencer Fullerton Baird took charge. Since 1850 he had been working for it, developing the National Museum. An indefatigable student of the collections, he trained a school of young men and was instrumental in organizing a system of international exchange of publications. He was a leader in the organization of the U. S. Fish Commission. Methods which he invented for fish culture, and the studies of natural history of our water inaugurated by him were epoch-making. It was he who originated the marine biological station at Woods Hole, Mass., modeled on the famous station at Naples. Following him was Samuel Pierpont Langley, pioneer in the new astronomy, inventor of the bolometer, an extraordinarily sensitive electrical thermometer which advanced the science of astrophysics. He applied it to the study of the energy of the sun, and the radiation of the moon. He rescued aviation from ridicule and in 1896 conducted flights of nearly a mile. His interest in the preservation of rapidly disappearing forms of the larger animals in the United States led to the establishment of the National Zoological Park.

His successor, Dr Charles W. Walcott, a researcher in the earliest forms of animal life, has had an important influence on the development of forestry and reclamation. He was the moving spirit in the establishment of the Carnegie Institution and under his administration the National Gallery of Art and the Freer Gallery were opened as branches of the Smithsonian. Private individuals of wealth have become interested in its work and provided endowment funds so it could expand.

A bureau of American Ethnology was organized in 1879 to study Indian tribes. The astrophysical observatory is making a general study of the reasons for the habitability of the world. The variability of the sun was discovered in 1903 through its work. The Institution and its staff have participated in the work of numerous expeditions so that archaeology, astronomy, botany, ethnology, geology, zoology, paleontology, and other sciences have benefited.

As a foundation it is small in financial resources but its work is of far-reaching importance and it has demonstrated that politics need play no part in guiding the direction of scientific research.

Faith in its work has been attested by a large number of endowment gifts made to it, most of them restricted to specific

use. The total endowment is now only $1,106,803. The
Freer endowment is separate, and its funds, used to support the
gallery, are administered by the Institution, but are still invested in the original securities left by Mr Freer. Appropriations are made by Congress, amounting in 1935 to $1,132,073,
chiefly for maintenance and the preservation of the National
Museum. John A. Roebling provided funds for the continued
operation of the Mount St Katherine Observatory in Egypt.
The PWA allotted $680,000 for the erection of much-needed
buildings at the National Zoological Park. Field work, greatly
limited by lack of funds, has been carried on through the generosity of outside individuals and the assistance of the PWA.

Thus it may be seen that important scientific work can be
done under governmental auspices by a foundation which is a
ward of the government. The Carnegie Institution and the
Rockefeller Institute are semi-public institutions. A scientist,
Dr Vannevar Bush, is president of the Carnegie Institution,
but the financial strings are held by such trustees as W. Cam-
eron Forbes, Walter S. Gifford, Homer L. Ferguson, and Frederic A. Delano. Another eminent scientist, Dr Herbert S.
Gasser, is director of the Rockefeller Institute, but the board of
trustees is headed by Raymond B. Fosdick, and includes John
D. Jr and John D. 3rd. The work and the scope of these
foundations are so definitely pitched in the direction of human
betterment that they cannot do other than work on the theory
that they are indeed public institutions. Their direction, however, is in the hands of individuals appointed by those who provide the funds and their income is from investments in private
corporations, usually those in which their trustees are directors.
The Smithsonian, however, is a governmental and public institution, responsible to the government and ultimately to the
people of the United States, dedicated forever to scientific advancement, whose directors are chosen by the government and,
most important, whose funds are protected and guaranteed by
the government. Herbert Hoover paid it tribute by saying,

"The Smithsonian has been peculiarly the architect of scientific investigation in this country." Andrew Carnegie wanted to create the Carnegie Institution along the same lines, and Theodore Roosevelt, then President, was ready to recommend this in a special message to Congress. However, Nicholas Murray Butler was unfortunately consulted. He sent for Elihu Root and together they spiked the scheme by winning Mr Carnegie and Roosevelt to their view.*

Nobody can underestimate, of course, the work of the Carnegie and Rockefeller institutions, but for that very reason, because the importance of their work cannot be underestimated, it is all the more vital to point out the difference in the economic bases between them and the Smithsonian. Someday it may be seen that the Smithsonian is more enduring, built on firmer ground. To many it seems a preferable means of carrying on scientific work on which the advancement and happiness of the human race depends. Distrust of everything remotely connected with the government will probably incline wealthy donors to set up their own foundations, perpetuating their names, and thus withhold possible private contributions to the Smithsonian.

As long as capitalism lasts the work of the private foundations will be a magnificent justification for capitalism and a noble tribute to its willingness to further scientific progress.† Yet we still have a right to complain that its contributions are not greater. They are negligible in the field of pure science compared to the sums it spends on applied science. Apologists

---

* Revealed by Dr Butler in his autobiography, *Across the Busy Years*.

† Of course a time may come, if it has not already arrived, when there will appear a conflict between the advancement of science and the stability of the capitalistic system. Discoveries may be made which if used would upset the whole economic system, making factories and whole industries obsolete. Inventions may be made which capitalist production cannot use profitably. Then they must be suppressed in the interests of profits. Thus the present system supports science only where it may be useful and not harmful to it ; it furthers scientific progress in those spheres where this conflict is not yet apparent.

for the present economic system may point to the foundations as splendid indications of how capitalism fulfills its function in promoting the progress of the world. But if capitalism falters, if the economic fabric should weaken so that the important work which it at present supports should be interrupted, then it may be said that the foundations have assumed a responsibility far too great for any group, other than governmental, no matter how philanthropic in purpose or how financially powerful, had any right to assume. Since scientific progress is so closely tied up with the economic system, it is but a step to argue that the status quo, the inequalities inherent in present-day capitalism must be maintained in order to guarantee human progress. That is an impossible position.

With far greater pertinence it may be said that because of the very value and importance of the work it is doubtful if the foundations should be permitted to carry on an obligation which they cannot guarantee, an obligation so vital to human progress. While all praise must be given to the work they do, the work they do not do must also be pointed out. Philanthropies must pick and choose their projects amongst the vast number of possibilities, all needful. One cannot criticize the Rockefeller International Health Board for combating yaws in Jamaica and hookworm in Egypt because more money should be spent on child-bed fever in Chicago or syphilis in New York. You must admit that all these projects should be pressed : diphtheria should be fought in China and infantile paralysis in America. It may be called Utopian but it is none the less true that one project should not be sacrificed for another : they all need support, they all need funds for research, for medical and public health work. All the more reason therefore why a national drive is imperative, led by the government, so that the advancement of science does not depend upon the dollars of the foundations, but upon a nation aroused and aware of the necessity for this moral substitute for war.

CHAPTER VII

AN ENDOWMENT FOR WAR

THE CARNEGIE ENDOWMENT FOR INTERNATIONAL PEACE

Mr Carnegie got his idea for an endowment for international peace while looking at the Grand Canyon of Colorado. He had read in a New York newspaper that President William Howard Taft had said that matters of national honor, as well as other disputes between nations, should be referred to a court of arbitration. Reflecting upon this while gazing at one of the most spectacular scenic wonders of the world, the little Scotchman said to himself : "Mr Taft has bridged the chasm between war and peace." Always anxious to draw his native and his adopted countries together, the philanthropist, in telling his trustees December 14th, 1910, the genesis of his inspiration, declared : "As sure as you draw the breath of life, gentlemen, you can consolidate the English-speaking race in a treaty that would render war impossible."

So, three and a half years before the outbreak of the World War, he set aside ten million dollars' worth of Five Per Cent Mortgage Bonds of the United States Steel Corporation to establish the Carnegie Endowment for International Peace. "Although we no longer eat our fellow men, nor torture prisoners, nor sack cities, killing their inhabitants," he wrote, "we still kill each other in war like barbarians. Only wild beasts are excusable for doing this, in the Twentieth Century of the Christian era, for the crime of war is inherent, since it decides not in favor of right, but always of the strong. The nation is a criminal which refuses arbitration and drives its adversary to a tribunal which knows nothing of righteous judgment."

On that principle the Kellogg-Briand Pact was drawn up. By outlawing war, August 27, 1928, the peace advocates

thought they had abolished it.   Mr Carnegie had dreamed of
that happy moment.   "When civilized nations enter into such
treaties and war is discarded as disgraceful to civilized men, the
Trustees will then consider what is the next most degrading
evil or evils, whose banishment would most advance progress
and happiness of men and so on from century to century without end my Trustees of each age will determine how they can
best aid man in his upward march to higher and higher states
unceasingly.   Let my Trustees therefor ask themselves from
time to time, from age to age, how they can best help man in
his glorious ascent onward and upward and to this end devote
the fund."

In accepting the gift the trustees declared that they "were
not unmindful of the delicacy and difficulty involved in dealing
with so great a sum for such a purpose wisely and not mis-
chievously in ways that are practical and effective.   So it began
as an association, with Elihu Root as president, James Brown
Scott as secretary, and Nicholas Murray Butler in charge of the
division of "intercourse and education."   A bill was introduced in Congress for national incorporation, but it was never
acted upon.   Not until 1930, twenty years after its establishment, did the association become incorporated, and then it was
under the laws of the State of New York.   In the original bill
the aims of the Endowment were said to be : to promote a thorough and scientific investigation and study of the causes of war
and of the methods to prevent it, to aid in the development of
international law and its acceptance among nations, to diffuse
information and education influencing public opinion, to establish a better understanding of international rights and duties,
to cultivate friendly feelings between the inhabitants of the different countries, to promote the acceptance of peaceable methods, and "to maintain, promote, and assist such establishments,
organizations, associations, and agencies as shall be deemed
necessary or useful in the accomplishment of the purposes of
the corporation, or any of them."

The last declaration whetted the appetites of all professional pacifists. The $10,000,000 seemed intended for them and they all begged for a slice of it. This was something the little Scotchman had not anticipated, so it was decided that the Endowment was to be not a money-granting, but an operating body. Peace societies must look elsewhere for support. The Carnegie Endowment set up its own machinery and began to work in its own way. It soon relented, however, and made grants to the American Peace Society and several other organizations. One of the first things it did was to list all institutions, agencies, or societies engaged in peace work, with a statement of their character and value. Following this, a list of all persons in the United States engaged in peace work was compiled.

Offices were established in Washington, New York, London, and Paris. Baron Paul d'Estournelles de Constant was placed in charge of the latter. $24,000 was appropriated as the annual contribution to the Permanent International Peace Bureau at Berne, Switzerland. It was discovered that this constituted 91 ½ % of its income, so other contributors were sought. Viscount Haldane's speech on *England and Germany, A Study of National Characters* was printed and 250,000 copies distributed in Germany. Norman Angell's book, *The Great Illusion*, proving that wars do not pay, was distributed in France, Germany, Italy, Japan, Spain, the United States, India, and China. Financial support was given to the Franco-German Interparliamentary Conference at Berne in May, 1913. In 1912 the department of intercourse and education spent only $100,425 and the department of history spent only $40,000. However, these appropriations were doubled the following year.

During 1913–14 an inquiry was made into the Balkan Wars. Baron d'Estournelles, chairman of the committee, on account of other business, could not go to the Balkans. Neither could Francis Hirst of London nor Professor Josef Redlich of Vienna, two other members. Professor Walther Schücking of Marburg tried to find the committee in Belgrade, but he arrived too late, and returned home. Later it was discovered that the committee had adjourned to Salonika. Among those who did serve were Professor Paul Milioukov of Russia, H. N. Brailsford of London, and Dr Samuel T. Dutton of Teachers' College, New York. Their findings were made public in May, 1914. No rule of international law applicable to land warfare, they concluded, was not violated by all belligerents. Soldiers and noncombatants were shown to be equally responsible for discreditable actions. Dr Butler observed that the "finer instincts were temporarily wiped out and the beast in man controlled his actions."

The trustees of the Endowment put themselves on record against preferential treatment of American coastwise vessels in Panama Canal tolls, and distributed 1,200,000 copies of a statement taking the side of Great Britain in protesting against exemptions. Research was begun on a scientific study of the causes of war and a conference was planned, to meet in Lucerne, Switzerland, August 5, 1914, of those engaged in this work, but the outbreak of the World War interfered so that only four out of the nineteen members appeared. However, the report for the year declared that the "war has not interrupted the work of the Japanese members of the committee, and in South America prospects look brighter than ever." The Interparliamentary Union conference at Stockholm, scheduled for August 19, 1914 had to be abandoned also. Only one American delegate arrived there, Congressman William D. B. Ainey, who made the trip to Sweden by way of Japan and the Trans-Siberian railway.

The various offices and departments had only just been organized, and the work of the Endowment started, when the nations went to war. Since there seemed to be no way to stop it, those in charge of the association began to make a record of it. Under Dr John Bates Clark the division of economics and history started the accumulation of documents and data, while the division of international law studied the repeated violations.

Dr Scott, in charge of this department, remarked, "Entry into war made it evident that our activities must be ineffective until the restoration of peace." Through the American Association for International Conciliation the official documents were published : the German White Book, the Russian Orange Book, the Belgian Grey Book, the French Yellow Book, etc. Norman Angell and B. N. Langdon-Davies were brought to the United States to lecture on "The Great Illusion." In fact, a long list of distinguished lecturers were sent around the country to discuss the international situation. The Endowment's largest contribution, however, was $100,000 for the expenses of the Second Pan American Scientific Congress.

Many people criticized the association for not stopping the War, but the executive committee replied that that was something beyond its powers. "Frequent letters suggesting that the Endowment do this or that" are received, it reported, "and the suggestions are often accompanied by the assurance that the writer is just the person to undertake it." Stung by criticisms, the trustees declared on February 16, 1915 : "We wish to say to all friends of peace that the dreadful war now raging affords no just cause for discouragement, it reflects no discredit to past efforts and no reason to doubt that still greater efforts in the future may be effective and useful. . . It seems incredible that after this the stricken peoples will set their feet in the same old paths of policy and suspicion which must lead to the same result." Dr Butler, however, looked on the brighter side : "War itself is so powerful an educator of public opinion," he wrote, reporting on his division, "that it will advance by years if not by decades instruction which it was in part the duty of the Division to originate and carry on."

Prior to the American entry into the War the Endowment concentrated chiefly upon the publication of books, the arrangement of lectures, and the entertainment of distinguished visitors, many of whom were Allied propagandists. Among the books published were Professor William A. Dunning's *The*

British Empire and the United States, Dr Charles W. Eliot's *Some Roads Toward Peace,* an account of his trip to China in 1912, a study of Balkan wars previous to 1914, a report of the trip of Robert Bacon (one of the trustees) to South America in 1913, and a study of the loss of life in modern wars published by the Clarendon Press of Oxford at the expense of the Endowment in 1916. One of its most successful publications was a pamphlet, *Problems About War for Classes in Arithmetic* by David Eugene Smith of Teachers' College, which led to a contest, with prizes for pupils and teachers.

Those in charge of the Endowment were militantly pro-Ally in their sentiments. Elihu Root was largely responsible for Robert Lansing's appointment in the State Department, and the recent publication of portions of the letters of Mr Lansing and Senator Root clearly indicate their lack of neutrality. Frank L. Polk, counselor to the State Department and trustee of the Endowment, was also anxious for the United States to join the Allies. Dr James Brown Scott, secretary of the Endowment, was appointed chairman of the Neutrality Board, whose rulings were notably favorable to France and Great Britain. Even Andrew Carnegie, saddened as he was by the War, wrote letters to President Wilson urging that the United States join the war "to end war." * Among the propagandists entertained by the Endowment between 1914 and 1917 were : Eugene Brieux, the Marquis and Marchioness of Aberdeen, M. Homberg of the French Ministry of Finance, Sir Johnstone Forbes-Robertson, Sir Walter Raleigh of Oxford, George M. Trevelyan of Cambridge, Marquis de Polignac, Sir Herbert Beerbohm Tree, Captain Ian Hay, John S. Haldane of Oxford and Stephen Lauzanne of Paris. In 1916 $2500 was given to the France-America Society to promote friendship, a trifling sum, perhaps, but significant of the sympathies of those in charge of the Endowment.

* See Dr Charles C. Tansill *America Goes To War,* Little, Brown and Co., 1938.

When America poised on the brink of war and there was much talk of "preparedness" and contempt for "pacifists," the Endowment was criticized by those who did not know the feelings of the trustees, as a subversive society agitating for peace. Aroused by such remarks, the trustees issued a statement on February 23, 1917, declaring that "the Carnegie Endowment for International Peace has no part in any effort to hinder timely and adequate preparation of the military and naval forces and material necessary to defend national rights and liberties of the American people against forcible foreign aggression. . . Mutual respect for international rights is an essential basis of durable peace and a nation which does not insist upon that respect fails in its duty, not only to its own liberty, but to the peace of the world."   The association had its funds invested in one of the biggest and fastest growing of the war babies : the United States Steel Corporation.   The trustees were directors and investors in big business then booming with war orders.   Mr Root was head of a firm of corporation lawyers.   Dr Butler was president of a university several of whose trustees were munitions makers.   It is not to be wondered therefor, that the sentiments of these men, at first perhaps confused, soon clarified into a conviction that peace could be achieved only by a victory of the Allies.

So, as the war fever mounted in this country, the Endowment strove to be on the side of prevailing public opinion.   Within a few years of its establishment the association for international peace met the first crisis in its career by crying for a relentless prosecution of the War as loudly as any jingoist.   No sooner had the United States entered the conflict than the trustees resolved, April 18, 1917, that "the most effective means of promoting durable international peace is to prosecute the war against the Imperial German government to the final victory of democracy."   Leading the stampede, noisiest in his demands, most arbitrary in his insistence on the regimentation of minds in his own university, was Nicholas Murray Butler, director of the department of intercourse and education, and later chosen president of the Endowment. The income from $10,000,000 which to some people might seem to encourage independence of opinion, had the very opposite effect. The pacifists in charge of the association could not resist the frenzy of the mass mind. Indeed, they contributed to it. Apparently they did not seriously believe in their own propaganda. Whether they realized it or not they had been paving the way to war. Associated, as they were, with big business identified with Allied success, their investments made them less, rather than more independent than those less richly endowed. No more than the average man in the street, who was soon to be drafted, could they resist the pressure of the very propaganda they professed to oppose.

The enthusiasm of the trustees for war was so great, in fact, that they repeated their resolution at their meeting of November 1, 1917. The division of international law, which had been collecting data on all known examples of international arbitration under the supervision of Dr John Bassett Moore, was turned over to the State Department and its staff, paid by the Endowment, prepared a large number of volumes to be shipped to France for the enlightenment of the peace conference. Dr James Brown Scott accompanied this material as official technical advisor, but like the other experts, he was ignored. Meanwhile Dr Butler was beating the drums and shouting for universal military service.

It is true that some books were published during these years : a treatise on the biological effects of war, *The Growth of Liberalism in Japan*, *The Early Effects of the War upon Women and Children in Great Britain*, Hugo Grotius' *The Freedom of the Seas*, from the text of 1633, and many others of a similar nature. A gift of 9,000 American books, typical of the political and intellectual life of the United States, was made to the Museo Social Argentino in Buenos Aires. In the first year of its existence the association spent only $114,151 but by 1916 it had appropriated $550,595 for the year, a figure seldom lowered since and usually surpassed. Up to 1918 the administrative expenses were $427,874 out of a total expenditure of $3,241,179.

For the pacifists who stood out against the war hysteria, who were consistently loyal to their convictions, or for the conscientious objectors to war, either in this country or in Europe, the Endowment had no sympathy. During the War the officers looked toward the restoration of peace for their great opportunity. As early as 1916 they began begging the Carnegie Corporation for additional funds, asking for an additional endowment of five million dollars for the expansion of activities when the War ended. They did not get it, but they did get $100,000 a year for several years to finance the economic and social history of the War. In 1920 the association reported proudly that it "had taken no part in the controversy on the Treaty of Peace." Dr Butler sided with his friend Henry Cabot Lodge against Woodrow Wilson. As long as the League of Nations was associated with that Democrat in the White House, he would have nothing to do with it. However, Elihu Root in 1920, although he spoke disparagingly of "the so-called Covenant of the League of Nations," asked for $50,000 to send himself, Dr Scott, and three assistants to Europe to help set up a permanent court of international justice. They remained for six weeks and spent only $15,000 so the balance was presented to Westminster Abbey for its restoration fund.

As early as 1914 Mr Root had suggested that the association prepare a social and economic history of the War and a beginning was made by the department of economics and history. Not until 1919 was the project fully launched, however, on a grand scale under the editorship of Professor James T. Shotwell of Columbia. American and foreign scholars prepared, in all, 152 volumes. Those in foreign languages have been published abroad first, and then translated into English. The original estimate that it would cost $605,000 proved much too modest, but the Carnegie Corporation paid the bill which finally amounted to $896,000. In March, 1937, Professor Shotwell announced that the job had been completed. "I believe," he said, "that the wealth of data covered in these volumes would, if read and understood by the people of the world, be a real preventive of war." Other after-War projects were the reconstructions of the universities of Louvain and Belgrade, contributions to the restoration of Rheims and the support of scholars engaged in cataloguing the Vatican library. Professor Shotwell is now directing a study of Canadian-American relations.

The Endowment has always carefully refrained from anything so controversial that it might lead to unfavorable criticism. It has concentrated on scholarly pursuits which would not challenge the existing order. It has arranged for the international exchange of students, professors, experts, lecturers, and journalists. It has established "International Relations Clubs" and placed "International Mind Alcoves" in many libraries. Invariably it has associated with the best people. Every summer Dr Butler has made a trip to Europe ; usually he is given a dinner in Paris and a lunch in London, and sometimes he visits Geneva. He has then returned to report what the best minds in Europe are thinking. In the first ten years of its existence the association spent $658,627 on administrative expenses, $2,273,485 on the division of intercourse and education, $557,143 for the department of economics and history, $840,121 for international law, a total of $4,842,377. It loaned $70,000 to the Republic of China, and in 1922 it built a model public square at Farginers, France, at the cost of $150,000.

Throughout the twenties, while victorious nations tried to enforce an unenforceable treaty, while France dominated the Continent and Great Britain used the League of Nations as a branch of the Foreign Office, while statesmen divided up the world's oil reserves, Dr Butler and his associates reported their activities with enthusiasm and optimism. The masses do not want war, they repeated confidently. In 1923, the year France marched into the Ruhr and Germany inflated the mark, Dr Butler insisted that for the sake of the peace of the world France should be guaranteed security. Soon after he succeeded Mr Root as president of the Endowment in 1925, the association purchased a building in Paris, at 173 Boulevard St Germain, costing $150,000, to serve as the European headquarters. An annual appropriation of $60,000 a year is made for its maintenance. A permanent representative is stationed at Geneva where complete information about the League of Nations is provided American tourists. Representatives are sent to all international conferences and reports sent home, sometimes as often as twice a week.

The Disarmament Conference arranged by Mr Hughes and President Harding, now completely repudiated, cheered the officers of the Endowment considerably and a number of pamphlets were published concerning it. The Nine Power Treaty guaranteeing the territorial integrity of China seemed a great achievement. The Locarno pacts, since disregarded, gave the peace promoters grounds for encouragement, and the Pact of Paris, for which Dr Butler has been given the credit for arranging, with the help of Mr Kellogg and Mr Briand, seemed to him in 1928 a fruition of years of labor. "Now," he exulted, "a nation cannot remain neutral without at the same time being immoral." Mr Carnegie's dream was coming true, it appeared, and soon the trustees would have to look for the "next most degrading evil."

Apparently it did not occur to Dr Butler that many nations, including his beloved France and Great Britain, might prefer to be considered immoral than to go to war over Manchuria or Ethiopia. To the promoters of peace, however, it was a triumph to arrange an international pact which, if adhered to, would turn every minor conflict into a major one. By the time he received the Nobel Prize in 1931, all these pacts had been discarded. "The spirit and temper of those days," Dr Butler reported sadly, "have been forgotten as though they did not exist." Reviewing the violations of Japan, a profound melancholy weighed upon him. It did not occur to him to question the reasons for the ineffectuality of the Endowment or the causes of the complete lack of realism which permeated all its efforts.

Unwilling to expose the profits of the munitions-makers, those in charge of the Endowment imagine that what they are doing has some relevance to the modern world. Its activities and methods have been so innocuous that radicals have raised the question of its sincerity. Apparently it searches for well-meaning tasks which by some stretch of the imagination can be related to the cause of peace. Medieval books are published, lectures, luncheons, dinners, speeches, conferences are arranged. A man is brought from Vienna to Washington to prepare a cattle map of the world. A model tariff walls map was built and exhibited, 2436 books are sold and 22,482 are given away in a single year. Dr Butler extended his trip in 1931 to visit Vienna, Budapest, and Prague. He met Dolfuss and Goemboes. The following year he had a nice talk with Mussolini.

Dr James Brown Scott assured the readers of the yearbook that the organization in 1933 was making progress. "The Endowment is becoming an unofficial instrument of international policy," he observed, "taking up here and there the ends and threads of international problems and questions which governments find it difficult to handle and through private initiative reaching conclusions which are not of a formal nature but which unofficially find their way into the policies of governments. . . The resurgence of ideas of exaggerated nationalism makes it difficult for governments to deal officially with their international problems, opportunities are correspondingly increasing for quiet, unobtrusive, but effective use by the Endowment and its offices of good will and friendly advice, developing a role as surprising as it was unexpected." In other words, the annual trips of Dr Butler are supposed to influence the course of history.

After the collapse of the London Economic Conference in 1933, Dr Butler called his own conference at Chatham House in 1935. The American delegates were Dr Butler, Malcolm W. Davis, the Endowment's representative in Paris, Leon Fraser, now president of New York's First National Bank, C. O. Hardy of Brookings, Henry S. Haskell, one of Dr Butler's assistants in New York, Phillip C. Jessup of Columbia, Peter Molyneaux, a trustee of the Endowment, and Frederic M. Sackett, former U. S. Senator from Kentucky. A long list of recommendations resulted, including the stabilization of currencies on a gold basis, the limitation of armaments, and a number of noble but wholly impractical suggestions to the governments of the world.

Commenting on Dr Butler's 1935 report the *New Republic* remarked on its "spirit of melancholy acceptance of our plenetary antagonisms." The Italian conquest of Ethiopia discouraged him and the report was issued the week Hitler marched into the Rhineland. Even more despondent was Dr Butler's 1936 report. "Public opinion simply cannot trust the word of some governments unless it be when they are planning or executing something wholly selfish or minatory." As if speaking of himself, he speaks of "popular sentiment" as being "hopeless and helpless when confronted by the task of lessening and then removing the causes of war." The economic interpretation of history he abhors as smacking of Marxism and Bolshevism. It was the Women's International League for Peace which instigated the Senatorial investigation of war profiteering. As for neutrality Dr Butler says, "There can be no neutrality in the nineteenth century sense without complete and immoral neglect of national obligations." He cannot forget his idea of an international police force.

The Chatham House conference left in its wake the usual

residuary committees. If Dr Butler could not have a conference he could always have a number of committees. So a joint committee was appointed in conjunction with the International Chamber of Commerce to study trade barriers and monetary stabilization — which happen to be problems that worry international bankers. The committee called upon a committee of experts for help, resulting in a two-volume report, presented to the joint committee, which approved of it, and passed it on to the various foreign offices and committees of the League of Nations. This work cost $12,500.

Attempts were then made to publicize the findings throughout the United States. The Director of the League of Nations Association was sent on a lecture tour, and with the help of several leaders "in the field" propaganda was carried on in the Middle West and on the Pacific Coast. Study outlines and discussion groups were organized among the farmers, concentrating in forty-two counties in Iowa. Dr Butler painted a glowing picture in his 1936 report : "The reader should visualize a group of from fifty to seventy-five farmers, who have worked hard all day, gathered with their wives and children in a farm home, the neighborhood schoolhouse or the country church for discussions of such subjects as 'The Farmer's Stake in World Peace.' . . . These hard working, intelligent and alert people often prolong their interested discussion until after eleven at night, or even longer, fortified by a good farm supper."

Such activities are typical of the work of the Endowment. Dr Butler made his usual trips abroad in 1936, 1937, and 1938, but in 1936 the sit-in strikes "made travel and hotel service so uncertain that the usual visit to the Centre Européen in Paris was omitted." In 1937 he ventured as far as Geneva, where a luncheon was given in his honor, but he was back in New York within a month. Of course, much of the work of the Endowment, particularly in its studies in international law, has value from an academic point of view. The exchange professors unquestionably get opportunities to learn much and they may even impart something in their lectures.   The books and pamphlets published and distributed spread a thin layer of information over many minds.   It is heartening to know that 9,508 people abroad have requested books and that so many foreigners enjoyed *The Adventures of Tom Sawyer*.   When one thinks of the ravages of civil war in Spain it is pleasant to remember that two Spanish librarians were brought to the United States to study library service.   The International Mind Alcoves in 493 libraries undoubtedly broaden the views of many high school students and club women.   The 1103 International Relations Clubs certainly must have provoked considerable amount of discussion among small groups in the colleges and stimulated some thinking.   But how these things contribute to "the substitution of judicial processes for appeal to armed force" remains a little difficult to understand.   A few individuals may be encouraged to stand out against war when it comes, but can the Endowment itself, considering its record, and the things it stands for, be trusted to back them up ?

Carleton Beals in *Glass Houses* * says of the Endowment : "It is a very equivocal organization, careful never to air any of the root causes of war in any way to endanger vested interests or profit-making, and is always pro-British.   Every so often it sends a good-will representative through Latin America.   It also gives assistance to the Pan American society, for years little more than a closed corporation of powerful American interests having investments in Latin America.   As might be expected, the good-will envoys selected have been utterly incapable of promoting good-will, have actually been persons who have definitely promoted American aggression toward Latin America. . . In 1938 it sent David P. Barrows, of the Political Science Department of the University of California, my own Alma Mater.   Barrows has always been a big stick imperialist.   It just so happened I was in Central America when

* Published by J. B. Lippincott and Co., 1938.

Barrows went through there.   As I was just one jump ahead of Barrows I gave the reporters his complete record.   In this I was also helped by a clipping my mother had sent me by chance in which Barrows made the statement that the United States was privileged to intervene militarily anywhere, anytime, in Latin America.   The reporters all quoted this gleefully when Barrows went through. . . Time and again he had come out in support of the grossest aggressive measures toward Latin America.   Such was the first Carnegie Peace foundation good-will emissary. . . More recently the foundation has chosen Dana Munro . . . a consistent apologist . . . for the old-style armed intervention policy, for everything of the worst imperialistic odor in our relations with that part of the world."

Let us look at the trustees : Wallace McK. Alexander, sugar tycoon of Hawaii, vice president of the Matson Line ; Arthur A. Ballantine, corporation lawyer in Root's old firm ; David P. Barrows, just mentioned, major general in the National Guard ; William Marshall Bullitt, lawyer and trustee of the Mutual Life Insurance Co. ; John W. Davis, Morgan counsel, now vice president of the Endowment ; Frederic A. Delano ; D. S. M. Colonel in the Transportation Corps during the World War ; Howard Heinz of the 57 varieties ; Alanson B. Houghton, chairman of the board of the Corning Glass Works ; Frank O. Lowden, former governor of Illinois ; Roland S. Morris, lawyer of Philadelphia and former Ambassador to Japan ; Henry S. Pritchett, Chevalier of the Legion of Honor of France, Gold Cross Commander of the Order of George I of Greece, director in A. T. & T. ; Edward L. Ryerson Jr, banker and independent steel magnate ; James R. Sheffield, lawyer of New York ; Silas H. Strawn, of the First National Bank of Chicago ; Robert A. Taft, director of banks and corporations ; Eliot Wadsworth, banker ; and Thomas J. Watson, president of International Business Machines, decorated by Hitler in 1937. All these men are involved in big business, all share the same ideas.   They are members of the group, considered in Chap-

ter XIII, which rules America through their interlocking directorates, not only in banks and corporations but in foundations
and organized private charities. Of those who whooped it
up for war in 1917 only three remain, but their points-of-view
are the same, for the board is a self-perpetuating body which
elects friends and business associates.   The public has no voice.

Speaking of Fascism and Communism in his 1936 report Dr
Butler asked : "How can a democratic people be indifferent or
neutral when a fellow democracy is forcibly attacked by one of
the philosophies of compulsion ?   What is being attacked is
that democracy's own outpost, and if the attack on that outpost be successful, it will be followed by an attack on democracy itself."   That is not a plea for peace, but a call to arms.   It
is precisely the argument which got us into the last war.   In
October, 1937, Dr Butler helped matters along by calling Japan
an "assassin" and on December 14, 1937, the trustees of the Endowment called upon this country to face its responsibility for
the maintenance and defense of "solemn covenants between
nations."   On an international broadcast sponsored by the Endowment on Armistice Day, 1937, Dr Butler said : "To call
police work war is a contradiction in terms.   It is the instru-
mentality for the rule of law, and to the rule of law there is absolutely no alternative but the rule of force."   Lord Lothian
followed him with a plea for a "world constitution" and a "government of supernational affairs."   At a luncheon for Lord
Cecil on November 20, 1937, Dr Butler repeated : "There has
been a complete breakdown in public morals, a complete turning of backs by governments upon their plighted words, and
when that is done there is no alternative but force."   Hence he
called for "collective action" and a "world police."

Of course Dr Butler was enthusiastic about President Roosevelt's Chicago speech calling for a "quarantine" on aggressor
nations.   "Isolation," declared the head of the Endowment, "is
a folly only exceeded by its immorality."   He seems determined that the United States shall go to the aid of France and

Britain should either need our help. Through the International Relations Clubs this sort of propaganda is encouraged. The Endowment tells Americans about international problems and urges us to do something about them. It appeals to the idealism and high-mindedness of youth and advocates a foreign policy which would mean that the American navy would be used as an international police force. It encourages British and French propaganda. The Carnegie Endowment might be considered an expensive luxury which we, as a rich nation, can afford, since it supports a number of people doing work of possible academic value, but it becomes a menace to our peace, and to the peace of the world, when it agitates for international agreements demanding that we go to war for the sake of the peace of the world. If the nations of Europe should start a holy war against fascism or communism it is easy to imagine the Carnegie Endowment crying for another crusade to make the world safe for democracy. Just as the Endowment helped in building sentiment favorable to France and England from 1914 to 1917, so it is building up the same sentiment today. Of course the Endowment believes that international questions should be solved by judicial discussion. But if a nation refuses that means, then, according to Dr Butler, we are immoral if we remain neutral.

No one can read the Endowment reports or yearbooks without a disheartening sense of complete futility and utter ineffectuality. It has done nothing toward taking the profits out of war ; it has never attacked the bases of economic imperialism, it has made no attempt to show the populations of war-like countries today how their leaders are driving them into war. It might investigate the world-wide struggle for oil and its connection with foreign policies. It might look into the influence of international bankers on diplomacy. It might investigate the international ramifications of the steel industry, the scrap iron industry, the shipping industry, and the part these play in making inevitable another war. It might inquire into the role of newspapers and newspaper proprietors, or into the active foreign propaganda in this country. It has done none of these things, for it believes in war under certain circumstances, under the very circumstances in which it is most likely to come. It diverts the energies of those anxious for peace into futile and ineffective channels; it encourages earnest people to imagine that by joining clubs and reading pamphlets they are preventing the next war. It dares make no effort to combat the psychological build-up created by statesmen and journalists. Indeed, it actively contributes to it. The most richly endowed institution dedicated to the promotion of peace is thus turned into an aggressive agent for the promotion of war. For many it has become a polite society of academic minds, a sincere, well-intentioned, but completely futile racket for professional pacifists. As a result the agitation for peace has become a well-paid profession for glib-talking idealists who deliver lectures under quite a number of auspices. By repeating the same old ideas to each other they think they are making progress.

These auspices are well known. The Church Peace Union, founded by Mr Carnegie with a two million dollar endowment paid by the Carnegie Corporation, it is supposed to promote peace through the churches. It is now headed by Dr William H. Merrill of the Brick Church of New York, with Henry A. Atkinson as general secretary. It appropriated $112,614 in 1936 and was helped by the Carnegie Corporation to the extent of $20,000. At its meeting of January 21, 1937 it appointed a committee on "policy and outlook" to find out just what it was doing. Until that committee reports it will do no good to inquire. Apparently it holds a number of conferences every year in this country and abroad. It has a subsidiary known as the World Alliance to work with the World Christian Student Federation and the International Christian Student Council for Life and Work. These hold sessions in Prague, Avignon, and Cambridge. Like most peace organizations these have a fondness for holding conferences, preferably abroad.

A somewhat more realistic organization is the Foreign Policy Association to which the Endowment contributed. The Rockefeller Foundation gives it $25,000 annually and an additional $25,000 for "popular education." At its lectures, discussions, broadcasts, luncheons, and debates throughout the country a genuine effort seems to be made to get at the roots of the problems under discussion. It pretends to be neutral but its officers favor "collective action," and its speakers tend to encourage or to promote British and French propaganda. (Of course, there is always somebody taking the opposite view on hand to answer them.) The direction of its propaganda must necessarily be colored by the personal opinions of those in charge of it.

More closely associated with the Endowment is the very active League of Nations Association directed by Clark M. Eichelberger, one of the Endowment's busiest lecturers in the field. It stands frankly for "a universal League of Nations functioning effectively to promote international cooperation and to achieve international peace and security." Through its offices in Geneva, Washington, and New York it tries to influence the foreign policy of the United States and, by means of publications, lectures, and radio broadcasts, to arouse the American people to demand a foreign policy which will promote "the development of the world community centered in Geneva." The Endowment contributes substantial amounts annually to this organization. Dr Butler said of Mr Eichelberger in his 1936 report: "He has been the outstanding speaker upon whom the field workers counted for assistance in addressing a great variety of audiences. The Director is happy to record his appreciation of this able cooperation in the work of the Endowment." An attempt has been made to achieve cooperation amongst the many peace organizations through the establishment of the National Peace Conference, toward which the Endowment contributed $12,500 in 1937. Dr Walter W. Van Kirk, in charge of it, declares "the Conference is not another peace organization. It is the agency of the bodies represented in it.   The aim of the Conference is not to diminish the activity of any of the constituent agencies but to unite their voices, when they can be united, into a single expression of the best thought of the nation."   A central clearing house was established and a number of committees organized.   Other "conferences" which have been given contributions by the Endowment are : the conference of university men on Ways of Staying Out of War held by the Council on Foreign Relations in New York, the International Textile Conference in Washington, the Conference on Church, Community, and State at Oxford, England, and the second International Catholic Conference in Dublin, Ireland.

Another project mentioned in Dr Butler's 1937 report is one for "peace education with children and youth under the auspices of the Greater New York Federation of Churches . . . under the following divisions : Youth Department, Drama Department, Children's Division, Work with Parents in Sunday Schools, Weekday Church Schools, and Metropolitan Federation of Daily Vacation Bible Schools.   A manual, *Junior Teachers Guide on World Peace*, was prepared and published, and a new project was successfully undertaken under the name of Table Talks for Parents."   Toward this the division contributed $5000.   Considering the projects accepted and supported, it would be of great public interest to know what projects, because of the timidity and lack of vision of those in charge of the Endowment, were rejected.

Beginning his annual report for 1937 with an idea that a college freshman would reject as too hackneyed, Dr Butler supposes that an "intelligent inhabitant of the planet Mars should look across space to see what is happening on this Mother Earth."   Such a spectator would see many things which distress the president of the Endowment, but no hint is given of what such an observer would think of the Endowment itself and its activities.   He might suggest that the trustees ask themselves now, this year, whether the Endowment as at present directed by Dr Butler is showing any sign of an intelligent understanding of its responsibilities. If this citizen from Mars should make a detached and critical study of the Endowment, the result might be a thorough house-cleaning of the organization and the installation of a more aggressive and intelligent leadership.

It may not be true that the Endowment sets about futile and useless activities because it does not want peace propaganda to get too strong a hold on the American people. But it is definitely committed to international policies which will lead to war more certainly than to enduring peace. A genuine, realistic investigation of the causes of war might imperil the financial interests of some of the trustees and it might involve harsh criticisms of the foreign policies of France and Great Britain. Consciously or unconsciously, it is fooling the public and itself, but it would be a ghastly joke if it is discovered that while ineffectual in the promotion of peace, this endowment should be successful in the perpetuation of war.

CHAPTER VIII

THE PROMOTION OF EDUCATION

THE GENERAL EDUCATION BOARD

Although the Rockefeller General Education Board was started January 15, 1902 and was incorporated a year later by an Act of Congress for "the promotion of education within the United States without distinction of race, sex, or creed," it was twelve years before it made public a report of its activities. John D. Sr gave the Board a million dollars in 1902, $10,000,000 in 1905, $32,000,000 in 1907, and another $10,000,000 in 1909, but reserved to himself and his son the right to designate the spending of a large part of it. Six years later the first report declared : "Because, as the Board's work was felt to be experimental in character, premature statements respecting the scope and outcome of its efforts were to be avoided." However, "after something more than a decade tangible results have begun to appear."

As a matter of fact, the General Education Board was largely an outgrowth of the American Baptist Educational Society. As Mr Rockefeller's fortune increased, the educational interests of his advisors broadened. He was prepared to give larger sums than it seemed expedient to allocate to a sectarian organization. Baptist ministers continued to be his advisors in philanthropy, but a bigger, more resounding name was desired for the dispensing agency. The entire field of education in the United States was open. Anything might be done. For more than a year ex-Baptist preachers, acting as Rockefeller's agents, "made thorough studies of" the possibilities. They concluded, after what we are expected to believe was diligent research and long deliberation, that the most effective means of promoting education in the United States was to aid agriculture in the South.

So the first work of the General Education Board was to finance demonstrations designed to teach Southern farmers how to grow more crops.

If you follow the Board's line of reasoning you will see how it justified this decision. In 1903 the state of public education in the South was incredibly backward. Free schools were unknown in the South before the Civil War and very little was done in ante-bellum days to establish a public school system worthy of the name. High schools were rare. In Georgia the school term was a little more than five months out of the year, in Mississippi four months, in Virginia one hundred days. In Alabama white teachers received an average salary of $151.84 a year, and Negro teachers $95.53. The total state school expenditure in Alabama in 1903 was only a little more than a million dollars.* Georgia spent less and prescribed no qualifications for the state superintendent. Mississippi spent a little less than $2,000,000 a year on public schools and Tennessee a little more. North Carolina paid her state superintendent $2000 a year and South Carolina paid hers $1900. Virginia merely demanded that hers be an "expert educator." Only forty schools in Virginia offered two to three extra grades doing what might be called high school work ; North Carolina had thirty-five such schools. In Raleigh the public school consisted of seven grades. In several states the state constitution expressly forbad counties voting taxes for high schools.

This was the problem which the General Education Board faced. But why did it face that particular problem ? Of the seven original incorporators only one, Daniel C. Gilman, first president of Johns Hopkins and later first president of the Carnegie Institution in Washington, was an educator. One was a railroad president, one a clothing merchant, one a banker, one a publisher, one an ex-Baptist minister, and the sixth was Jabez L. M. Curry of Georgia, a lieutenant-colonel in the Con-

---

* The state superintendent in Alabama was elected and could not succeed himself.

federate Army, president of the Board of Foreign Missions of the Southern Baptist Convention, and author of *Struggles and Triumphs of Virginia Baptists*. When he was chosen for a place on the General Education Board he was an agent for the Slater and Peabody funds, working in the South. The Peabody Fund had been creating sentiment and promoting legislation in the South favorable to popular education. Many Southern states relied upon it. In Alabama the legislature permitted the superintendent of education to hold "institutes" for teachers every summer in each Congressional district and to spend "not more than $500 but not in any case to exceed the amount paid for such purpose by the Peabody Educational Fund." The Slater Fund was devoted to Negro education, particularly in the rural schools. The work and experience of these funds suggested to the Board what it might do.

Daniel C. Gilman was a trustee of the Peabody Fund. Robert C. Ogden, partner of John Wanamaker and author of *Pew Rents and Christ, Can They Be Reconciled?* had long been interested in education in the South. He was a trustee of both Hampton and Tuskegee, and he originated the Southern Education Board which made studies resulting in the conclusion that no fund by direct gifts could contribute a system of public schools to the South. With such interests on the part of its members it is natural that the Board should select as secretary ex-Baptist minister Wallace Butterick, who had worked for both the Slater and Peabody funds. The Board was simply following a path already explored, doing on a larger scale the work in which the other funds had been pioneers.

Although possessing funds many times larger than either the Peabody, which had $2,000,000, or the Slater, which had a little more than a million, the Rockefeller Board had no intention of being left holding the bag. It was determined not to do work or to make appropriations that should be done or made by the states. Progress could not be forced from the outside, agents working in the South declared ; it must come through com-

munity initiative.   The fundamental difficulty was the poverty
of the South.   Even the Rockefeller millions could not build
or support a system of public education in the Southern states.
The money must come from taxes, and taxes could not be collected until the farmer's income was increased.   Eighty-five
per cent of the population of the South was rural and the average earnings in agriculture were $150 a year.

A suggestion was made that the General Education Board
support the teaching of agriculture in the common schools.
This was rejected, as it was thought it would be imposing something from the outside.   First of all, the Board was convinced,
the Southern farmers had to be persuaded of the feasibility of
superior farm methods.   They didn't believe that better methods would produce more crops or that it would do them any
good to raise more.   In order to induce them to make the effort
to improve their lot, the Cooperative Farm Demonstrations
were started.   The boll-weevil plague had begun.   A man was
found in Texas, Seaman A. Knapp, who was giving farm demonstrations for the U.S. Department of Agriculture.   In 1906
the Board made an agreement with the government to use Dr
Knapp for educational work in farm demonstrations.   This
was done in infected states with government funds and in non-
infected states with Rockefeller funds, while the control of
both demonstrations was left with the Department of Agriculture.   Dr Knapp trained others to give the demonstrations.
Twenty-four agents went out in 1906 ; the following year there
were thirty-six agents, twenty-one supported by the government and fifteen by the G.E.B., in 1908, 156 agents, 71 by the
government and 85 by the G.E.B.   As the experiment demonstrated its success, the Board increased its quota of agents.
Then the Southern legislatures woke up and began making appropriations, for the demonstrations doubled the crop where
the new methods were applied.

Meanwhile the Board started its campaign for more and better public high schools.   It offered the states to pay the salaries

of "Professors of Secondary Education" who were accredited to the state university and who traveled through the state organizing high schools. The first of these officials began in Virginia in 1905 and the last in Kentucky in 1910. They were high school evangelists, making speeches, holding conferences, playing one town against another. They combated all kinds of obstacles and prejudices in establishing publicly supported high schools. Public schools were thought of as "charity schools." Class concepts in regard to education persisted. Many Southerners believed that only the wealthy or the well-to-do should get a high school education. However, with the help of the Peabody Fund and the Southern Education Board, a high school system was created that was practically non-existent before 1905. This had to be done in the most tactful and diplomatic manner lest the Southerners become offended and set up active opposition. Only in this way could the outside instigation be effective. Looking at the record of what it accomplished, one wonders how long, without the help of such organizations as the General Education Board, it would have taken these states to set up free public high school instruction.

At the same time a survey was made of the institutions of higher learning in the United States. Higher education in Europe, it was noted, was a government concern, but in the United States neither the national nor the state governments took the initiative in providing adequate colleges. Our universities have usually been founded by religious bodies and supported mainly through endowments from the wealthy. The number of denominational colleges was astonishing. Ohio, with a population of less than five million, had forty colleges, twice as many as the whole German Empire with eight times the population. Many of these "colleges" were not even good secondary schools ; they robbed local high schools of pupils. "Local institutional, or denominational pride, vanity, or self-interest propped up tottering, feeble, or superfluous institutions," the Board reported. Only twenty-five colleges in seventeen states had in 1913 an income of $500,000 from all sources and 176 had an income of $25,000 or less.

With his second gift, $10,000,000, Mr Rockefeller directed the Board to assist such institutions of learning as it deemed "best adapted to promote a comprehensive system of higher education in the United States." With his third gift, $32,000,-000, he specified that one-third of it should go toward endowments and two-thirds toward purposes he would later select. The Board saw no reason for assisting tottering institutions ; it looked for colleges which would draw further funds from other sources. Following the Rockefeller policy, the gifts were contingent, on the condition that at least equal and usually greater sums be raised. In most cases the Board gave a third or less of the total sum sought.

In order not to make any bad investments in colleges that were on the downgrade the factors governing college growth were examined. Healthy colleges with an assured future were favored. Those near large population centers were considered the strongest. But the Board was not satisfied to stop there. The business management of the colleges was scrutinized, and those institutions which applied for contributions were always required to supply a financial statement.

Chaos shocking to business men was uncovered. There was no uniformity in college accounting systems. The Board's searching questionnaires startled many institutions into financial reform. One college, it was found, kept no record of the bonds given it for endowment ; its files were an accumulation of valuable and worthless papers, and it was necessary to appeal to the memories of the oldest officers to get an approximate notion of its financial condition. In many institutions endowment funds were not kept separate, and so that without being aware of it, the officers were spending capital funds for current expenses. Bookkeeping systems were installed and auditing required in the institutions aided, as a result of these inquiries.

Up to June 1914 the Board had pledged to 103 colleges and to nineteen secondary schools $10,582,591 and these institutions had undertaken to raise elsewhere another $40,000,000. Not all of this was actually paid because many colleges failed to meet the Board's conditions. Nevertheless, the Board declares that $50,000,000 was added to the endowment reserves of American education. The resources of the G.E.B. at that time amounted to $33,939,156, giving a gross income of $2,417,079 annually. Appropriations up to June 30, 1914 were : to medical schools $2,670,874, Negro colleges and schools $699,781, miscellaneous schools $159,991, "professors of secondary education" $242,861, Southern Education Board $97,126, rural school agents $104,443, farm demonstrations $925,750 (in the South), $50,876 (in the North), rural organization service $37,166, educational conferences $18,108. The administrative expenses for the first twelve years were $304,794, making a total of appropriations of $15,894,364.

Although William H. Baldwin Jr, president of the Long Island Railroad, served as chairman of the Board from 1902 to 1905 and Robert C. Ogden, the clothing merchant, succeeded him for one year, the moving spirits of the organization, creating its plans and policies, were two Baptist clergymen : Frederick T. Gates and Wallace Butterick. Gates was the Minnesota preacher who, while soliciting funds for the University of Chicago, sold John D. Sr on large-scale philanthropy. When he withdrew in 1916 after nine years as chairman, the Board resolved that "to Mr Gates the creation of the Board was due ; in a large sense he formulated its purposes and shaped its policies." He was succeeded by Wallace Butterick who had served as secretary from the beginning. After graduating from a normal school and a theological seminary, he began his preaching career in Minnesota and was later called to Albany, N. Y. for a short while before joining the Rockefeller forces in 1902. He it was who traveled in the South until he found a field in which the board could be "helpfully cooperative" — the same field, coincidentally, in which he had served as an agent for the Peabody and Slater funds. From 1916 until his death in 1926 he was chairman of the Board, shaping its policies, and in charge of spending the largest single fund ever devoted to education. Yet Mr Butterick, although he received many honorary degrees, was not a college graduate.

From 1915 to 1925, when it was announced that it had largely finished its work "in this part of the field," the Board made contingent gifts to many colleges. Between 1902 and 1925 it appropriated $60,000,000 toward the endowment of 291 colleges, not including medical schools. When the requisite supplemental sums are included this meant that a grand total of $200,000,000 was probably added to the permanent funds of American universities. The Board then concluded that public interest no longer needed a stimulus to give to university endowments. Before the Board paid its pledges certain requirements were insisted upon : the supplementary sum must be in cash or in sound securities ; it was not permitted to include legacies, and the university had to be free from debt. The total gifts of the G.E.B. toward endowments today amount to more than $150,000,000, which has helped to bring about nearly a tenfold increase in the endowment held by colleges and universities since 1902.

With a few exceptions (in the case of medical schools) the Board maintained its policy, announced in 1915, that it did not give buildings, grounds, or apparatus, nor make gifts to specific departments, chairs, or lines of research "because such gifts might operate as a restriction on the freedom of the institution and might in practice amount to interference with policy." It cannot be proved that the Rockefeller Board has in any specific instance influenced colleges or universities in their "policies," or acted as a restriction on freedom of speech, research, or opinion. Yet it has been obvious to many, those within and those outside universities, that the power implied in this tremendous sum inevitably has had the tendency to influence in subtle ways the opinions and policies of professors, university presidents, and trustees. Controlling such an enormous sum, invested in American railroads, corporations, and oil companies, it would hardly be necessary for the Board to speak any word on the subject of economic orthodoxy or radicalism.

When Congress began to make appropriations for farm demonstrations in the South, the G.E.B. then sent its agents to Maine and New Hampshire, not so much to promote education or agriculture as to advance agricultural education. State colleges were aided. Meanwhile the Southern states began to submit to popular vote amendments to their state constitutions permitting taxation for rural high schools. Teacher training classes were introduced into high schools because the normal schools gave training not adapted to rural conditions. Jackson Davis was appointed general field agent in charge of work of Negro education. Home-maker clubs for Negro girls were organized. In 1916 a study of the public school system of Maryland was made at the request of the state and recommendations made by the Board's agents were put into law after a year's survey. A start was made toward adult education in Mississippi by organizing "folk schools" for all the people in connection with the "agricultural high schools." Since it was found that teachers had no suitable places to live, "teachers' manse" were built in connection with consolidated rural schools where teachers could live and share expenses cooperatively.

The Board thus engaged in many varied activities, but the emphasis after 1915 centered more and more upon medical education. A study of the problem of training public health officials, begun by the Rockefeller Foundation in 1913, completed in 1915, recommended a plan for an Institute of Public Health and Hygiene. With the help of the G.E.B. it was decided to establish this at Johns Hopkins, to open in 1917. The Rockefeller Institute for Medical Research had been at work since 1901, and on January 1, 1916, in accordance with John D. Sr's stipulation that he might designate personally two-thirds of the amount of the appropriations drawn against his $32,000,-000 gift, he directed that $1,000,000 worth of securities paying 4½% interest be delivered to the Institute. The following year the medical school of the University of Chicago appealed for $5,300,000 for the McCormick Institute and the Presbyterian Hospital. S. A. Sprague gave $2,000,000, the G.E.B. and the Rockefeller Foundation gave a million each, and in ninety days the citizens of Chicago subscribed the remainder.

It is interesting to see how the big funds matched gifts to their favorite institutions. The Yale Medical School was reconstructed with the help of the G.E.B. and others. Vanderbilt University got $1,000,000 from the Carnegie Corporation, so the G.E.B. appropriated $4,000,000 for a medical school. Mr George Eastman gave a dental dispensary to Rochester costing $750,000 and an endowment of $1,000,000. He also gave the University of Rochester $4,000,000 for training in dentistry provided another $5,000,000 was raised. The G.E.B. promptly appropriated this sum. Mr Brookings helped Washington University in St Louis, so the G.E.B. appropriated $1,250,000 toward a total of $1,600,000 for endowment and $70,000 annually for current expenses ; $350,000 was earmarked for the Harvard Medical School and $400,000 for the study of obstetrics at Johns Hopkins. Even with these contributions, designed to help make medical teaching and research safe careers, a study made under the auspices of the Board in 1920 asserted that there were still lacking medical schools properly equipped on the clinical side in this country and that no medical school in the United States could equal the two smallest and weakest in Germany. In that year Edward S. Harkness gave $1,300,000 to the Presbyterian Hospital in New York, Joseph De Lamar gave $5,000,000 for a laboratory building, and $3,000,000 more was needed to complete the program. Thereupon the G.E.B., the Rockefeller Foundation and the Carnegie Corporation gave a million each while a "private donor" gave another million for the site. For the Columbia Medical Center the G.E.B. and the

Carnegie Corporation gave a million each in 1929. The Woods Hole Laboratory, another favored institution, got $750,000 from the Rockefeller Foundation, $100,000 from the Carnegie Corporation, and the G.E.B. gave $50,000 for a library and $750,000 for a dormitory.

As a Christmas gift to American education, John D. Sr announced in December 1919 that he would give $50,000,000 for the endowment of colleges to be applied toward raising of teachers' salaries. An investigation of faculty salaries showed that 75% of them received between $600 and $2500 a year. Capital appropriations went to selected institutions and annual grants were made to others for a limited period. By 1922 most of the Christmas gift had been appropriated but not disbursed, for in that year the total resources of the Board reached their peak : $135,047,056.

Early in 1916 the G.E.B. became interested in experimental education, appropriating $46,750 for the purpose. The studies made of the Gary schools, when considered by the New York City Board of Education, became an issue in the mayoralty campaign in 1917 when John F. Hylan deliberately confused in the public mind the plan for shifting of classes instituted by Dr Wirt in Gary, Indiana, with the labor shifts in the steel mills. When an attempt was made to make it seem as if the Rockefellers were trying to foist a special theory of education on the helpless children of New York, the Board withdrew itself from the picture as quickly as possible. Attention was then turned to the Lincoln School where, in connection with Teachers' College, experiments in a new curriculum might be carried out. In 1917, $192,000 was appropriated for it. Beginning on upper Park Avenue with 116 pupils, including the youngest Rockefeller grandchildren, in 1918, it had six grades of elementary school and three of Junior High. The following year $300,000, was paid for the ground at 425 West 123rd Street where the school was built, endowed with $500,000 by the Board and turned over to Teachers' College.

When the National Research Council was founded at the
suggestion of Woodrow Wilson in 1918 both the Carnegie
Corporation and the G.E.B. agreed to contribute annually to it
for research and scholarships.   This work broadened in 1922
and the G.E.B. and the Rockefeller Foundation said they would
contribute $50,000 each for fellowships and an additional $25,-
000 for the work of American scientists abroad. $60,000 was
set aside in 1923 for the American Classical League, and $240,-
000 for studies of honors courses in American universities.
$50,000 went to the study of reforestation in Europe by
American experts.   Legal education elicited an appropriation
of $750,000 in 1926 and an additional $30,000 was used to persuade Professor Josef Redlich of Vienna to lecture at Harvard
Law School for three years.   Princeton got $1,000,000 toward
a $3,000,000 fund for teaching and research in science.   When
Mr Eastman gave Rochester University $12,900,000, which
raised $10,000,000 more and announced that it needed another
$10,000,000 for its medical school, the G.E.B. responded with
$1,000,000 in 1923 and $750,000 in 1925.

It is interesting to watch the careers of the personnel connected with the foundations and the universities.   Dr Wickliffe Rose, who began as a teacher of philosophy in Peabody
College, was later an agent for the Peabody Fund, became
secretary of the Rockefeller Sanitary Commission in 1910 and
joined the General Education Board the same year.   When Mr
Butterick went into semi-retirement in 1923 Dr Rose became
president of the Board and following the custom of big corporations, Mr Butterick was retained as "chairman of the board."
The year before that Dr James R. Angell, who had been president of the National Research Council, later president of the
Carnegie Corporation, and after that president of Yale University, joined the Board, as did Raymond B. Fosdick, who was
later to become president of the Rockefeller Foundation and
serve on all the Rockefeller philanthropic boards.   Jerome D.

Greene, later secretary of the Rockefeller Foundation, joined the Board in 1912 and George E. Vincent, who became president of the Rockefeller Foundation, had been a member of the G.E.B. since 1914. In 1924 Trevor Arnett, who had written studies of the financial conditions of the colleges, resigned from the Board to become vice president of Chicago University but rejoined it later as its president, succeeding Wickliffe Rose.

The career of Dr Abraham Flexner is a story in itself. While his brother Simon was in charge of the Rockefeller Institute, he taught Latin and Greek in a Louisville, Kentucky, high school until he published a book in 1908 severely criticising American colleges. This led to a job with the Carnegie Foundation for the Advancement of Teaching, where he remained until 1925, serving as its secretary for the last eight years. Meanwhile he wrote a report on *Prostitution in Europe* in 1913 for the Rockefeller Foundation and investigated the Gary schools in 1916 for the G.E.B. He directed the studies in medical education for the G.E.B. from 1925 until he retired in 1930 to direct the Institute for Advanced Study at Princeton endowed with $5,000,000 by Louis Bamberger and his sister, Mrs Felix Fuld.

The first year a report was made, in 1915, the total funds of the G.E.B. were $46,116,929 (Book value). In that year it made a profit of $19,472 on its investments, chiefly railroad bonds, and it purchased $2,114,801 worth of new securities : railroad bonds, U. S. Steel bonds, 500 shares of Bankers Trust stock and 200 shares of Guaranty Trust. Since the Western Pacific Railroad failed to meet its 5% payments a "protective committee" was formed on which Starr J. Murphy, Rockefeller lawyer and Board member, represented the G.E.B. The Board's investments included more than $9,000,000 worth of oil stocks in Rockefeller companies and more than $7,000,000 in "miscellaneous" stocks, chiefly railroads and International Harvester, which probably profited by the improved agricultural methods promoted by the Board. Its bond portfolio included Interborough Rapid Transit of New York, Jones and Laughlin Steel, and Republic Iron and Steel.

In 1916–17 the Board lost $310,302 on Missouri Pacific bonds and $431,830 on Western Pacific, but showed a profit of $691,-479 on other investments. Its administrative expenses that year were $88,304 and its income $2,864,961, with disbursements of $2,309,720. Its annual appropriation then averaged about a million and a half a year. In 1928 a new item appeared on the financial statement among the assets : "secured demand loans, $60,400." Apparently this tax-free philanthropic institution went into the banking business temporarily to conserve its assets during the boom and crash, for in 1929 the "secured demand loans" jumped to $16,575,169. This was at a time when call money on Wall Street was paying very high interest rates. What could be shrewder, therefor, for those in charge of the investment portfolio to do than to sell securities at unnaturally high levels, loan the proceeds at several times higher interest rates than the securities paid, and take for collateral these same securities ? The worst that could happen, if the borrowers could not pay the interest, would be that the Board would get the forfeited collateral, amounting, probably, to about twice the amount loaned. There is nothing reprehensible about this unless you feel that a tax-free philanthropic foundation should not go into the banking business. In 1930 the secured demand loans dropped to $10,488,426 and in the following year disappeared altogether.

Although the quotations on the common stocks held by the G.E.B. fell off in 1929, the crash did little to harm the total market value of the investments held, since its investment officers followed the policy of the wealthy and invested in high grade bonds or kept their funds liquid. But when these funds were threatened in 1932–33 the G.E.B., like other foundations and millionaires, began to feel the pinch of the depression. An excellent income had been derived from the interest on unpaid appropriations : in 1928 these amounted to $46,741,474, which brought in $5,272,667.   On June 30, 1931 the Board reported undistributed income of $13,032,232 with unpaid appropriations reduced to $11,890,832.   An excellent cash position was maintained after the "secured demand" loan item disappeared from the assets, for then Chase Bank certificates of deposit amounting to $3,000,000 were held.   In 1932 this was halved but the Board had on hand $2,280,842 in cash.   According to its financial statement in 1929 the Board owned $43,393,476 worth of stocks and $26,456 in bonds.   In 1930 the bond portfolio jumped to $34,000,000.   After that the disbursements began to decline.   In 1931 the Board paid out $4,419,290, in 1932 $3,961,338, and in 1933 the expenditures were reduced to $3,725,414, so that the principal was not drawn upon.   Reducing disbursements still more in 1934, to $3,028,723, it revealed that this sum was $530,451 in excess of current income.   The reduced appropriations were made chargeable to income, it was explained, because it was decided to keep expenditures down until securities had regained some of their former value.   (See Chapter XII for their market value.)

By 1936 the bond holdings of the Board were reduced to $17,884,251 and its stocks to $31,175,148.   The income was $2,658,104.   Appropriations were $3,253,608 from income and $6,253,750 from principal, a total of $9,730,740.   Actual payments made during 1935–36 were $4,323,864.   The undisbursed income on hand June 30, 1936 was $8,688,467.   There remained unpaid appropriations from the principal, $13,865,481 and unpaid appropriations from the income accounts, $7,732,-197.   Cash of more than $3,000,000 is listed in the investment column and more than $8,000,000 in the "income accounts assets" as of June 30, 1936, indicating at that time unprecedented liquidity.

The present members of the board are those in the "Rockefeller family" who have long been closely associated with the philanthropic and business interests, such as Winthrop W. Aldrich, John W. Davis, Walter W. Stewart, and Owen D. Young. Both John D. Jr, and John D. 3rd are on the Board, as are Raymond B. Fosdick, Max Mason, former president of the Foundation, Jerome D. Greene, former secretary of the Foundation, and Trevor Arnett, long associated with the philanthropies. Its work is divided into five departments : social sciences and general education, ($1,252,460 appropriated), Natural Sciences ($12,200 appropriated), Medical Sciences, ($3,550,000 appropriated), and the Southern program ($1,345,735 appropriated).

In 1934 the Board made a grant to the American Council on Education for the establishment of an "American Youth Commission." $10,000 was spent on an analysis of how the needs of youth are being met in a small city (Muncie, Indiana), $19,200 for a similar analysis in a medium-sized city (Dallas, Texas), and $78,700 in a representative state (Maryland). An "Inventory of Oncoming Youth," originally set up by the Committee on Higher Education of the Pennsylvania Department of Public Instruction was furthered and $77,800 appropriated for a survey of the Civilian Conservation Corps. $250,000 was earmarked for a five-year study of the Educational Policies Commission inaugurated by the National Education Association. The annual grant to the Progressive Educational Association was raised from $10,000 to $15,000. This society also has a commission, "On Relations of Schools and Colleges," studying curriculum changes, which received $22,000 annually for a three-year period, and $270,000 was set aside over a period of three years for a Commission on Secondary School Curriculum for an intensive study of the characteristics of adolescents.

The Board also assisted in the launching of a monthly magazine, *Building America*, by the Society for Curriculum Study, which was guaranteed $30,000 for a three-year period when it is hoped the periodical will be self-supporting. A "Commission on Human Relations" is editing material on how to teach "human relations" in the schools ; surveys are being made on the teaching of English, Music, Art, and a committee is at work developing "criteria for identifying a good secondary school." A grant of $140,000, expendable over five years, was made for a study of students' success in college, particularly the students who come from the thirty schools cooperating with the Commission on the Relation of School to College. A clearing house for information regarding the use of motion pictures in education was set up and investigations made in the subject. Experimental films are being produced for which $75,000 was appropriated for a two-year period.

A limited number of fellowships (six in 1935–36) and grants in aid are made to individuals engaged in work closely connected with these projects. A larger number are granted through the Social Science Research Council. Two hundred and one such scholarships, costing $329,678 exclusive of administration, were granted in 1935–36, to "develop leaders in areas insufficiently manned for effective teaching and research." One hundred and twenty-two scholarships were granted for improving the "quality of educational leadership" in the South. Most of the recipients are connected with colleges and universities and will return to their positions. "For all these awards," the Board reports, "the first requirement was that the help be given to individuals having assured prospects of usefulness within a program now under development by the Rockefeller Foundation. Appointments are not open to application; choice of individual is determined by his direct relationship to a developing plan. . . The cooperation of the Board with other agencies in the training of personnel is due to the necessity of providing men and women trained for such special duties within an *accepted* * plan of action."

In the South the Board has concentrated on helping selected universities to undertake more aggressive "leadership" in "fields of special interest," on improving a small number of colleges "of regional influence," on aiding state departments of education in

* This word is not italicized in the Board's report.

training personnel, and on developing Negro education through public and private agencies. Libraries have been assisted at Birmingham, Southern College, the College of William and Mary, Davidson College, Furman University, Hendrix College, Mercer University, Southwestern College, the Universities of Texas, North Carolina, and Virginia, Vanderbilt and Duke Universities. A number of curriculum studies were helped. $136,500 was appropriated for state agents and assistants for Negro schools. Special teacher-training projects have also been financed, including one for teacher-librarians. A number of Negro schools and colleges were given emergency grants during the depression. $75,000 has been granted annually to Fisk University and a million and a half has been appropriated toward a three million endowment fund, which was completed by a grant from the Rosenwald Fund and $150,000 from the citizens of Nashville. Special appropriations were made to Atlanta University in Georgia, Talladega College in Alabama, Benedict College in South Carolina, Prairie View State Normal and Industrial College in Texas, and the Louisville Municipal College for Negroes in Kentucky. $130,000 was appropriated for the medical school at Fisk and $100,000 for Howard, while 46 fellowships were granted through various Negro schools and colleges.

Among its "emergency grants" during the depression the Board gave additional support to many projects financed in the main by governmental agencies in education. So much was done, in fact, by the combined agencies that the 1936 report quotes a worker as saying, "what might have been a disaster was turned into a constructive opportunity." $500,000 was appropriated by the Board to these emergency programs of which one-fourth went to nursery schools and parent-education work, and a little less than one-fourth to educational aid for unemployed youth. Over half went to adult and general education projects. Youth was helped by a $30,000 grant to the American Council on Education for investigations conducted by the

Committee on Youth Problems of the U.S. Office of Education, $40,000 to prepare suitable study materials, particularly in the social sciences, for young men of different levels of training, and $4000 to the New York State Department of Education to prepare materials for the New Era colleges established by federal relief funds. $70,000 was placed at the disposal of the Affiliated Schools of Workers, which is sponsored by a number of universities, to help in the education of women in industry, of which $14,000 went to evaluate its own work. Allied to this is the Workers' Education Bureau, which works through the American Federation of Labor. It got $65,250 to organize workers' educational classes in industrial centers.

These facts and figures not only give an indication of the scope and influence of the Board, they also suggest in how many ways American education is being colored and directed by agencies drawing upon Rockefeller money for their support. To document this completely would entail a catalog of thousands of projects listed in the annual reports since 1915. Only those engaged in education or whose interests are in some way related to it appreciate the pervasive effect of the Rockefeller millions on American education. The Board has appropriated $247,392,112 since 1902. A sum of this size represents a tremendous power. But most of the gifts of the G.E.B. are contingent on other sums being raised from other sources. In the public mind the Rockefellers and the General Education Board have often received credit for philanthropy in which thousands of unheralded donors also contributed. The state and national governments have spent as much or more on many of the projects in the South instigated by the General Education Board. When it was established it was hoped by the Rockefellers that other philanthropists would give large sums to the Board for it to administer. Only one such contributor has done so, Anna T. Jeanes, who gave it $200,000 to spend for Negro rural schools in the South. This has been administered and the fund kept separate. Other millionaires, apparently, have preferred not to place the spending of large funds in the hands of the Rockefeller Board.

However, without getting any additional funds, the power of the Board is incalculable. Not only does it control the direction of its own large funds, but its policy of contingent giving places it in position to control the direction of nearly all large expenditures in the field of American education. The power of a quarter of a billion dollars is tremendous, but the power of a half a billion dollars is more than twice as great. By giving $250,000,000 to American education it is probable that more than $500,000,000 was raised. Thus, the policies and ideas of the Rockefellers, their board, and their agents control and permeate American education. It is not necessary for anybody connected with the Board to suggest policies or to express ideas. Everybody related to American education knows very well what they are. Today every teacher, professor, student is touched in some manner by one or more projects financed by the Board. To do educational research, or indeed research of any sort, one comes into contact with commissions, reports, conferences, investigations, helped in part by the Board. The whole educational community in the United States lives in a refulgent glow generated by the Rockefeller millions. A career in education is unthinkable without drawing at some point upon these vast resources. The possibility of getting a stipend, a fellowship, a grant in aid, inevitably conditions the direction and thought of every educational worker or researcher in the country. No university president, trustee, professor, or instructor is so stupid as not to realize the actual and potential help that the Board can be to him or his university.

And in a capitalist democracy this must be so : the South did not create a free educational system until instigated by the Board, secondary school education could not have progressed so rapidly without the G.E.B., Negro education would have remained primitive were it not for these philanthropies, medical education in the United States was shockingly backward until Rockefeller and other millionaires began to give great sums to it.   Only through the efforts and contributions of the Board were teachers' salaries raised and adequate endowments obtained for hundreds of schools and colleges.   This is one of the functions of a foundation.   If it has been at a price in loss of independence, if it has meant an insidious influence upon research, thought, and teaching, if it has given a potential control over education to a giant educational trust, these are payments we, as a people, have had to make for undeniable benefits.

"In due time the objects of the General Education Board will have been achieved," the report dated February 11, 1932 declared.   "The General Education Board will then have ceased to exist. . . It will not go on forever.   The statesmen and benefactors of the next age will invent the organization and provide the means they require."   Mr Rockefeller gave the Board power over its own life : the principal as well as the interest may be spent at its discretion.   Since it has embarked upon a number of policies and projects it must feel bound to see them through.   In 1927 it was spending its principal but the depression gave it such a shock that it decreased appropriations within income limits.   It is not probable that the Board has any definite ideas regarding its length of life : it may decide to spend the principal as quickly as would seem to it advisable, or it may take measures to extend its tenure indefinitely.   The tendency of Boards of this sort, unless a definite time limit has been placed upon them, is to continue indefinitely since those engaged in its work are usually apt to see constantly widening horizons of usefulness.

It is possible that another and worse depression may deal to its securities a knockout blow which would bring its activities to an abrupt termination.   The plan is now to liquidate it within eight years, although it is possible John D. Jr or some other member of the Rockefeller clan may decide to further its projects by additional funds when the present capital becomes depleted. The financial condition of colleges and universities have, since the depression, been the source of considerable worry in educational circles, for upon them depend not only the education of millions but the livelihood of thousands. Dr Trevor Arnett in 1936 made a study of this subject, showing what the diminishing rate of interest on investments has done to the college endowments. He found that endowments had increased from $166,000,000 in 1900 to a total of over a billion and a half in 1934. One fourth of the institutions had 88.8% of the total endowment. "In 1928 sixteen institutions (the larger ones) secured a return on their funds of more than 5%, running from 5.01% in one instance up to 5.64% in another. One university secured a return of 6.5% while three institutions reported a return of 4.68%, 4.90%, and 4.99%, respectively. In 1935 only one of these institutions reported a return above 5%, viz., 5.02% while eight reported a rate between 4 and 5% and eleven reported a rate between 3 and 4%." Another authority gives the rate on $1,305,000,000 endowment as 3.8%. In 1890 the endowment of $74,000,000 paid 5.35%.

Whether you admit that the capitalist system is running down, the fact remains that there has been a decrease in income on the large investments of the universities, notwithstanding the additional increments in their capital, and it is a problem causing considerable anxiety to educators. More and more capital funds must be given, paying less and less income, in order to keep our great universities running. Remember that most of these endowments were given in "gold dollars" and their present resources are counted in "Roosevelt" dollars. They must raise student fees, making higher education a luxury for the few, or look for support from millionaires or the government. Since the millionaires are in a financial condition similar to the universities, they hesitate to part with large capital funds, and the government is not disposed at present to make large appropriations for education. Here, perhaps, with augmented funds, the G.E.B. and other foundations may step in and keep in operation privately endowed universities. Large endowments have meant great expansion in departments and buildings. Greater and greater income must be found to keep these enormous plants in operation. With increasing prosperity, of course, this problem will take care of itself, for the universities have their funds well invested in the American economic system.

But if the bottom should drop out of the values of bonds, mortgages, and stocks, and interest rates are again curtailed, then not only the universities but the foundations would be sorely hit. The Board has the same type of investments as the universities, the same type as, indeed, large, cautious, wise investors of large means are apt to have. It is composed of university presidents, bankers, and leaders of industry who are the trustees, directors, and financial advisors to large corporations, universities, and foundations alike. It is probable that those in charge of its investments are in as good a position as anybody in the world to get information on what investment policies to follow. It is logical to suppose that they can get such information from the Rockefellers themselves and their financial advisors, from the heads of such banks as the Chase, the Guaranty Trust, or the Bankers Trust, from the Morgan partners on the Rockefeller boards, from the far-flung empire of oil controlled by Rockefeller money. It is upon them and their interests that our educational and philanthropic as well as our industrial and financial fabric depends. If by their wisdom, their policies, and their ideas, they cannot keep it from going to pieces, then we must look elsewhere for leadership and support.

CHAPTER IX

PENSIONS AND EDUCATIONAL STANDARDS

THE CARNEGIE FOUNDATION FOR THE
ADVANCEMENT OF TEACHING

Having reached the conclusion that "the least rewarded of all professions is that of the teacher in our higher educational institutions," so that "able men hesitate to adopt teaching as a career, and many old professors whose places should be occupied by younger men, cannot be retired," Andrew Carnegie transferred to the trustees of the Carnegie Foundation December 1, 1905, $10,000,000 worth of 5% First Mortgage Bonds of the United States Steel Corporation, "the revenue of which is to provide retiring pensions for teachers of Universities, Colleges, and Technical Schools in our country, Canada, and Newfoundland under such conditions as you may adopt from time to time. Expert calculation shows that the revenue will be ample for the purpose."

Within four years it was evident that the revenue would not be "ample" nor even sufficient. No "expert calculation" was made in 1905, but only a rough estimate, resulting in much confusion, embarrassment, and disappointment later. What caused considerable worry at the time, however, was Mr Carnegie's exclusion of what he called "Sectarian" institutions. "Only such as are under the control of a sect or require Trustees (or a majority thereof), Officers, Faculty, or Students to belong to any specified sect, or which impose any theological test, are to be excluded." * Since most of our colleges were denominational in origin and still had sectarian connections, this provision caused much gnashing of teeth. "Should we," the trustees of colleges asked themselves, "free ourselves from the denomina-

* State universities were also excluded at first.

tion which founded us in order to make our faculty members eligible for Carnegie pensions ? By doing so would we lose denominational support ? Which would mean most in financial returns in the long run ?"

Mr Carnegie announced his gift April 16, 1905, in a letter to the twenty-four trustees he selected, headed by Charles W. Eliot and including David Starr Jordan, Nicholas Murray Butler, Jacob Gould Schurman, Frank A. Vanderlip, and Woodrow Wilson. The Carnegie Foundation was incorporated in New York State May 8, 1905, the securities were transferred to it December 1, 1905 and it was reincorporated by Act of Congress as the Carnegie Foundation for the Advancement of Teaching March 10, 1906. During the summer of 1905 questionnaires were sent to the colleges to obtain information the Foundation would need. Data were received concerning educational standards, relations of colleges to the states and to denominations, the compensation paid professors, and maximum and minimum pay. Six hundred and fifteen institutions were queried ; 421 replied. The average salary of 6969 professors was found to be $1376, the maximum $1783, and the minimum $726. The average age was thirty-eight years and the average length of service eight years. A not unimportant aside was noted : the committee was particularly impressed by the large place small colleges filled in the American system of education.

Since one of the most important objects of the Foundation was to raise educational standards, institutions were graded according to their apparent eligibility for what was to be called the "accepted list" : A, universities with graduate schools and professional departments, B, college or technical schools with good entrance requirements, C, those chiefly preparatory in character. From the very moment the idea was conceived the Foundation was never thought of by anybody connected with it as a mere insurance or annuity scheme. The act of incorporation stated that it was to "do all things necessary to encourage, uphold and dignify the profession of teaching and the cause of higher education" and from its inception those in charge tried to make it a means of advancing teaching and raising educational standards. By classifying colleges as eligible or ineligible, by granting to some and withholding from others, by making public its findings and demanding higher and higher standards in entrance requirements and scholarship, those in charge of the Foundation believed that they could use the power of the $10,000,000 to advance the cause of education.

On the basis of the information obtained, the Foundation on April 6, 1906 drew up an "accepted list" of fifty colleges in the United States and two in Canada. Twenty-five were in New England and all except one was in the North. In the first year a total of $122,130 was paid in annuities to 88 persons. Professors having reached the age of 65 were eligible to retire with annuities amounting roughly to 80% of their average active pay. This averaged $1387 per person. Widows got half what their husbands would have received, averaging $833 annually. Professors had to be active for fifteen years previous to retirement to be eligible. They might retire earlier than 65 if they had had 25 years of service. Those whose pay averaged below $1600 got 90%. If the pay averaged more than $1200 the retired professor got $1000, plus $50 for each $100 of active pay in excess of $1200, but none were allowed more than $3000.* These figures were reduced somewhat for those who retired on the basis of long service rather than age.

Immediately, as professors brought pressure to bear upon trustees, there was a scramble of colleges to become eligible. It was realized at once that colleges on the "accepted list" were thereby distinguished and more apt to get endowment funds from wealthy donors than those who were not "accepted." If a professor were eligible for a pension he would prefer to teach in an accepted college for less pay than to work for higher pay

* Professor William James of Harvard received this maximum for several years before he died.

at a non-accepted institution without prospect of an annuity. Denominational colleges which had planned to cut their sectarian apron-strings in 1905 feared to do so because of the probable accusation that they did it merely to get on the "accepted list." Randolph-Macon College was accepted in 1907 but retired from the list in 1909 because the Methodists insisted on choosing the trustees. George Washington University was dropped for a time because it had insufficient endowment. A number of institutions, such as Boston Museum, which considered themselves educational in character, were refused. Five hundred individual applications of professors who thought they should be helped had to be refused the first year. Ministers, editorial writers, teachers in normal schools, and many others pleaded to be included. Need had nothing to do with eligibility and many heart-rending individual cases of retired professors, old, blind, destitute, and in poorhouses had to be turned down.

Soon the question of including tax-supported universities arose. Mr Carnegie declared in 1905 that he could not "presume to include them." However, in 1909 he relented, and said that if the legislatures and the governors approved, he would add another $5,000,000 to the Foundation's endowment so that state colleges could be included. The Commonwealth of Massachusetts acted at once and thirty-two other states promptly followed. In that year the first actuarial studies were made for the Foundation. It was found that if the professors' salaries should increase and every professor in the eligible list should claim his allowance the endowment would be inadequate. However, the annual report dismissed this cloud on the horizon by remarking that it was really a problem of "common sense" and "fairness" and only partly an actuarial problem since the trustees in Rule X, reserved the power "to alter these rules in such a manner as experience may indicate as desirable for the benefit of the whole body of teachers." They demonstrated this by permitting retirement after twenty-five years only in cases of disability, although what constituted disability was a matter of considerable disagreement.

Confronted by the imminent probability of having more colleges on the "accepted list" than the endowment could provide for, the Foundation announced in 1910 that mere "compliance with the requirements" was not enough to get on the list. The question of exceptional cases was also a source of worry. College presidents who had been let out of their jobs considered themselves automatically eligible for Carnegie pensions. Even though they had been fired for incompetence, they were always ready to prove the extremity of their need and their meritorious service to the cause of education. This was before universities had set up any pension systems of their own and many college boards of trustees saw in the Foundation a heaven-sent agency to rescue them from embarrassing dilemmas. They thought that they could obtain Carnegie pensions for unpopular professors or university presidents and thus ease them out of their jobs with no ill-feelings or loss of dignity. "Few business houses," commented Dr Henry S. Pritchett in 1911, president of the Foundation, "would be as heartless with their old servants." Some were so hard-hearted that they contemplated retiring professors of long service without annuity if the Foundation could not take care of them. The trustees of many colleges maintained that they could not use college funds for pension purposes.

Dr Pritchett, who resigned from the Massachusetts Institute of Technology, where he had been president for six years, to become president of the Foundation in 1906, used the annual report for lengthy dissertations on the state of American education. "What proportion of students in the colleges are really of college grade?" he asked in 1910. "Are professional schools of creditable service to the professions?" It is not recorded that he has yet obtained satisfactory answers. After the Civil War, he noted, the people of the United States turned to education with a "veritable passion." The problem, as he saw it, was one of articulation between the college and the secondary school. The colleges complained of the superficial knowledge of the students who came to them, their unreadiness to apply themselves in any prolonged or concentrated way. The secondary schools complained of the difference between what the colleges advertised and what they actually performed. Dr Pritchett quoted a report on the American Rhodes scholar who finds difficulty in doing his work, arising out of the superficiality and diffuseness of his previous training in American secondary schools and colleges and the failure of this training to give him intellectual power. "It is," commented Dr Pritchett, "the characteristic of our whole American life."

Commenting on the appointment of a president to the University of Kentucky, Dr Pritchett remarked that this was "one of the most backward of all states in education" and that this appointee "had no qualifications for the educational duties to which he was called." The political control of education in Oklahoma, he noted, "excites more than ordinary regret." Later he criticised college catalogs, quoting one of a tiny Ohio college as saying, "Our reputation for educational effort is world-wide. . . In the past year a new factor has entered our school life : We have an endowment fund started !" And Iowa State Teachers' College advertised proudly that it "never refused to receive a single student," a boast many others might acknowledge also. Pacific Union College devoted the cover of its catalog to an advertisement for biscuits.

Meanwhile Dr Abraham Flexner delivered to the Foundation his sensational report on medical schools which did more than anything else to induce the General Education Board and other philanthropic agencies to make large contributions to medical education. "It is impossible to print the truth respecting all of our 150 medical schools without damaging some of them," the report declared. "It is impossible to maintain the standard of the report without endangering the very bases upon which many of the schools rest." The state of medical education in the United States was found to be deplorable, particularly on the Pacific Coast. California had all varieties of medical schools. San Francisco had two strong schools but Los Angeles had "no educational institution able to deal with medicine on a sound or fruitful basis." A "College of Medical Evangelists" was found where medical subjects were studied from a Biblical point of view. It required 900 hours of Bible study, 540 hours of medicine, 250 hours of evangelistic field work, and 240 hours in care of the sick for an M.D. degree. Ohio was involved in a political fight on homeopathy versus allopathy, as a result of the state university's plan to take over the Starling-Ohio Medical College at Columbus — a city, by the way, which in 1914 had "no public clinic for the poor, no city hospital, and no hospital for infectious diseases."

In addition to these two studies of medicine made between 1910 and 1913, costing $57,500, the Foundation also financed studies into the organization of educational institutions, college entrance requirements, agricultural colleges, the financial status of the teacher, legal education, and admission to the bar. This was an activity not specifically included in the original endowment from Mr Carnegie, although he approved of it. The research showed promise of such important results, however, that Mr Carnegie, as president of the newly founded Carnegie Corporation, offered a million and a quarter of its funds to the Foundation for a Division of Educational Inquiry.* Soon after that the state of Vermont requested a study made of its school system. The report recommended a reorganization of the public schools and suggested a withdrawal of subsidies to three Vermont colleges on the ground that they led to "educational politics." A howl went up from the colleges and from

---

* $1,000,000 in Chicago and Northwestern Railroad Co. 4% Mortgage Bonds and $250,000 in Westchester County Bronx Valley Sanitary Sewer District 4% Bonds.

patriotic Vermonters who resented the Carnegie investigation, but the recommendations were carried out.

Dr Pritchett devoted a section of nearly every annual report to a discussion of various pension systems. As early as 1906 a study was made of Army pensions. By 1911 he affirmed his belief in a contributory system as being most just and least harmful. The following year he discussed state pension systems and the systems put in by a few colleges and universities for themselves. Actuarial estimates, he declared, were of no help, for the problem was insoluble on an actuarial basis. By experience the Foundation had learned not to make exceptions. "It would astound the public as it did the Trustees," he wrote in 1918, "to discover year by year how many university presidents and teachers, men in their early fifties and sound health, persuaded themselves that for one reason or another, the cause of education or the public good would be advanced if they were endowed with a pension under some special ruling." A few hundred adequate pensions, he said, were better than thousands of very small ones. After all, the policy of the Foundation was not merely to pay pensions, but to dignify the profession of teaching through such pensions. In 1913 the Foundation announced that the pensions granted would be on the basis of average salary of the last five years regardless of the service rendered, even if part-time. A professor therefore found it better to retire altogether and get a pension than to work part-time and draw a smaller pension when he did retire. Many retired professors continued to lecture occasionally, a few obtained remunerative jobs in business, and there was considerable discussion of what constituted "retirement." It was finally decided that a professor might still get a retirement pension no matter what he did so long as he did not teach.

In 1915 the Foundation received a report on the weakness of its pension system which showed conclusively what was wrong with the Carnegie system. A non-contributory system will not work in the long run for the economic betterment of a group, it said. A pension system should receive the support of the teacher and his employer. "No system can be secure unless a reserve is set aside year by year. Only thus can the cost be determined." The original conception of paying pensions for professors in a limited number of institutions, it was seen, ten years after beginning it, was neither adequate nor fair. Teachers refused jobs in colleges which had no retiring allowance, thus the colleges on the "accepted list" could pay lower salaries and still hold their professors. A non-contributory system thus always had the effect of reducing or holding down salaries. "It is not possible for the Foundation or any other endowment," the report declared, "however large, to undertake the burden for all the colleges in the United States and Canada." The endowment, it was discovered, was inadequate to provide the retiring allowances for all the teachers then in the "accepted" colleges.

This was a situation that might have been foreseen and there were those who had seen it. Nevertheless the Foundation continued a policy that brought it to the brink of bankruptcy. The only thing it could do, when it finally faced the problem, was to change the rules. In 1917 it reiterated its right to change the conditions under which annuities were granted and it pointed out that no "free" pensions were possible which did not affect pay. Some teachers, the Foundation discovered to its surprise, considered the rules granting pensions as contracts. Those administering the Foundation had learned much. "It is to be regretted that this knowledge was not available when the Foundation began," Dr Pritchett observed. However, he assured the pensioners that the Foundation was trying to deal sincerely with its obligations and its mistakes. The estimated cost of the annuity system then in operation, if continued, would be $69,000,000 in the next forty-five years. The income of the endowment was not nearly sufficient, and it was estimated that in forty-five years there would be a deficit of $37,000,000. Evidently something had gone wrong with the "expert calculation" mentioned by Mr Carnegie in 1905.

Faced with that situation the Foundation turned to the wealthy Carnegie Corporation for aid, asking it to supply capital for a Teachers Annuity Association. Though called "sister institutions" the Carnegie Foundation for the Advancement of Teaching has behaved more like a spendthrift son toward the Carnegie Corporation than an older sister. The Corporation agreed to do so on the condition that the Foundation begin at once a reserve fund, using its surplus of $1,000,000 as a starter. The Corporation then would contribute $5,000,000 at once and $600,000 annually up to a total of $13,000,000. $1,000,000 of this was for the capital of the Teachers Annuity Association, $1,000,000 for the assistance of teachers getting pensions or due to get them, and $11,000,000 for a reserve, the income of which would be available in ten years for the discharge of the obligations of the Foundation. At the same time the Corporation gently advised a revision of the rules in such a way that the pensions would not exceed income.

The Foundation had made, it seemed, a study of life insurance and had discovered that very few college professors carried life insurance policies. So it was decided to set up the Teachers Insurance and Annuity Association. The Foundation, with the help of the Corporation, would provide the overhead cost so that the teachers could get insurance at cost, which meant at rates lower than those offered by commercial or even mutual companies. "How much speculation had occupied the attention of teachers," Dr Pritchett remarked in 1917, "it is impossible to say, but probably to a larger extent than is generally supposed." Many professors, it was known, had invested in weak insurance companies. After a questionnaire had been sent to the colleges with an explanation of the Foundation's pension problem, a study was started by a committee composed of six trustees, two members appointed by the American Association of University Professors, one each by the Association of American Universities, the National Association of

State Universities, and the Association of American Colleges.

This committee reported that 40% of the male teachers in the universities were in their thirties. The estimated annual cost of pensions would be $1,753,073 annually if all the professors eligible retired at 65. The grants to female teachers and widows would bring the annual total up to $2,226,422. "Any pensions system supported by a fixed income," the committee concluded, "is a continually growing load which in the end will be too heavy for any fixed source of support." The cost of retiring allowances to the Foundation was $570,214 in 1916 and the income available was $800,322, so the immediate problem was taken care of: the calculations of the committee indicated, however, grave doubts about the future. Furthermore, the Foundation could not undertake annuity contracts because the moment payments were accepted it would become an insurance company and subject to the New York State regulations for insurance companies.

So, somewhat reluctantly, the original idea of giving teachers a new sense of security through the granting of annuities had to be abandoned. The original estimated cost of $410,000 annually had been completely exploded by the growing number of colleges, the number "accepted," the increase in the number of professors, and the apparently unanticipated increase in their salaries. 564 allowances had been granted in the first twelve years. Dr Pritchett remarked that the effect of non-contributory pensions was "demoralizing." With the approval of the committee the rules were changed. Professors were thus classified : Group A : All connected with "accepted" institutions on November 17, 1915, and who reached the age of 65 before June 30, 1923, would get the full retiring allowances they had been led to expect, as would also those in Group B, who had not reached 65 on June 30, 1923. Group C, however, those who had become associated with "accepted" institutions after November 17, 1915, would merely be eligible to get disability annuities after five years as a teacher. As for pensions they were advised to take out insurance for themselves with the Teachers Insurance and Annuity Association.

There was considerable criticism of these revisions which led several colleges to set up their own pension systems. But the Teachers Insurance and Annuity Association got off to a good start. Without agents it began signing up college professors with insurance and annuity policies. So successful was it that by 1925 the expense of management exceeded the income from $1,000,000 which the Foundation had set aside from funds supplied by the Corporation to pay overhead,* so that it had to apply to the Carnegie Corporation for further grants in order that the policyholders would not be called upon to bear any of these expenses. Furthermore, the discovery was made that although by 1928 the reserves of the Foundation would be more than the $13,000,000 anticipated, the cost of retiring allowances, because of the continued rise in salaries, had risen far beyond the actuarial estimate of 1916. An increase of $100 a year to professors' salaries, it was pointed out, meant an additional load of $2,000,000 for the Foundation. It seemed to be impossible to get an accurate list of the number of professors eligible. Apparently the Foundation left it to the colleges to compile the lists and permitted them to make additions from time to time which threw calculations off balance. New names kept cropping up which had been omitted for one reason or another from the list compiled ten years previously. War service, for example, counted as professorial service, and it seemed unjust to deprive professors of pensions because a careless officer neglected to include their names. In 1925–26 alone 97 new names appeared. Many of these were declared ineligible but those remaining added $200,000 to the annual load. 3700 teachers had expectations of annuities. But,

---

* Income on $1,000,000 was $50,000. The excess overhead cost amounted to $65,000.

the report for 1926 pointed out, it would be unfair to be generous to a limited number for a few years and then reduce the annuity later.

Such a remark was usually a warning that pensions would be reduced. By 1929 the annual cost of retiring allowances and annuities reached $1,445,690. The income from the general fund was $1,524,208, but the cost of pension studies and administration brought about a difference of more than $100,000 over income. It was obviously necessary to revise the rules again. The allowances, the report for 1929 declared, were originally $1500, then they were for $2000 for a long period, and recently they had risen to $2500. The level of professorial salaries, it noted, had risen beyond any expectation that would have been reasonable in 1916, due in part to the stimulation given by the General Education Board. The retirement age was therefore set at 70 instead of 65. Maximum allowances were established at 70 for those who were 65 in 1929 at $3000, in 1930 at $2300, in 1931 at $1600, in 1932 at $1000, which would be the maximum thereafter. A teacher retiring at 70, it was pointed out, who was 65 in 1931, thus had seven years to add to his accumulations to take care of him the rest of his life. It did not say that he would have to work five years longer and then get a smaller pension than he had been led to expect. The Carnegie Corporation once more came to the rescue, however, to make some of these provisions less harsh by granting a fund of $5,400,000, which was to be used to supplement the retiring allowances given by the Foundation. A number of colleges joined in supplementing the annuities.

Of course a howl of protest went up when these reductions were announced May 1, 1929. William Macdonald wrote in the *Nation* :

"It is bad enough to be reminded from time to time that corporations are not supposed to have souls but when a corporation that is not operated for profit calmly announces that it does not any longer propose to keep faith in the beneficial social enterprise in which it has long been engaged, the reminder seems to be rubbed in with peculiar harshness and brutality. When it appears that the corporation in question has been run on a low plane of intelligence and that policies which would have done discredit to an amateur in merchandising or finance have produced their natural fruit in virtual bankruptcy the most sympathetic critic may well wonder whether the boasted efficiency of American business possesses, after all, the high virtues claimed for it.

"It would be idle for the Foundation to insist that the data available in 1905 were insufficient to enable it to make a reasonably accurate forecast of its probable obligations. The information was abundant. . . It was for the Foundation to say within its own discretion what academic standards entitle an institution to a place on its approved list, what age limits or previous terms of service. . . Ordinary business intelligence dictated that such matters be examined and determined. What the Foundation did, on the contrary, was to blunder from the beginning. It has continued to blunder throughout its twenty-four years. Now with three times the principal fund with which it started, it is virtually bankrupt if by bankruptcy means the inability to make good its financial assurances, and the professors must stand the loss. . . It does not seem it would have been a crushing intellectual feat for the Foundation with every facility for obtaining information and expert advice to have made these elementary requirements."

Edwin W. Patterson, writing in the American Association of University Professors' *Bulletin* in March 1930, said :

"The reduction from $3,600, the prior maximum, to $1,500 raised a serious problem for those who have relied upon the Carnegie retiring allowance as a provision for old age. It is no sufficient answer to say that they should not have relied upon the rules of the foundation because those rules did not make a legally enforceable contract. . . In a public statement made last Spring as well as in a letter to President Crew, Dr Pritchett stated that 'free pensions had been found to be, like most free gifts, demoralizing.' These reasons for saying that the free pensions are demoralizing boil down to the view that each college teacher should look out for himself and provide his own retiring allowance. One might point out that this was not Mr Carnegie's view when he inaugurated the free pension scheme. . . If the free pensions system was demoralizing in 1916, if it is demoralizing in 1929, may it not be even more demoralizing in 1932, and may not the Trustees determine to make a further reduction in the free pension in order to devote the Foundation's funds to some less demoralizing objective (e.g. further investigations of college athletics ?)."

Nor is this the end of the story. The Foundation began in 1906 with $10,000,000 worth of U. S. Steel bonds. In the early years the income was not spent, the accumulations were invested, so that by 1910 the Foundation had $11,114,056 in total assets, and an income of $543,881. But expenditures rose so that by 1911 they were within $10,000 of the income. The additional $5,000,000 promised by Mr Carnegie was then paid in installments increasing the assets, which had been growing in value, so that by 1917 the Foundation owned $12,000,000 worth of U. S. Steel bonds and $2,164,000 in other securities in addition to $1,250,000 for the Division of Educational Inquiry. By 1929, as a result of further grants from the Carnegie Corporation and appreciation in the value of the securities held, the total funds amounted to $32,257,500. But there still remained a variable factor which could not be estimated in advance : the rising cost of overhead of the Teachers Insurance and Annuity Association.

The 1929 report reminded its readers that "the benefits accruing under the rules are based upon a conservative actuarial estimate of the resources of the Foundation. It is to be clearly understood that they are not contractual and that the obligations of the Foundation do not go beyond the resources now guaranteed to it." That was probably intended to warn the professors not to expect too much in the future. Everything seemed to be going well. The Teachers Insurance and Annuity Association reported an income of $3,870,522 and assets of $14,099,955. Its invested securities yielded 4.93% interest. For this the Association "gratefully acknowledges the wise and courteous guidance which men of large interests and experience have accorded to its finance committee and Board of Trustees."

But the item for overhead expenses had risen to $85,000 annually.

This was a growing burden which could not go on forever unchecked. It was estimated by Henry James, president of the Teachers Insurance and Annuity Association, in 1936 that a total of about $508,000 was contributed by the Foundation for the overhead of the TIAA. In that year arrangements were made to "terminate the period of the Association's tutelage." By 1935 the Association had outstanding more than 22,000 contracts for annuity and insurance with more than 15,000 teachers and others engaged in educational work. It paid in 1936 more than $500,000 in retirement benefits and up to that year more than $1,400,000 in life insurance policies. Its assets were $58,000,000 and they were growing at the rate of $7,000,000 a year. This was a rather big baby to support by way of overhead expenses. When the burden grew too great for the Foundation, the ever-ready younger sister across the hall at 522 Fifth Avenue * took it over. The Association's annual draft for these expenses mounted year by year until in 1935 it reached $160,000. The officers of the Corporation realized that this drain must in some way be "liquidated." Henry James remarked that year that the relations between the Association and the Corporation were "far from satisfactory."

Hopefully the Association expressed its appreciation through its trustees in 1935: "The Carnegie Corporation has never disappointed the Association in this relationship. It has apparently concluded that the money was being spent judiciously, and has agreed to the estimates without haggling over details. . . But none the less the Association's dependent status is not one that the Association can regard as business-like, suitable, or consonant with its own permanent interests." Looking

* The Carnegie Foundation for the Advancement of Teaching and the Carnegie Corporation occupy jointly the 10th floor of the Guaranty Trust Building.

for a way out of the difficulty, the Corporation had meanwhile sought independent actuarial advice and laid the problem before the Insurance Commissioner of the State of New York. The chickens, incubated so hopefully and hatched with optimism, had come home to roost.   The beautiful idea of paying the overhead expenses of the TIAA did not look so beautiful in 1935 as it had in 1918.

Dr Frederic P. Keppel, president of the Corporation, remarked in his 1936 report : "For sometime it has been recognized that the existing arrangement between the two did not furnish a satisfactory *modus vivendi* for the future." Speaking in tones which sound startlingly like those of Dr Pritchett, Dr Keppel declared that the understanding by which the Corporation agreed to provide for the Association's annual operating expenses "was moral rather than legal and was too vague to be comfortable for either organization." On its side, the Corporation could not control the annual drafts except by interference in its internal decisions, and the Association "was conscious of certain dangers unavoidably associated with its dependent status." For more than two years committees tried to solve the problem. It was finally decided that all policies and contracts of the Association outstanding on January 1, 1936 should be carried to termination without cost of administration to the policy-holders. Policies written subsequently included in the premium rates a moderate charge, sufficient to assure to the Association the "means of servicing an indefinite volume of new business without embarrassment on the score of overhead expense." *

The Corporation, however, had to part with another lump sum which would also "reinforce the capital and surplus structure and thus assist it to write business at a low cost." * The sum pledged was $6,700,000, which the Corporation agreed to pay to the TIAA. $2,700,000 was paid before December 31, 1935, but not included in this payment were the expenses of

* Dr Keppel's report.

administration for 1935 which the Corporation also paid. Further payments amounting to $4,000,000 were to be made before December 31, 1938 at the convenience of the Corporation. Until the full pledge is paid the overhead costs of the TIAA will continue to be borne by the Corporation.* Thus the Corporation "liquidates its indefinite involvement on terms which must be recognized as liberal and handsome. The grant of $6,700,000 on top of the million originally paid gives the Association resources more than equivalent to the yearly subventions upon which it has depended during the development stage." †

This stage is now said to be definitely passed, although the final payment by the Carnegie Corporation to the TIAA will not be until late in 1938 and the Corporation must bear the overhead expenses until that time. According to the 1937 report of the TIAA its total funds amount to $80,444,611 and its total income for that year was $13,343,821. It has 877 cooperating institutions which contribute premiums toward deferred annuities, which include some research organizations and secondary schools as well as colleges and universities. These institutions usually match dollar for dollar the premium paid by the teacher, deduct the teacher's contributions from salary, and forward the premiums monthly to the Association, which administers the plan. Each policy is a contract between the teacher and the Association ; the college is not a party to it. Up to October 1, 1937 no loan provision or cash surrender clause was included. These are now included in the life insurance policies but not in the annuity contracts. The passage of the Social Security Law which excludes non-profit-making institutions from its provisions gives the TIAA a new argu-

---

* Henry James' report.
† The story is not quite finished, even yet. The foundation made actuarial studies from 1933 to 1935 which show that in twelve years the pension load will again be greater than the income of the Foundation ! It is hoping to borrow the money from the Carnegie Corporation and repay it when the load lightens after 1955.

ment in persuading college trustees to sign up with it. The list of pensionables with expectations from Carnegie sources is now closed. Hereafter the colleges must bear the expenses for retirement plans. The TIAA offers them the cheapest method by which to do it.

This ends the story of the experiment which showed that pensions cannot be a philanthropy but must be a business. The Foundation's major expenditure remains and will remain for sometime the payment of retiring allowances to which it has obligated itself. These amounted to $1,870,234 in 1935–36 and have been happily provided for by the generous grants made to the Foundation by the Carnegie Corporation. As long as sound investments continue to pay interest and the financial advisors safeguard its funds, there is nothing for it to worry about. The investment officers have done fairly well : the profit on the general fund on the sale of investments between 1906 and 1935 was $1,875,972 and for the year 1935–36 was $158,072. Having shifted its worries about the TIAA to the Corporation, the Foundation has been able to turn its attention to other matters.

One of its earliest activities, beginning in 1907, was to act as an agency for the exchange of professors and teachers in secondary schools between Prussia and the United States. The World War unfortunately put an end to that. Research studies into state systems of education showed that such inquiries might yield important results. The Division of Educational Inquiry then became an important function of the Foundation. College entrance requirements became an immediate subject of study, and by 1919 a number of other projects were under way. In that year a study was published, *Justice and the Poor*, which showed how the administration of the law has failed in the case of the poor, and in the following year a bulletin was prepared on the professional preparation of teachers for American public schools.

Since then the Division has been widening its vistas of possible activity. In 1921 a study of the training of teachers cost $36,509 and in 1924 a report was made on the possibility of readjustment of the relations of higher institutions in Manitoba, which had a "gratifying reception." In 1926 a special appropriation of $10,000 was obtained from the Carnegie Corporation for a committee to study, under the auspices of the National Education Association, the problem of uniform standards and curricula in public schools, and $5000 for the expenses of a cooperative bureau for women teachers. The Foundation spent $5000 that year for a *Handbook for American Students in France* and other publications for the Institute of International Education, which arranges for the exchange of students between the universities of the United States and those abroad.

A report on the relation of college pay to teaching and research disclosed that pay rises with age. A number of pension studies were made. Most publicized of the reports were those on American College Athletics in 1929 and 1931. Details of the recruiting and subsidizing of athletes were exposed in the first and the changes that had been made as a result were summarized in the second. Football was a boy's game, these reports pointed out, which was and is used to exploit the student in order to earn money and make a name for his institution. Although many people were aware of this, the disclosures created a minor sensation and the newspapers gave the impression that this investigation was among the chief activities of the Foundation.

During the year 1935–36 the Division of Educational Inquiry spent $65,746, including a study of secondary and higher education in Pennsylvania which had been begun in 1925 and up to 1937 had cost $166,500. These researches, under the direction of Dr William S. Learned, staff member of the Foundation, yielded interesting results. After testing prospective teachers, Dr Learned found that many high school pupils surpass the would-be teachers, and that teachers as a group rank far below the standard of other professions. "They exhibit inferiority in contrast with the non-teachers in nearly every department of study," he concluded, "and they show up badly when compared in the same tests with students four years below them which represent educational problems with which they must be prepared to deal. The ability and attainment of those selected and prepared in special centers for that purpose is consistently and conspicuously below the level of the group as a whole. . . The situation is deplorable and totally unnecessary." He asks : "Do the parents desire to have their children taught in high school by persons of demonstrably less general education than many of those children already possess ?" These conditions, he asserts, are not confined to Pennsylvania.*

Professional education, art education, the unit-credit system, and the examination problem in Europe were the subjects of other studies. The last cost $21,800 and previous grants in 1931–32 of $95,400 were made. English, French, Scottish, Finnish, and Swiss committees reported and a conference was held at Folkstone, England, which issued voluminous reports. The Corporation also paid $94,500 for eighteen special research projects carried on under the auspices of the Foundation. These included the work of the American Council on Education in Modern Language Studies, the Educational Records Bureau, the International Institute of Teachers' College, the University of Minnesota studies in art education and graduate instruction, and the American Association of University Professors' study of the effect of the depression on higher education. Sixteen thousand dollars completed the final payments of a $50,000 appropriation to the Progressive Education Association and $9700 went to the Psychological Corporation of New York for work in the preparation of a curriculum in English usage. To describe or evaluate these projects is a career in

---

* $3,081,000, supplied by the Carnegie Corporation, has been spent on this group of studies since 1915. It is important to notice that a large number of the projects of the Division of Educational Inquiry are paid for by the Carnegie Corporation.

itself and no part of the scope of this book. The activities of the present-day educational world supported by the Carnegie Foundation, the Carnegie Corporation, and by the General Education Board are enormously complicated by innumerable institutions, committees, associations, etc., so that even those involved in it can give no clear picture of what is going on.

In 1930 Dr Pritchett retired to become "president emeritus." Dr Henry Suzzallo of the University of Washington then became president. He died after a little more than three years in the office and was succeeded by Walter A. Jessup, who had been president of the University of Iowa. Dr Pritchett continued to contribute to the annual reports, however, and in 1934 produced an essay on the "Social Conscience in Relation to Government." As early as 1915 Dr Pritchett had begun to have his doubts about the place or function of the Foundation. Writing on the subject, "Should the Carnegie Foundation Be Suppressed?" he said : "I have even doubted at times whether the Carnegie Foundation was indispensable to the educational salvation of the country!" Considering its record for judgment and foresight, these doubts are certainly justified.

No wonder then that Dr Pritchett, in thinking things over in 1928 declared : "It is probable that charitable trusts in the United States will, as time goes on, come under sharper public scrutiny and perhaps under control of the national or state governments." Whether their endowments will always be exempt from taxation, he added, only the future can answer. As long as foundations perform useful and important functions, these questions are not apt to arise. Certainly the Carnegie Foundation for the Advancement of Teaching has made important contributions, notably in the field of research and medical education,* but usually in a blundering and curiously indirect manner. Mr Carnegie gave his ten million dollar endowment to the Foundation because he thought that the profession of teaching was "least rewarded." Without mak-

* Dr Flexner's report may be judged the Foundation's greatest achievement.

ing actuarial studies or an adequate survey of the problem, the Foundation went blithely ahead with a non-contributory system which it was soon found had the effect of keeping down salaries rather than increasing the "rewards." When the salaries were raised the Foundation would have gone bankrupt if it had not been able to count on the generosity of the Carnegie Corporation.

Mr Carnegie said that able men would hesitate to enter the profession of teaching because their future was insecure. By leading professors to expect a certain annuity when they retired and then disappointing them, the Foundation made for many the profession less secure than it had been. Before the Carnegie pensions began professors knew that they had to provide for their own old age. The Carnegie pensions, and the publicity attending them, led many to think that their old age would be taken care of. By changing the rules the Foundation forfeited that confidence. Fortunately, by this time the universities themselves saw the necessity for contributory pension systems. But the same effect might have been achieved if the early officers of the Foundation had been less ambitious to include so many universities on the "accepted list." They probably thought they were advancing the cause of education but by expanding the "accepted list" beyond the limits that the Foundation could go in making pension payments, they nearly wrecked the whole scheme. A small, restricted list, no larger than the income from the endowment could support, might have been just as effective in instigating colleges to put in their own systems.

Mr Carnegie said that old professors could not retire, but the Foundation made this doubly difficult by setting the retirement age first at 65 and then postponing it to 70. Furthermore the Foundation did not take care of the needy. They applied in vain. It was therefore much less "philanthropic" than it seemed, because it left it to the professors themselves whether they would apply for pensions. Need had nothing to do, necessarily, with eligibility. Many retired professors made comfortable incomes from their writings, many went into non-academic jobs and still drew Carnegie pensions.

As early as 1911 Dr Pritchett made clear in his report that he knew the non-contributory system would not work. The Carnegie Corporation would have to be called upon for more funds. But suppose there had been no such foundation to come to the rescue ? The twenty-five million dollars which the Corporation appropriated to the Foundation and to the TIAA may be called philanthropy, but it looks, upon inspection, more like the covering up of mistakes. The Carnegie Foundation for the Advancement of Teaching did something which no Rockefeller board would ever do : It obligated itself to pay indefinite sums which would be determined by a variable factor over which it had no control. The men who made this mistake were the trustees, almost all of whom were presidents of leading American colleges. It is almost enough to lead one to doubt the sagacity of university presidents.

It may be that college presidents have grown in wisdom. The present board is composed almost exclusively of such men, although Thomas W. Lamont is (in 1937) chairman. Frederick Carlos Ferry, however, is vice chairman. He is president, trustee, and professor of mathematics of Hamilton College ; formerly dean of Williams College, he has served as trustee of the TIAA (1910–21) and as president of the Association of American Colleges. Lotus Delta Coffmann, president of the University of Minnesota, is secretary of the board. Prominent on the board are : Frank Aydelotte, president of Swarthmore, American secretary of the Rhodes trustees since 1918, trustee of the TIAA 1923–27, chairman of the Guggenheim Foundation advisory board since 1925, member of the educational division of the National Research Council since 1922, trustee of the World Peace Foundation and of the Institute for Advanced Study. Of course Nicholas Murray Butler is on the board. Samuel P. Capen, former professor in Clark University and specialist in higher education for the U.S. Department of Education, 1914–19, who has also been a member of the division of educational relations of the National Research Council (1918–1933), secretary of the Educational Research Committee of the Commonwealth Fund, 1923–27, and now a trustee of Tufts College, is also a trustee of the Carnegie Foundation for the Advancement of Teaching.

Other college presidents now on the board are: James Bryant Conant of Harvard; George Hutchinson Denny of the University of Alabama; Harold Willis Dodds of Princeton; Edward C. Elliott of Purdue; Livingston Farrand, until recently president of Cornell; Frank Porter Graham, president of the University of North Carolina; James Hampton Kirkland, chancellor since 1893 of Vanderbilt University; Ernest Hiram Lindley, chancellor of the University of Kansas; William Allan Neilson, president of Smith College; John Lloyd Newcomb, president of the University of Virginia; George Norlin, president of the University of Colorado; Josiah Harmar Penniman, provost of the University of Pennsylvania; Kenneth C. M. Sills, president of Bowdoin; and Henry Merritt Wriston, president of Lawrence College.

These are the gentlemen who are responsible for the administration, not only of the universities which they head, but also this Foundation, whose power cannot be measured by its endowment, and, indirectly, for the $80,000,000 insurance company to which the Foundation has given birth. The trustees of this insurance association are: H. M. Addinsell, chairman of the executive committee of the First Boston Corporation (formerly with Harris Forbes); Waldron P. Belknap, vice president of the Bankers Trust Co.; Edmund E. Day, president of Cornell and formerly with the Rockefeller Foundation; Christian Gauss, dean of Princeton; Frederick A. Goetze, treasurer of Columbia University; Henry R. Hayes, investment banker, vice president of Stone and Webster; Robert

Henderson, vice president and actuary, retired, of the Equitable Life Assurance Society ; Henry James, chairman and president ; Pierre Jay, chairman of the Fiduciary Trust Co. of New York ; R. Baylor Knox, vice president of the City Farmers Trust Co. ; Joseph B. Maclean, associate actuary Mutual Life Insurance Co. ; George C. McDonald, of McDonald, Currie and Co. of Montreal ; Elihu Root Jr ; and George Whitney, partner in J. P. Morgan. Four others are nominated by the policyholders : Lloyd K. Garrison, dean of the University of Wisconsin Law School ; Harold G. Moulton, president of the Brookings Institution ; Professor William B. Munro of the California Institute of Technology ; and Professor William F. Ogburn, professor of the University of Chicago.

These names represent not only an appalling amount of brains but also a rather imposing amount of financial power. Here is a segment of the centralized interlocking directorate discussed at length in Chapter XIII. While college presidents do not, of course, control the investment of the endowment funds which they represent, they are the guardians, the watchdogs, as well as the collectors of these funds. Perhaps they would not use the power that this money may exert to defend, to protect, to nurture the system which has made possible such capitalizations. Yet here is a group of college presidents gathered together on a board of trustees of a foundation with assets of more than eighteen million, which has, with the help of the Carnegie Corporation (assets more than $150,000,000), created an insurance company with assets of more than $80,-000,000. Add to this the endowment funds of the universities which the trustees represent and it becomes possible to visualize the amount of potential financial power in the hands of a relatively small group. Add to this the power of the Rockefeller philanthropies, whose representatives are to be found in this same pattern, and you begin to get a picture of the economic bases of American higher education.

The General Education Board, by designating not only

where its own funds, but the bulk of educational contributions
from wealthy donors should go, has had to an amazing degree
the power of life and death over the higher educational institutions of this country.   The Carnegie Foundation for the Advancement of Teaching, setting up an "accepted list," has
had a similar power.   It began by insisting that small colleges
cut their denominational apron-strings.   This had the effect of
compelling colleges to retie those strings to the big educational
endowments.   As Dr E. V. Hollis has pointed out, more than
70% of the endowments from the foundations has gone to a
group of only twenty colleges.   It cannot be denied that these
are the favored institutions.   Since, generally speaking, the two
largest foundations have worked together and prefer the same
institutions, their joint power over the educational life of the
country is greater than can be estimated.

CHAPTER X

"EDUCATING" THE PUBLIC

"Two things I can't understand," declared old Washington Duke, "one is the Holy Ghost and free grace, and the other is my son Buck." * He was referring to some of the business practices of James Buchanan Duke, who was not altogether clear about all the details himself, since he is reported to have remarked that he didn't understand dividends, he was satisfied with profits. Neither the old man, who sold Duke's Mixture to the Yankee army and began the Duke interest in education by luring Trinity College to Durham, nor young Buck Duke, who created the American Tobacco Company, the Duke Power Company, and the Duke Endowment, had any difficulty about comprehending the uses of philanthropy. Trinity College was the pride of the Southern Methodists, who were inclined to disapprove of cigarette smoking. But after Trinity got several hundred thousand dollars from cigarette profits, tobacco did not seem so vile a weed. Since the creation of the Duke Endowment with shares in the power company, there has been little criticism of public utilities in North and South Carolina. As Buck remarked shortly before his death, "What I mean is, I've got 'em fixed so they won't bother it after I'm gone."

After he had made his fortune in tobacco, Buck became so interested in electricity through water-power, that into the buying of rivers and building utilities he poured a large part of his profits. It has been estimated that the Duke Power Company and its subsidiaries may someday be worth a billion dollars. Certainly that is an investment worth protecting with all the ingenuity at the command of Buck Duke and his lawyers. To discover a way to protect the power company into per-

* *American Mercury*, August 1929.

petuity against critics and legislators was a serious problem, but it was solved by the creation of the Duke Endowment by means of a remarkable, and possibly historic indenture. This extraordinary legal document weaves together all the Duke interests. First of all, it created a fund consisting of 122,647 shares of the Duke Power Company, 100,000 shares of the British-American Tobacco Company, 75,000 shares of the R. J. Reynolds Tobacco Company, 5000 shares of the common stock of George W. Helme Company, 12,325 shares of Republic Cotton Mills, 7935³⁄₁₀ shares of Judson Mills. Secondly, this fund was to exist into perpetuity and be used for specific purposes. Thirdly, Mr Duke forbad the trustees to sell any shares of the Duke Power Company, except by unanimous consent, and to invest only in the Duke Power Company, its subsidiaries, or in U. S. Government, state, or municipal bonds. Six million dollars, he directed, should be paid Duke University "as soon as reasonably may be . . . if Trinity within three months or such time as the trustees may allow be changed to Duke as a memorial to Washington Duke." This university, he declared, should eventually include not only an undergraduate department, but schools of "religious training," schools for "the training of teachers," for chemistry, for law, a "co-ordinate college for women," a school of business administration, a graduate school of arts and sciences, a medical school, and an engineering school.

Twenty per cent of the income of the fund is to snowball by reinvestment until the total capital is equal to the original, so that the endowment in time will amount to about eighty million. Thirty-two per cent of this main fund was to endow the university, thirty-two per cent was to go to hospitals in North and South Carolina, five per cent to Davidson College, five per cent to Furman College, four per cent to Johnson C. Smith College, ten per cent to orphanages, two per cent for needy and deserving superannuated Methodist preachers of North Carolina, six per cent for building Methodist churches, four per cent for the operation of these churches. Ben Dixon MacNeill, the only newspaperman with whom Duke spoke freely, quotes Mr Duke indirectly, interpreting these gifts : "Public thinking and public attitudes toward private business are determined primarily by lawyers who dominate the government, by preachers who dominate religion, by doctors who dominate life and death." * Thus the sources of public opinion were woven into Buck Duke's great plan, safeguarding his public utility. In the seventh clause of the indenture he declared : "I recommend the securities of the Southern Power System (Duke Power Company and its subsidiaries) as the prime investment for funds and I advise the trustees that they do not change any such investment except in the most urgent and extraordinary necessity, and I request the trustees to see to it that at all times these companies be managed and operated by men best qualified for such service."

So, as J. W. Jenkins declared in his laudatory biography, *J. B. Duke, Master Builder*, the endowment is based "on a utility that will last as long as water flows and industry demands power," an endowment that is "not only perpetual but cumulative." Having achieved that magnificent job of master-building, Buck then created the Doris Duke Trust with 125,000 shares in the Duke Power Company. When he died he left ten million dollars to Duke University for a medical college, seven million to it for other purposes, and one third of the residuary was to be used to pay his widow $100,000 a year and on her death to revert to the Duke Endowment. The fortune he left to his heirs is thus well protected by the endowment. As one critic says, "the university is the tail of the utility kite."

Louis Graves reports,† however, that all the people of the Carolinas do not feel that way. He says that there is nothing insidious or sinister about the endowment. "Not to communities in North and South Carolina where it builds and supports hospitals, nor to Methodist ministers who are pensioned,

* *American Mercury*, August 1929.
† *World's Work*, March 1931.

nor to Methodist congregations helped for maintenance of churches, nor the orphan asylums, nor to Duke University." On the other hand, Dr Abraham Flexner, whose experience with both the Rockefeller and the Carnegie philanthropies should entitle him to be considered an authority on foundations, while praising and defending private initiative in philanthropy in the *Atlantic Monthly*,* wrote : "A conspicuous example of the abuse of private power under the guise of rendering a public service is furnished by the so-called Duke Foundation." In 1933, he said, the Duke Power Company paid four million dollars in dividends ; of this less than one-half went to philanthropic purposes : one half went to the Doris Duke Trust and the remainder to other persons and institutions.

Ernest Seeman, for ten years manager of the Duke University Press, reported † what happened when the Duke Power Company was threatened by plans for a publicly owned power plant to be erected by a loan from PWA. "Propaganda was piped out to editors against it, to educators, churches. An orator warned the South Carolina Legislature 'if rates are cut the sick and orphaned, churches and hospitals, student and preacher would have to pay for it.'" Furthermore, Mr Seeman gives other illuminating examples of how the endowment operates. William B. Bell, endowment trustee and president of the American Cyanamid Company, objected to a scientific article on the tobacco beetle in *Ecological Monographs* because the scientist did not praise his company's products. The chemistry department of the university, Mr Seeman declares, is a research laboratory for the Liggett and Myers Tobacco Company. (The endowment owns 17,175 shares of A, and 8451 of B, common.) Dr Edmund Soper, pacifist friend of labor unions, was encouraged to resign. (The endowment owns 164,115 shares in the Aluminum Company of America, of which George G. Allen, chairman of the endowment, is a director.) Mr Seeman also

---

* August 1935.
† *New Republic*, September 30, 1936.

mentions several others who, he says, were forced out because of their opinions.

At the end of twelve years the endowment reported that 36.83% of its income came from the Duke Power Company. It received during that time $43,842,705 in dividends and interest. Its expenses, including compensation to Trustees, was $1,968,-148. (The Duke Endowment is one of the few foundations which now pays its trustees.) To the corpus of the trust was added $10,127,138. Available for distribution : $31,747,419. In twelve years distributions were :

Duke University	$13,004,787.65
Hospitals	9,462,092.82
Davidson College	712,977.78
Furman University	712,977.78
Johnson C. Smith University	554,860.19
Orphanages	1,304,378.11
Methodist preachers	278,541.50
Methodist rural churches	423,201.43
Operating churches	500,547.84
	$26,954,365.10

William R. Perkins, on the eighth anniversary of the establishment of the endowment,* made a speech which is particularly significant when one considers his position. He is vice-chairman of the endowment, counsel for the Duke Power Company and the British-American Tobacco Company, and vice president of the Duke Power Company. He said : "Of course there was pointed out to Mr Duke the possible danger of basing a large, perpetual charity on a business that might change, indeed, upon a public utility that was subject to popular regulation and already being made a target by those who wished to put the government into business. But such arguments caused him no dismay, so full was his confidence that he could entrust his benevolence to the people whom it served." He added, perhaps not in a tone of warning, yet with unmistakable mean-

* The Duke Endowment and the Duke Power Company share offices in Rockefeller Center, N. Y. American Cyanamid is across the hall.

ing as a reminder, that Mr Duke authorized the trustees of the endowment "to withhold the benefits from Duke University should that institution in their judgment be not operated in a manner calculated to achieve the results intended." He then quoted Mr Duke as saying : "If I amount to anything in this world, I owe it to my Daddy and the Methodist Church." Mr Perkins closed his speech confidently on this note : "God is still in His Heaven and all will be right with the world if we only give God a chance !"

Blessed with the vast endowment, Duke University has expanded rapidly, obtained many important teachers, a football team, many new buildings, and it has recently achieved fame through a book by one of its professors on extra-sensory perceptions. God has been given a chance to provide waterpower to the Duke utilities and the people of North and South Carolina have left the power companies alone. The endowment pays hospitals one dollar per day per bed for charity patients and it has built a few new hospitals, but the Rosenwald Fund reports a shocking shortage of hospital facilities for the white population as well as for Negroes.* However, the main objective of Buck Duke seems to have been achieved. Ben Dixon MacNeill quotes him : "I'm the last Duke, but I don't think anybody will bother this thing I'm leaving. What I mean is that I've got 'em fixed now so there won't be any more meddling with it by legislatures and courts and newspapers like I've been bothered with all my life. But I've got 'em now and it's going on making profits. Not even Joe Dan'els † will cuss me now."

Julius Rosenwald was a very different type of man. While Buck Duke could barely read and write, had a mania for monopoly and created a foundation whose perpetuity was guaranteed by all the devices his lawyers could invent, Julius Rosenwald was a cultured, intelligent, far-sighted business man,

* Negro Hospitals 1931, Rosenwald Fund Report.
† Josephus Daniels was one of Mr Duke's most persistent critics.

who, although he has been criticised for paying low wages, never sought to relate the prestige of his philanthropies, at least consciously, with his mail-order business, nor tried to protect his family's investment in Sears, Roebuck by setting up the Julius Rosenwald Fund. He tried to persuade other philanthropists not to make their foundations perpetuities but to spend the principal as well as the income, insisting that future generations be permitted to take care of themselves. He admitted that making a lot of money was chiefly a matter of luck and he had the social consciousness to try to find a field where his wealth would do the most good. It may be said that by spending vast sums for Negro education he was encouraging the states to be negligent in their duty, but he tried to avoid that by giving only one third the cost of the Rosenwald schools. Even this share may have led public authorities to rely too much on philanthropy. He must, in any event, be given credit for lofty intentions. It is sometimes said by humanitarians that it would be better if millionaires, instead of setting up foundations, raised the living standards of their employees through higher wages. Mr Rosenwald understood the economic system well enough to know that that would not work. If he paid low wages it was because the logic of business demanded it ; he did not exhibit any hypocrisy about it, nor try to justify low wages on moral or patriotic grounds.

As early as 1912 he became interested in bettering the condition of the Negroes through education and improving race relations. Through Booker T. Washington and the Tuskegee Institute he agreed to contribute to the building of any school house for Negroes in the vicinity of Tuskegee provided that it were made a unit of the regular school system, and that Negroes made substantial contributions either in money or labor. In 1913 the first "Rosenwald School" was erected, toward which he contributed approximately one-third, white citizens contributed one-third, and Negroes by labor and money gave one-third. On that basis the "Rosenwald Schools" have been built.

He did not ask or insist that they be named for him and it has
sometimes been erroneously supposed that he paid the full
amount.   Hence others have declared that he has obtained
more than his share of the glory for something for which anonymous whites and Negroes contributed two-thirds.

In twenty years 5,357 public schools, shops, and teachers'
homes were built in 883 counties of fifteen Southern states at a
total cost of $28,408,520, toward which Mr Rosenwald con-
tributed $4,366,519.   This program was stopped in 1932 "lest
by continuing it longer the southern states might come to rely
too heavily on outside aid and so be delayed in assuming full responsibility for the schools of this section of the population as a
regular and integral part of the public provisions for the education of all the people."   A quarter of a million has been given to
university centers in Washington, Atlanta, Nashville, and New
Orleans, chiefly since 1928.   Public health needs have been
emphasized.   "The needs of the Negroes in health are fully as
great as in education and the neglect of this group in all forms
of health service is appalling," it reports.   The Fund has tried
to stimulate public agencies and to create institutions which
would serve as models and offer professional training for doctors and nurses.   It has spent $857,507 on this work.   Those in
charge of the fund have felt that change is dependent on "economic forces."   "The need has been so great that we have been
forced to take an interest even though we have not made any
large financial contributions."   So the Fund has "called public
attention to the unfortunate position of the Negroes in certain
economic situations, particularly in farm tenancy and in the
trade unions ; we have shown to public authorities the economic
plight of this group and have tried to see to it that in the government provisions for relief and recovery Negroes were given
adequate consideration and fair treatment."   The reports of
the Fund indicate something of the overwhelming magnitude
of the problems of health, education, and economic security the
Negro faces, and in relating what the Rosenwald Fund has done

suggests how little any philanthropic fund can do and how much remains to be done. No one, after reading these reports can say : "Oh, that problem is being taken care of by the philanthropies." No foundation or group of foundations can do much more than call attention to the problem.

The Rosenwald Fund was one of the first to become interested in the problem of syphilis, in 1930, in cooperation with the U. S. Public Health Service. Studies have been made of medical services to persons of moderate means through group insurance. Support has been given to a few demonstrations of pay clinics, hospital services at low cost, and other forms of organized medical services. It contributed to this approximately one million dollars. Officers of the Fund took a substantial part in the initiation, organization, and researches of the Committee on the Costs of Medical Care. Even today Negro schools are inadequately supplied with books ; often they lack even textbooks. So the Fund has tried to get some reading material into the Negro schools ; it has given a total of $653,118 to general library service, aiding library schools for both white and colored librarians, and supporting in part state library commissions. Notable also have been the fellowships granted the unusually talented. James Weldon Johnson was enabled to devote two years to writing ; Marian Anderson, the concert singer, was given a year in Europe at a turning point in her career ; Langston Hughes, Claude McKay, and W. E. B. DuBois have held fellowships.

The Julius Rosenwald Fund was incorporated in Illinois as a philanthropic corporation "for the well being of mankind," in 1917. During its first ten years Mr Rosenwald administered it himself. In 1927 it was enlarged into a general foundation under the control of eleven trustees and administered by officers who give full time to the work. About four million was expended in the first ten years and about nine million in the second decade. Mr Rosenwald's gifts were chiefly in the form of stock in Sears, Roebuck (227,874 shares) which in 1928 had

a market value of more than forty millions. He insisted that it
must spend the principal as well as the income within twenty-
five years of his death. Between April 1928, and September
1929, the trustees therefor appropriated more than five millions
while the paper profits of the stock increased by three times this
amount. Commitments made when the stock was quoted at
200 fell due when the stock was worth only a fraction of that,
while the needs in the fields of the Fund's interest multiplied.

It was then that the Rockefeller General Education Board
and the Carnegie Corporation came to the rescue. Mr Rosenwald's idea of spending both principal and income almost
wrecked his foundation, and to be saved he had to turn, it
might be noted, to endowments which operated under no such
compulsion. When the Rosenwald Fund was reorganized in
1927 Edwin R. Embree, who had received his philanthropic
training in the Rockefeller Foundation, was obtained as President of the Rosenwald Fund. Beardsley Ruml, then a member of the General Education Board and now a trustee of the
Spelman Fund, became a trustee in the Rosenwald Fund. Thus
two important Rockefeller philanthropic agents were obtained
who were of special service in time of need and thus the Rockefeller interests reached out to take a hand in the administration
of another important foundation. When Mr Ruml retired
from the Rosenwald Fund to become treasurer of R. H. Macy
and Company, Robert M. Hutchins, president of Rockefeller's
University of Chicago, became a trustee in his place. The
General Education Board made emergency grants totaling
$257,000 to various Negro schools and colleges. Some of
these were on a repayment basis, so the Rosenwald Fund later
reimbursed the General Education Board for some of its contributions. The Carnegie Corporation's assistance, however,
was an outright gift of $200,000 directly to the Fund. Hence
the Rosenwald Fund was able to continue its work, helped also
by bank loans and the spreading out of some pledges over a
period of years, maintaining an average of $840,000 in disburse-

ments each year. For the year 1936–37 the payments were slightly more than one million.

Recently the Fund made an investigation to find out what sort of teaching was being given in the "Rosenwald" schools, and discovered a shocking number of ill-trained teachers. In one Louisiana school rote teaching had gone to an incredible extreme. "When do the robins come ?" the teacher asked one little boy. "In the Fall," he answered. "Read the lesson again," commanded the teacher. The boy read the textbook again, and again he said that the robins came in the Fall. Exasperated, the teacher made him read it a third time. Almost weeping the child said : "The robins come in the Spring." In Louisiana, of course, the robins do come in the Fall, but the textbook written and published in New England said they came in the Spring. Against all his experience and observation the boy was compelled to answer from a book which he felt was untruthful. In a Negro school children were asked why they must wash their hair. The answer which they were taught was that they must wash their hair so that it would not become long and stringy and get in their eyes. No doubt many of these Negro children wished they could make their hair long and stringy.*

Although undistinguished as a legislator, Senator Simon Guggenheim purchased immortality by establishing in 1925 in memory of his son, the John Simon Guggenheim Memorial Foundation, which will probably have a more enduring influence on American life than any legislation he might have sponsored. From 1925 to 1936 it has assisted 525 scholars and artists by means of fellowships granted for varying periods, usually one year, to citizens and permanent residents of the United States and citizens of several South American countries. These are chosen, usually upon application, by a Committee of Selec-

* "Little Red School House 1936 Model" by E. R. Embree, *Atlantic Monthly*, November, 1937.

tion on the basis of the quality of the applicant's past work, and a judgment of the quality of his future accomplishment. Financial need is not considered in the selection, although the size of the stipend is usually determined by the Fellow's own financial resources. Allotment is not made by fields of work, for the Foundation is primarily interested in individuals of promise. Those holding fellowships are not restricted in any way ; they do not even have to make reports on the progress of their work. It is rumored that one fellow used the stipend to get a divorce. That may have set him free to do better work. Known chiefly in the newspapers as a Foundation which helps artists and writers, it has granted twice as many fellowships for research as to those engaged in creative work in the arts. One hundred and sixteen of the fellows had no college degrees. Harvard, it appears, is the leading training ground. Three hundred and thirty four had academic positions at the time of their appointment, 191 were free lance scholars and artists. The University of California leads all educational research institutions in the number of fellowships appointments.

It is frequently whispered that "you need pull" to get a Guggenheim fellowship. Such a suspicion is inevitable where judgments must be made about individuals, judgments inescapably colored by personal opinion. The biennial report of 1935–1936 published brief biographies of the fellows appointed in the first decade. Henry Allen Moe, the secretary of the Foundation, commented : "No person could judge — nor, for that matter could a score of persons — of the *quality* of the productions mentioned ; and for the Foundation nothing else matters." There are two committees of selection under the chairmanship of Dr Frank Aydelotte, who has had much experience in charge of the Rhodes scholarships. One committee selects fellows from South American countries and the other selects fellows from the United States. For 1935 the committee for selection for the United States consisted of Dr Aydelotte, President of Swarthmore, Dean Guy Stanton Ford of the University of Minnesota, Dean Charles B. Lipman of the University of California, Professor Marjorie Nicholson of Smith College, and Professor Edwin B. Wilson of the Harvard University School of Public Health. The first two served also in 1936, assisted by Dr Florence R. Sabin of the Rockefeller Institute and Dr Carl Sauer of the University of California. Dr Aydelotte was also chairman of the committee for Latin America, assisted by Dr Thomas Barbour, director of the Museum of Comparative Zoology of Harvard, Dr Elmer Drew Merrill, administrator of Botanical Collections, Harvard, Dr Antonio Garcia Solalinde, Professor of Spanish, University of Wisconsin, and Dr Richard P. Strong, Professor of Tropical Medicine at Harvard. These committees serve without compensation. In 1934 the Trustees removed the previous restriction that fellowship work must be done abroad, and in 1936 twenty-seven, or almost one-half of the fellows appointed from the United States, elected to work in this country.

Among those who held fellowships in 1936 were John Bakeless, to complete his book on Marlowe ; James T. Farrell, to do creative writing ; Granville Hicks, for writing an interpretation of English literature since 1890 ; Zora Neale Hurston, for gathering material for books on authentic Negro folk-life ; Donald Culross Peattie, for writing the story of the rise in the wilderness of an idealistic American community ; Robert Turney, for creative work in the drama. Renewals were granted to Peter Blume, Yasuo Kuniyoshi, Peppino Mangravite, Doris Rosenthal, Antonio Salemme and Carl Walters, artists ; to Abram Lincoln Harris, economist ; Dante Fiorillo, musician ; Morris Moore, scientist ; Isidor Schneider, writer ; and John Webster Spargo, student of law and literature. From Argentina Carlos Eugenio Dielefait was appointed for studies in the problems of statistical theories at Massachusetts Institute of Technology, from Chile Adalberto Schaeffer Steeger came to study infectious diseases as related to pediatrics, from Mexico Andres Henestrosa was designated for studies in the significance of

Zapotecan culture, and three reappointments were made : Enrique Savino, studying public health at Harvard, Hernandez Pedro Bermudez in Cuba, and Alfredo Banos Jr., from Mexico, studying theoretical physics and cosmic radiation at M.I.T.

Among those who have had fellowships in the past have been Louis Adamic, Conrad Aiken, George Antheil, Peggy Bacon, Carleton Beals, Hart Crane, Hallie Flanagan, Mordecai Ezekiel, Stephen Vincent Benet, Kay Boyle, William Henry Chamberlain, Angna Enters, Paul Green, Albert Halper, Lewis Mumford, Nathaniel Peffer, Katherine Anne Porter, Evelyn Scott, Edmund Wilson, Thomas Wolfe. It is interesting and perhaps significant to notice in the list of fellows the number, too many to be listed here, of those who have held fellowships from other foundations, notably the Laura Spelman Memorial, the General Education Board, and the Rosenwald Fund, or are connected with universities as instructors or professors. It is an indication of the dependence of distinguished artists and writers upon the patronage of the wealthy, either directly from the foundations or indirectly through educational institutions. Criticism of the Guggenheim Foundation has been frequently made that it chooses individuals already well known, already "arrived," and overlooks the promising unknown. To some extent this may be justified, since by appointing people who already have a reputation the Foundation is taking few chances, while an unknown is very much of a gamble. But the fact is that so far as financial aid is concerned, those who have "names" may be in just as great need of assistance as those as yet unheard of ; the mere fact that the name is known is no indication that she or he has attained adequate security in which to do good work.

The financial statement for 1936 shows total assets of $6,060,-368. Interest on securities and dividends amounts to $154,213. Fellowship payments were $79,826 ; the total administrative expenses were $45,142, of which $30,487 went to salaries. The John Simon Guggenheim Memorial Foundation is not to be

confused with any of the three other Guggenheim philanthropic foundations : the Daniel Guggenheim School of Aeronautics at New York University, started by Harry Guggenheim, endowed by his father, first with $225,000 and in 1925
with $500,000. Later Daniel Guggenheim gave $2,500,000
for the promotion of aeronautics, chiefly through research at
M.I.T., the University of California, and the University of
Washington. Daniel, Murry, and Leonia Guggenheim also
established a foundation of four million dollars to support the
Goldman Band concerts in Central Park, and Murry and Leonia
Guggenheim have endowed with two million a dental clinic
costing a million dollars, and have given additional sums.

A different approach to the problem of educating the public
is that of the Maurice and Laura Falk Foundation, established
by Maurice Falk of Pittsburgh as a memorial to his wife, with
ten million dollars to be spent in thirty-five years. "Convinced that the constructive use of its funds for the promotion
of an orderly and sound economic progress would aid broadly
in achieving social progress," it declares in its 1936 report, "the
Falk Foundation has been concentrating its funds in the economics field. . . Hope of magic short cuts or quick results was
never entertained. From the first, research and education were
indicated as the only sure paths of progress — research which
would gradually extend the frontiers of economic knowledge,
and education which would disseminate that knowledge widely
among the people and their leaders as a basis on which, through
the process of public discussion, lines of policy in time take
shape. . ."

"Foundations are charged with a public trust," it continues.
"It is incumbent upon them, therefore, to support those studies
which are so broad that they cut across the limits of individual
business groups. . . Not limiting itself to research, the Falk
Foundation has attempted to acquaint the general public with
the conclusions and recommendations of these studies. . . On

that account the Falk Foundation has made it a cardinal point in its program to have its studies interpreted to the public in clear and non-technical language adapted to the layman." It does not conduct research itself, but makes grants to "reputable outside organizations for the specific budgets of definitive research studies." Once the grant is made, it refrains from any control over the conduct of the study. Hence its resources have gone to the support of "organizations which have a high reputation for outstanding achievement in producing impartial studies in economics. On that account, the Falk Foundation grants have gone chiefly to organizations like the Brookings Institution, the National Bureau of Economic Research, and the business research bureaus of leading colleges and universities."

To Brookings it granted in 1936 $158,013 for the study entitled *The Distribution of Wealth and Income in Relation to Economic Progress*, in two volumes : *The Formation of Capital* and *Income and Economic Progress*. Two preceding volumes in the series appeared in 1934 : *America's Capacity to Produce* and *America's Capacity to Consume*. These volumes have been thoroughly discussed and analyzed by economists, politicians, editorial writers and the general public. Among the points made by these studies which the Falk Foundation emphasizes as being of particular importance are : "The United States has not reached a stage in its economic evolution at which it is possible, in terms of present productive capacity, to provide an adequate standard of living for everybody. Production curtailment programs — whatever their merit in meeting temporary maladjustments — can lead in the long run only to national impoverishment. The nation's inability to find markets to absorb the full output of its productive establishment, is explained, in large part, by the unequal distribution of the national income and the consequent restricted flow of purchasing power through consumptive channels. The successful operation of the economic system in the United States requires that back of each unit of productive power there be placed a corresponding unit of consumer power. The economies of mass production cannot be realized unless the nation has a corresponding mass consumption."

It is possible that quite a number of people had come to similar conclusions before these studies were published. However, the Falk Foundation points out : "The study has served not only to show the shortcomings of such programs as those of the Technocrats, the share-the-wealthers, and similar 'movement-makers' who have proposed short cuts to prosperity, but also to point out, in constructive terms, the means by which the traditional capitalistic economy of the United States can be made, under wise and responsible management, to yield increasing benefits to the masses of the people. . . Observers like David Lawrence, Walter Lippmann, and Alfred P. Sloan have put high estimates on the value of the study." . . . So information about these findings was disseminated by means of news releases, special articles, speeches to "key audiences," and drama-logues for radio broadcasting. Special editions of the summaries were published and a paper-bound edition of the four volumes, for class-room use, was issued to colleges and universities, while 100,000 copies were sent free of charge to the clergy of the country through the Federal Council of the Churches of Christ in America. "The experiment has shown that there are great possibilities for creating in the United States an enlightened public opinion on economic matters." $104,524.98 was spent on this effort, of which $5,140.85 was assigned to Brookings. Possibly it was this demonstration that led Alfred P. Sloan to set aside ten million dollars for a foundation for economic research.

The Foundation also supported the Brookings study entitled "The Recovery Problem in the United States" with a $70,000 appropriation and the study entitled "Prices and Profits" received a grant of $35,000. Other grants made were : to the National Bureau of Economic Research, $15,000, for the study by Eugene Altschul and Dr Fritz Strauss on "Agriculture and the Business Cycle" ; to the University of Pittsburgh, $33,500, for a study of "The Economics of the Iron and Steel Industry." * This was undertaken on the request of the Brookings Institution which was then engaged, under a grant from the Rockefeller Foundation, on a concurrent appraisal of the effects of the Recovery Act on American business in general.

In the summer of 1935 Raymond Leslie Buell, president of the Foreign Policy Association, proposed the formation of a committee to serve as a medium for disseminating research and expert knowledge regarding public questions. Supported by a grant of $25,000, the Public Affairs Committee was organized and has since issued many pamphlets based on studies by research organizations. So successful was its work that the Falk Foundation granted a total of $45,000 to it, $10,000 of which was conditional on grants from other sources.

The Alfred P. Sloan Foundation for Economic Research, endowed with $10,000,000, one-third of which is in common stock of General Motors, has Mr Sloan as chairman, and his brother, Harold S. Sloan, former Associate Professor of Economics at State Teachers College, Montclair, N. J., as executive director. It was established July 6, 1936, as a non-profit corporation under the laws of Delaware, but was not announced until February 25, 1937 because the founder was too busy with labor troubles. It has an office at 30 Rockefeller Plaza, New York City. "This particular foundation," Mr Sloan announced in the *New York Times* December 13, 1937, "proposes to concentrate to an important degree on a single objective, i.e., the promotion of a wider knowledge of basic economic truths generally accepted as such by authorities of recognized standing and as demonstrated by experience, as well as a better understanding of economic problems in which we are today so

---

* Ernest T. Weir, steel magnate, is vice-chairman of the Board of Managers of the Falk Foundation.

greatly involved and as to which we are so importantly concerned." It has granted fellowships to five young industrial
executives for a year's graduate study at Massachusetts Institute
of Technology, and it has financed a number of excursions to
Washington and to industrial areas for students and teachers.

For twenty-five years Robert S. Brookings was in the wood-
enware business with Samuel Cupples in St Louis : everything
from clothespins to willow-baskets, from brooms to toothpicks.
Speaking of the business practices of the time, he later admitted : "Today they would put us in jail for things we all did
then." His biographer, Hermann Hagedorn, declares that he
insisted that the government not interfere with "the processes
of free competition" while he tried at the same time to prevent
any competition at all through monopoly and trade agreements.
He established near St Louis the Cupples terminal warehouses
since imitated by Bush terminals and others. In 1897 he retired
from active business to devote himself to the interests of George
Washington University in St Louis, of which he was president
of the board of trustees. Of all the forms of philanthropy, he
and old Samuel Cupples agreed, "education alone was free from
the palsy of pauperism." "You cannot pauperize the intellect," they said. He not only gave generously to the university, he obtained large sums for it from the Carnegie Corporation and other foundations. Mr Carnegie took such a fancy to
him that he made him a trustee of the Carnegie Endowment for
International Peace. Shocked by the revelations in Abraham
Flexner's report on medical education, he studied the subject
thoroughly, and with large grants from the Carnegie Corporation he rebuilt the medical school. Always interested in economic problems, writing a number of books on them himself,
he established in 1922 the Institute of Economics in connection
with George Washington University, and he obtained a ten-
year appropriation of $1,650,000 from the Carnegie Corpora-
tion. Already, in 1916, he had created the Institute of Gov-

ernment Research, and later he established the Brookings Graduate School. These three divisions were incorporated in 1927 as one : "The Brookings Institution," each carrying on its work under the unified auspices in Washington.

The personnel connected with the Brookings Institution is worth noting. The Institute of Government Research had the following founders : Charles D. Norton, secretary to President Taft, Jerome D. Greene, Raymond B. Fosdick, Frederick Strauss, of the Rockefeller Foundation, James F. Curtis, deputy governor of the Federal Reserve Bank of New York, Anson Phelps Stokes of Yale, Frank J. Goodnow of Johns Hopkins, Charles P. Neill, director of American Smelting and Refining, Martin A. Ryerson, banker, of Chicago,* and Robert S. Brookings. Its purpose was to make "an expert and objective study of administrative problems," particularly budget studies, and a publication of the Brookings Institution declares : "its work of placing the nation's finances on a more satisfactory basis ranks as one of its notable achievements."

In answer to inquiry it gives its present board of trustees : Dwight F. Davis, chairman, ex-governor of the Philippine Islands ; Leo S. Rowe, vice-chairman, economist, assistant secretary of the Treasury 1917–19, director of the Pan-American Union ; Robert Perkins Bass, ex-governor of New Hampshire, president of the New Hampshire State Jersey Cattle Club ; Clarence Phelps Dodge, publisher of Colorado Springs *Gazette*, trustee of the University of Beirut, Turkey, member of the International Committee of the Y.M.C.A., president of the Washington, D. C. Community Chest 1934–36 ; Marshall Field, trustee of the estate of Marshall Field, director of the Chicago and Northwestern Railroad and the New York Philharmonic Society ; Jerome D. Greene, Alanson B. Houghton, John C. Merriam, Roland S. Morris, Harold G. Moulton, Lessing Rosenthal, Anson Phelps Stokes, Harry Brookings Wallace, nephew of Mr Brookings, and John G. Winant, another

* Also trustee of the Carnegie Endowment for International Peace.

former governor of New Hampshire. Frederic A. Delano was previously a trustee and chairman of the board. Harold G. Moulton of the University of Chicago was obtained as director of the Brookings Institution in 1927.

The Brookings Graduate School is empowered to grant Ph.D. degrees but does not make a practice of doing so. It offers a supergraduate research training which provides students "with special facilities somewhat similar to those furnished hospitals by internes." "The Institute," it goes on to explain, "has no claim upon a fellow's time or the results of his work, nor does it attempt to determine the character or study he is making. It does, however, accept responsibility for advice, counsel, and suggestion for each student and for surrounding him with a stimulating intellectual atmosphere." One of its first research jobs was on German reparations, incorporated in *Germany's Capacity to Pay*, 1923, which furnished the groundwork for the Dawes Plan. Its staff also studied the French debt problem, Italy's international economic position, and the subject of "War Debts and World Prosperity."

For a study of the Agricultural Adjustment Administration the Rockefeller Foundation in 1936 appropriated and paid $11,-367, and appropriated $7616 for a concurrent study of the NRA. Since 1928 the Rockefeller boards have supported the Brookings Institution general program "at a level of $75,000 a year." In 1936 the Rockefeller Foundation appropriated $225,000 to be available over three years. Before Mr. Brookings' death he obtained generous grants from the Spelman Fund; $50,000 a year for seven years from George Eastman, and from others smaller amounts. It does not send all its publications to members of Congress, but once or twice a year the president of the Institution addresses a letter to each Congressman with a list of publications stating that any of them will be supplied upon specific request in writing. The demand for them, it is said, is large and increasing. The matter of the impartiality of the Brookings reports has been a subject of wide discussion ; even a long and detailed analysis of them would merely add to the debate, and no digest would give a fair or accurate picture.   The reader must refer to the reports and decide the question for himself.

The point of view of those behind the Brookings Institution may be sampled by a brief quotation from a speech by the president of the Rockefeller Foundation on the occasion of the dedication of the Institution's new building on Jackson Place, Washington ; a gift of the widow, Isabel Valle Brookings.   At that time Mr Fosdick declared : "We must face the fact that the social mechanism can be kept from cracking under the strain only as we develop the sciences that relate to man. . . Unless our generation can make some appreciable progress toward this goal of social control, then pessimism has the better of the argument and the chances of our keeping the train on the track are exceedingly slight."   By reading the Brookings reports it will be seen how its experts are trying to keep the train on the track.

Another important agency working in the social sciences supported by the foundations is the Social Science Research Council, formed in 1922, the same year that the Brookings Institute of Economics was organized.   It exists, according to its statement, for the "one comprehensive purpose of advancing the study of man in his relations to man."   Not even Mr Fosdick could phrase it better.   It was chartered by the State of Illinois with twenty-eight directors and incorporators of which twenty-one are elected for three year terms by the seven national scientific societies : The American Anthropological Association, the American Historical Association, the American Economic Association, the American Political Science Association, the American Psychological Association, the American Sociological Association, and the American Statistical Association.   The other seven directors are appointed by this board for two year terms.   It was started by the American Political

Science Association to provide for students of government adequate support for research and publication. The Council is run by committees on all of which representatives of the Foundations usually play an important role.

In 1923 the Council received a grant from the Laura Spelman Memorial to carry on work started by the National Research Council on human migrations. Between February and May, 1924, it got $18,000 for this project and $2500 for an international news study. In 1925 the Council got $82,500 for projects, fellowships, and administration. In 1926 it obtained $226,-000, of which $135,000 was for projects. It then established a regularly paid staff. In 1927 it got $1,958,000 to be available for a term of years. As of June 30, 1933, the amount of all grants from the beginning was $4,197,605 of which $1,401,038 was for use after July 1, 1933. For these contributions the Council acknowledged in its report a deep debt of gratitude to the Carnegie Corporation, the Carnegie Foundation for the Advancement of Teaching, the Russell Sage Foundation, the Maurice and Laura Falk Foundation, the Spelman Fund, the Rockefeller Foundation, and the Rosenwald Fund. The financial support, it was said, far exceeded expectations.

The contributions up to June, 1933, to the Council, were :

The Carnegie Corporation	$ 75,000
The Carnegie Foundation for the Advancement of Teaching	10,000
The Commonwealth Fund	5,000
The Falk Foundation	3,000
The General Education Board	45,000
Revell McCallum *	1,500
The Spelman Fund and the Rockefeller Foundation	3,871,105.91
John D. Rockefeller Jr	16,000
The Rosenwald Fund	66,000
The Russell Sage Foundation	42,000
Income from fees	13,000
	$4,197,605.91

* Secretary of the Spelman Fund, 1928.

It seems unnecessary to point out the Rockefeller share in this total. In 1936 the Rockefeller Foundation appropriated $115,-000 to the Council for public administration studies, $25,000 for the general program. The Carnegie Corporation contributed $25,000 for administrative expenses.

Let us glance at the committees that run it. Shelby M. Harrison of the Russell Sage Foundation has been chairman of the executive committee since 1925. He is also on the Committee on the Social Aspects of the Depression and on the Committee on Social Security. Edwin G. Nourse of the Brookings Institution is chairman of the Committee on Problems and Policy. He succeeded Harold G. Moulton of Brookings who was the previous chairman. Beardsley Ruml was on that committee for a number of years ; he is now on the Committee on Commission of Inquiry on Public Problems. Mr Nourse is also on the Committee on Appraisal of Research and on the Committee on Social and Economic Research ; he was formerly on the Special Committee on Graduate Training in Agricultural Economics and Rural Sociology and on the Committee on Population Redistribution. The Committee on Government Statistics was headed for a number of years by E. C. Day, in charge of social sciences for the Rockefeller Foundation ; he was also chairman of the Committee on Social Science Personnel ; he is now chairman of the Committee on Appraisal of Research. The Committee on Social Statistics was headed by Ralph G. Hurlin of the Russell Sage Foundation. Until 1937 the Committee on International Relations consisted of Owen D. Young, chairman, Newton D. Baker, Raymond B. Fosdick, S. Parker Gilbert, (Morgan partner), Jerome D. Greene, Thomas Nelson Perkins, (banker) — and Norman Thomas. For 1937–38 it consists of William Lingelbach, of the University of Pennsylvania, Philip Jessup of Columbia and Robert Warren, of Case, Pomeroy and Company. The chairman of the Committee on Investments, — $91,941 in securities, "book value" — is Oswald Knauth of the Associated Dry Goods Company. Louis Brownlow, of the Public Administration Clearing House in Chicago, a Rockefeller-supported agency, is chairman of the Committee on Public Administration ; he is also on the Committee on Conference Procedure, and the Committee on Social Security. The chairman of the Committee on Grants-in-Aid is Willard Thorp of Dun and Bradstreet.   Leverett S. Lyon of Brookings is also a member of this committee.

The names of these committees give a picture of the fields of research covered by the Council.   The other members of the committees are heads of departments in universities or colleges. It is easy to see why no criticism of the Social Science Research Council is likely to come from the colleges.   During 1933–34 the Council got new grants amounting to $207,500 ; during 1935–36 the new grants amounted to $319,250 ; in 1936–37 new grants amounted to $515,250, of which $225,000 was for fellowships,* $78,750 for general administration, and $105,-000 for work in the field of social security.   It has published forty bulletins of which twenty-one are related to agricultural problems and thirteen to the social aspects of the depression.

The Spelman Fund was chartered by the State of New York December 27, 1928 with a capital of $10,000,000 provided by the Laura Spelman Memorial Foundation before it was consolidated with the Rockefeller Foundation.   Its resources are expendable both of principal and income at the discretion of the trustees who were : Winthrop W. Aldrich, Cleveland E. Dodge, Raymond B. Fosdick, Thomas W. Lamont, Beardsley Ruml, and Arthur Woods.   Revell McCallum was secretary. It was formed, it said at the time, exclusively for charitable, scientific and educational purposes, including the advancement and diffusion of knowledge concerning "child improvement and interracial relations in cooperation with public agencies."

* Fellows studying in Europe are requested to keep in touch with social science fellowship representative of Rockefeller Foundation.

The child life projects were soon liquidated and the interracial relations problems turned over to the General Education Board. It has concentrated chiefly on the social sciences, particularly on projects relating to public administration.

From its formation to the present day it has repeated in nearly every report that it "has no political objectives." It is interested, it says, "only in helping provide experience and wisdom in executing public programs already adopted and no longer matters of controversy." In addition to experience and wisdom, it also contributes money. It has made a number of appropriations to Brookings ; $50,000 for technical assistance in the Bureau of Indian Affairs, but most astonishing, in view of its supposed impartiality, are the appropriations for purchase of stock in David Lawrence's Washington newspaper, the *United States Daily*. There was purchased $330,000 in the name of the Brookings Institution, $330,000 in the name of National Institute of Public Administration, and $330,000 in the name of the University of Chicago, a total of $990,000 in stock purchases made by the Spelman Fund and turned over to these institutions. The *United States Daily* was founded in 1926 by Owen D. Young, Charles Evans Hughes, Bernard Baruch, John W. Davis, F. Trubee Davidson, James W. Gerard, Samuel Insull, Otto H. Kahn, Jesse H. Jones, Walter C. Teagle, Simon Guggenheim, Mrs Charles H. Sabin, George F. Rand, C. Bascom Slemp, Colonel E. W. House, Robert S. Brookings, and others to give "all the facts, no opinion," and "presenting the official news of the legislative, executive, and judicial branches of the Federal government and each of the governments of the states."

The newspaper, however, was not self-supporting. In 1931 the Spelman Fund "made $503,000 available to the *United States Daily*" and in 1932 it contributed $160,000 to it "in the hope that income from subscription and advertising might be brought reasonably close to a sharply reduced expense." This expenditure of $990,000 in stock and $663,000 in grants, a total of $1,653,000, was more than a tenth of the capital of the Fund and constituted more than half the appropriations in those years. Its income in 1931 was only $373,486. The hope of the Spelman Fund for the *United States Daily* was in vain ; in May 1933 it ceased to be a daily and became a weekly, the *United States News*, the chief loudspeaker for broadcasting the opinions of Mr David Lawrence.

The other favorite project and now the chief recipient of its funds is the Public Administration Clearing House in Chicago, whose director, Louis Brownlow,* it will be remembered, is chairman of the Committee on Public Administration for the Social Science Research Council. This agency was "organized as an exchange for information concerning administrative processes in government, and to foster cooperation among organizations of operating officials, research units, technical experts, and others in the field of public administration." Its board of trustees consists of Frank O. Lowden, chairman, Ralph Budd, vice-chairman, President of C. B. & Q. Railroad ; Richard S. Childs, corporation officer, director of Bon Ami Co. and American Cyanamid Co. ; Frederick M. Davenport, former college professor and Congressman ; Robert M. Hutchins and Louis Brownlow. It got $500,000 from the Spelman Fund to set it up, and in 1933 it got $56,750 for "special activities" and $55,000 in 1934. The 1936 report of the Spelman Fund says : "Over the past eight years a group of organizations working in the field of public administration has come together in Chicago." Apparently this happened by chance, each magnetized by the other, but it may be that the magnet was Rockefeller money.

This becomes evident when we notice the appropriations each received from the Spelman Fund in the single year 1936 : American Public Works Association, $39,000 ; Municipal Finance Officers' Association, $90,000 ; Civil Service Assembly,

* One of the authors of the original draft of the Roosevelt reorganization bill.

$15,200 ; International City Managers' Association, $21,000 ; Governmental Research Association,* American Municipal Association, $97,000 ; American Legislators' Association,† American Public Welfare Association, $57,500 ; Public Administration Clearing House, $42,500 ; Council of State Governments, $42,000 ; National Association of Housing Officials, $7750 ; Public Administration Service, $25,000 ; National Association of Assessing Officials, $33,500 ; and the American Society of Planning Officials, $44,000. It may seem at first a coincidence that all these are located in the same building at the corner of Drexel Avenue and Fifty-eighth Street, Chicago ; have the same phone number and share the same offices at 17th and H Streets in Washington. It seems, however, that the University of Chicago donated the site for this building and erected the building with funds appropriated by the Spelman Fund, $1,153,600, to the University of Chicago for this purpose. From the staff of these organizations nine have been appointed to the University of Chicago faculty and others are occasionally invited to give lectures.

"Each of these organizations has a separate and distinct field," Louis Brownlow explains, "but it has been possible for their secretariats to cooperate in many helpful ways. These organizations share the belief that government in the United States can be made more satisfactory if administrative organizations, techniques, and methods are improved ; and that the responsibility for such improvement rests primarily upon the public officials."

The Spelman Fund also makes contributions to a few other organizations, such as $57,500 in 1933 for a Commission of Inquiry on Public Service Personnel to the Social Science Research Council, and an annual grant of $10,000 to the National Urban League, but its main interest is centered on the nine

---

* Robert M. Paige, secretary-treasurer of the Governmental Research Association, is also assistant director of the Public Administration Clearing House.

† Henry W. Toll, its executive director, is also executive director of Council of State Governments.

governmental organizations in Chicago. Its present trustees are : Cleveland E. Dodge, William Tudor Gardiner, Thomas W. Lamont, Charles E. Merriam, John D. Rockefeller, 3rd, Beardsley Ruml, and Arthur Woods. The late L. M. Dashiell, treasurer of the Rockefeller Foundation, was also treasurer of the Spelman Fund. Its funds amount to (ledger valuation) $6,790,251, including a $700,000 pledge from the Rockefeller Foundation, which apparently intends to contribute to the Spelman Fund when its capital decreases.

The National Bureau of Economic Research is another agency receiving material aid from Rockefeller philanthropy. The Rockefeller Foundation's program in the field of social security has, according to its 1936 report, two main objectives : "Research directed to the description and measurement of cyclical and structural change and to the analysis of the causes of instability," and "research directed to the question of protection against the main hazards that confront the individual, such as sickness, accident, old age dependency, and unemployment." The Foundation comments : "The program thus aims at both prevention and protection. On the protective side the Foundation has supported a special research committee of the Social Science Research Council. With respect to the preventive side, where patient, fundamental research is involved, the emphasis has been upon strong, well-staffed organizations such as the National Bureau of Economic Research and the Brookings Institution in the United States. . ." * Founded in 1920 as a "cooperative enterprise in economic research," it has, according to the Rockefeller Foundation, "contributed in an important way to the increasing exactness and reliability of measurements of national income and its component parts, and has done pioneer work on the more technical aspects of the business cycle. During 1936 the Bureau undertook to en-

* ". . . and the National research institutes in France, Belgium, the Netherlands, Norway, Austria, Sweden, Denmark and Bulgaria."

courage, in collaboration with the leading universities, systematic research in the fields of prices and of income and wealth distribution." It made two grants to this Bureau in 1936 : $7500 as "a supplementary budget item" and $255,000 toward the general research program and expenses of an executive director's office during 1937, 1938, and 1939.*

It is not surprising, therefore, to find the name of Beardsley Ruml on the board of directors, of which Chester I. Barnard, President of the New Jersey Bell Telephone Company, is chairman. Others on the board are : Henry S. Dennison, of the Dennison Manufacturing Company ; George M. Harrison,* president of the Brotherhood of Railway and Steamship Clerks ; Oswald W. Knauth, president of the Associated Dry Goods Corporation ; Harry W. Laidler, executive director of the League for Industrial Democracy ; L. C. Marshall of Johns Hopkins ; George O. May, of Price, Waterhouse and Co, (accountants) ; Shepard Morgan, vice president of the Chase National Bank ; George Soule † of the *New Republic ;* N. I. Stone, industrial and financial consultant. Six other directors are appointed from the universities, and seven by other organizations : American Engineering Council, American Economic Association, American Management Association, National Publishers Association, American Statistical Association, American Bankers Association, and the American Federation of Labor. Wesley C. Mitchell of Columbia is director of the research staff.

A study of real estate financing is going on, undertaken for the Committee on Banking and Credit for the Social Science Research Council. An agreement was entered into January 1, 1937 with the United States Bureau of Agricultural Economics "to collate and analyze pertinent data on agricultural and industrial changes." The measurement of national income and

* It also paid $80,450 from previous appropriations form the Bureau's "general budget."

† Both Mr Harrison and Mr Soule are on Social Science Research Council Committees.

wealth was one of "the first major areas in which the National Bureau initiated studies." National conferences have been called and committees appointed "to examine objectives of studies," "to explore the possibilities of cooperative action," and "to consider the formulation of a research program," in this field and in the field of prices in five industries ; textile, oil, steel, automobile, and coal. A third "area of cooperative effort," its report declares, is banking and credit, which "contains possibilities of unusual scientific and practical significance." A conference decided unanimously that "comprehensive studies are called for, if the bases for a wiser management of credit are to be discovered." Part of the support of the Bureau comes from its members, who pay $25 or more a year and receive all its publications before they are released to the public. Associate members pay $5 a year, receive the *Bulletin* (five issues annually), and may buy copies of the Bureau's books at a third off.

An eight-acre research center has been acquired at Riverdale, just beyond the New York City limits, called "Hillside," where conferences can be held. The annual report issued March 1, 1937 declared : "the guiding policy in the use of the property will be its gradual development as a center for the social sciences analogous in a modest way to 'Woods Hole' in the field of biology. The service that this unique institution has performed during fifty years for the advance of research and teaching in marine biology suggests the possible forms of use of 'Hillside' and perhaps also something of the goals of the entire cooperative program."

Independent of other foundations is Edward A. Filene's Twentieth Century Fund, although among its trustees are to be found Henry S. Dennison, who is on the board of directors of the National Bureau of Economic Research, Oswald Knauth, who is also connected with that organization and the Social Science Research Council, Charles P. Taft, and James G. Mc-

Donald, president of the Foreign Policy Association, which has
been assisted by both the Carnegie and Rockefeller philanthropies. Its economist is J. Frederick Dewhurst, who is on
the Committee on Industry and Trade of the Social Science
Research Council. Chartered in Massachusetts in 1922, for
the "improvement of economic, industrial, civic, and educational conditions, it shall be within the purposes of such corporation to use any means to such ends as may from time to
time seem expedient to its members or trustees, including study,
research, publication, publicity, instruction, and the organization of charitable and educational activities, agencies and institutions already established." Its chief interest in the first five
years of its life was the study and promotion of schemes for
consumer credit and cooperation, a subject which was one of
Mr Filene's major passions. To these studies have gone 48%
of its grants.

From 1919 to 1929 the Twentieth Century Fund acted solely
as a disbursing agency, making annual grants to outside organizations. In addition to consumer credit and cooperative organization studies, it aided investigations into "science in industry,"
"waste in distribution," unemployment, corporation finance,
and created and financed the committee on economic sanctions
headed by Dr Butler. Since Mr Evans Clark became director
of its activities, and, as the trend of the depression continued
downward, the trustees decided to abandon strict adherence to
conservative foundation tradition and "to search, through its
own operations, more deeply into the causes and cures of the
ills of our economic system." This meant further studies of
consumer credit, the organization of medical services, the security markets, the internal indebtedness of the United States,
labor and its relation to government, taxation, wastes in distribution, large corporations and their effect on American
economic life and old-age security." Not content with mere
research, it has tried to translate its findings into practical programs of "social action."

A study of "American Foundations and Their Fields" was made by the Fund in 1929, 1931, and 1934, which analyzed statistically the amounts, in terms of percentages, the foundations devoted to various fields. To Survey Associates the Fund has contributed $2500 annually. Its medical economics activities have been transferred to a non-profit, membership corporation, the Health Economics Association, which helps to promote voluntary, cooperative group payment medical service organizations. When it discovered that the insurance and corporation laws of several states made it illegal or impractical to set up genuine cooperative group payment agencies, except on a very limited scale, the Columbia University Legislative Drafting Bureau was retained to study this problem. The corporation study, designed to determine the place and effect of large corporations in American industry, has been published in the first of a series of booklets, entitled *Big Business, Its Growth and Its Place*. Willard L. Thorp is chairman of a committee investigating wastes, losses, and inefficiencies in our present mechanism for distributing commodities. Oswald Knauth was chairman of a committee which surveyed the relation between government debts and government credit, with particular reference to the United States Federal debt.* Thomas I. Parkinson, president of the Equitable Life Assurance Society, was chairman of a committee which sponsored a study covering the entire tax system of the United States.* With the help of Mrs Margaret Grant Schneider of the Social Science Research Council, a study was made of the Townsend Plan and the Social Security Act in relation to old-age security.

The Twentieth Century Fund is a comparatively small foundation. Its 1937 report shows capital assets of $474,577, but this does not include 150,000 shares of the common stock of William Filene's Company whose market value is not known precisely because there is no active market for it. During Mr Filene's lifetime it depended largely upon generous contribu-

* Published in 1937.

tions from him.   From 1932 to 1937 these payments came from a trust fund set up by him for the benefit of the Twentieth Century Fund which now has the entire principal.   On June 6, 1937 the trustees voted that the Fund would make no more grants to outside agencies, but will, in the future, use its entire income in carrying on its own activities.   Mr Filene died September 26, 1937.   Having deeded the trust fund he had established for the benefit of the Twentieth Century Fund to it before his death, he left the bulk of his estate to the Good Will Fund, Inc., of Boston, "organized for the following charitable and educational purposes ; scientific and educational purposes exclusively : Research and education in methods of applying scientific knowledge to the greater well-being of mankind ; the improvement of health and living conditions of wage earners and their dependents and all persons who have been or are likely to become public charges ; the improvement in methods of medical care ; and research and education as to the causes of poverty, methods for the elimination thereof, and as to the organization and operation of consumers' cooperative agencies." *   How much the Good Will Fund will have at its disposal remains undetermined until the final settlement of Mr Filene's estate.   Its directors are : Roy F. Bergengren, executive secretary of the Credit Union National Association, Percy S. Brown, executive director of the Fund and its secretary-treasurer, Robert Szold, lawyer, David K. Niles, Charles W. Wood, and Harland Allen, economist with Halsey, Stuart and Co.   No president has as yet been elected.

Although it is not legally a philanthropic foundation in the sense that the other endowments considered in this volume are, the Chemical Foundation deserves a passing mention for the contribution it has made to the creation of a billion dollar industry.   Before the World War the chemical industry of America, indeed, of the whole world, was largely in German

* From a letter to the author by Percy S. Brown, February 16, 1938.

hands. The chemists and industrialists of Germany dominated the manufacture of pharmaceutical chemicals and analine dyes. The United States had to rely upon German patents and manufacturers to get the bulk of our medicinal chemicals. Practically all our dyestuffs came from Germany. A. Mitchell Palmer, Alien Property Custodian, declared : "We had a plentiful lack of even such technical knowledge as was required to produce dyes in the laboratory, to say nothing of the vastly greater amount of similar knowledge required to translate laboratory into commercial production." In 1914 the German source stopped abruptly. We could no longer buy ; so we tried to manufacture equivalents. As the supplies held on hand by the German houses became exhausted small American manufacturers tried, through their laboratories, to find the secrets of German dyes. The results were discouraging ; it seemed virtually impossible to make those dyes in America. The secret appeared to be unattainable. But those patent secrets were not buried in German archives. For their self-protection the German firms registered their patents in Washington, thinking thus to protect themselves in case American chemists should happen upon their secrets. They waited hopefully for the end of the war that they might re-embark on the importing of German chemicals.

Such was the situation when America entered the war. The tiny American chemical industry, struggling with unsatisfactory results, saw its opportunity. The man who saw it most clearly was Francis P. Garvan. Already he had been assisting A. Mitchell Palmer investigating "hidden German property." The stock of the Bayer Company had been sold at public auction and its dye plants and patents were purchased by the Sterling Products Company for the Grasselli Chemical Company for $5,310,000 plus taxes and obligations. But there remained 4500 other valuable patents in the American patent office. On November 4, 1917 Congress amended the Trading with the Enemy Act so that the Alien Property Custodian could

seize these patents.   Thus, he announced, in a miracle of understatement, "a colossal obstacle was removed to the development of the American dyestuff industry."   "If German
chemical patents could be placed in the hands of an American
institution strong enough to protect them," Mr Garvan
pointed out, "a real obstacle might be opposed to German importation after the war."   Hence the Chemical Foundation,
not exactly a philanthropic institution, but yet one in which
every important American manufacturer of chemicals was a
stockholder.   For $269,850 paid to the United States govern-
ment, it acquired these German patents to hold them "as a
trustee for American industry."   Mr. Garvan, who thought of
this idea, became president, Colonel Douglas I. McKay, vice
president of J. G. White Company, vice president; and the
trustees were George L. Ingraham, Otto T. Barnard, Cleveland H. Dodge, B. Howell Griswold Jr, and Ralph Stone.
Joseph H. Choate was counsel and Ramsay Hoguet was patent
attorney.   Capitalized at $500,000 as a Delaware corporation,
it licensed these patents whose value it declared it was impossible to estimate to American companies, and it was prepared,
said Mr Garvan, "to fight at the customs gate against any vio-
lation of the patents owned by it."

Reviewing the present state of the American chemical industry, *Fortune,* December 1937, said: ". . . the War finally
brought U. S. chemical industry to its maturity.   And when
Francis P. Garvan as Alien Property Custodian seized the German chemical patents in this country and turned them over to
the Chemical Foundation, which had been created to receive
them, the United States began for the first time an independent
chemical life.   Then, and thereafter, the bankers heard of
chemical industry for the first time."   In January 1920, the
leading chemical stocks were not even listed on the New York
Stock Exchange, not even du Pont, Union Carbon and Car-
bide, Monsanto, or Dow.   Allied Chemical and Dye was only

just being formed. Since 1917 these companies, however, have paid $281,234,000 in dividends.

As *Fortune* observes : "U. S. Chemical Industry . . . was founded by the people of the U. S. In 1918–20 the people's government set the industry up in business as it practices business today. . . It was the government that wrote the tariffs that protected this 'infant industry' in the twenties." The Foundation boasts : "The establishment of a self-contained synthetic organic chemical industry in the United States is the only thing of substantial value which we got out of the war. Less than two months after the Foundation was organized President Wilson urged unusual tariff duties on dyes and related chemicals, and Republicans and Democrats joined together to give it unusual protection. In promoting, encouraging, and building up the chemical industry by educational means and otherwise, Mr Garvan, as president of the Foundation, served without pay. He considered it a public trust. The shareholders were divested of all voice in the business affairs of the Foundation by a voting trust placed in the hands of the trustees. A. Mitchell Palmer chose the officers.

Beginning, therefore, as a patent pool, the Foundation has worked for the advancement of the chemical industry by supporting research and education. It has spent $78,886 for work on biological stains, their development and marketing. It has financed research in a number of diseases and chemicals, although it does not tell what amounts have been spent on these projects. It has also assisted financially a number of chemical journals, distributed 300,000 copies of Edwin E. Slosson's *Creative Chemistry* and about 30,000,000 pieces of other educational literature including a series of booklets expounding the economic ideas of the late Francis P. Garvan in red-white-and-blue covers, entitled *The Deserted Village — American Political Economy*. In May 1935 the National Farm Chemurgic Council was formed at Dearborn, Michigan, "to advance the indus-

trial use of American farm products through applied science."
"Chemurgic," it was explained, meant putting chemistry and
related science to work in industry and for the farmer.   This
Council was incorporated in Michigan as a non-profit making
corporation "for scientific and educational purposes."   Its
president, coincidentally, was Francis P. Garvan, who led a
distinguished list of names on its board of governors.   Up to
May 1, 1937 the Chemical Foundation had contributed $201,-
101.79 to the Council for organization and "education." Henry
Ford has been much interested in it from its inception.

Mr Garvan said that he never drew a salary from the Chemical Foundation.   It has never declared a dividend.   Its income
from the licensing of patents, including the Strauss patents,
Numbers 1,316,817 and 1,339,378 for stainless steel manufacture, has never been revealed.   The size of the funds it controls is unknown.   No financial statement is given to the public.   A few criticisms of it have been made in Congress, but so
far it has resisted investigation.   Of all the many agencies
through which millionaires and business men by means of
philanthropic foundations, "institutions," bureaus, or councils
seek to influence and educate the American public, the Chemical Foundation seems the most questionable.

CHAPTER XI

PUBLIC HEALTH AND PRIVATE PHILANTHROPY

There is no such thing as a national Department of Health in the United States government. Any attempt to establish one would be balked by cries that it would be unconstitutional, since the Constitution grants no specific authority for such an office. What we have is the U. S. Public Health Service, a division of the Treasury Department, headed by a Surgeon General, Dr Thomas Parran, Jr, which is vaguely justified by the general welfare clause and, under the authority to make treaties and regulate commerce, is permitted to prevent the importation of disease, its interstate spread, and in a limited way to do some research on the cause and prevention of disease and the purity of biological products. Although we generally recognize that public health is a national concern, the Federal appropriation before 1932 for this service was less than five million dollars a year, and no one can examine the subject without realizing that public health in the United States is neither adequately nor satisfactorily organized.

Indeed, there is active, organized opposition to adequate public health measures. Drug and patent medicine interests killed in committee the Tugwell bill for regulating medicinal advertising ; real estate interests have consistently fought sanitary and housing improvements, and it has been charged that the American Medical Association thwarted the inclusion of health insurance in the Social Security Act. We do not believe in "paternalism" in government ; therefore it is considered better to let babies die than to permit the Federal government to intervene in such a vital matter as public health and thus be guilty of something which might be called "paternalistic." When the Committee on the Costs of Medical Care recommended community health centers, organized medical societies screamed that this was "socialistic." Millions of people cannot get proper medical attention while thousands of doctors make inadequate incomes because people cannot pay for the care the doctors are prepared to give. Yet, in spite of that, there is a wild, organized outcry against "socialized medicine" as something unspeakable whenever adequate measures are suggested for dealing with what is, after all, a national problem. Only now are we becoming aware of the necessity for a nation-wide drive against tuberculosis, syphilis, cancer, and infantile paralysis.

It seems that in a capitalistic democracy such things as decent health measures cannot be instigated by the national government. Local health boards are supposed to supervise sanitary conditions and hence we have the very minimum of health service unless the population is goaded into action. An outbreak of typhoid or diphtheria may stimulate action, or it may be started by the organized agitation and demonstration of health societies or philanthropic foundations. It is frequently declared that one of the greatest contributions of and justifications for philanthropic foundations is in the work they have done in behalf of public health. Where the Federal government has been negligent, and the state and local governments passive, the foundations, it is said, have gone into this field and demonstrated what necessary and beneficent work private philanthropy can do when faced by a problem that is a genuine challenge for effective action.

The largest single fund devoting itself to public health is the Rockefeller Foundation. Let us see what it did in one of its biggest years. According to Dr George E. Vincent, then president of it: "during 1928 the Rockefeller Foundation, in disbursing from income and capital $21,690,738 * (1) contributed to the development of medical sciences through provision for land, buildings, operation, or endowment for eighteen

---

* $12,000,000, or more than half of this, went to the China Medical Board.

medical schools in fourteen countries ; (2) provided for the support of the Peking Union Medical College ; (3) made minor appropriations for improving premedical instructions in China and Siam, for operating expenses of seventeen hospitals in China, and for laboratory supplies, equipment, and literature for European medical centers which are still feeling the after-effects of the war ; (4) through small grants assisted certain medical schools in France, Italy, and Ireland which offer exceptional facilities for graduate study ; (5) continued to contribute toward the biological science institutions in four countries ; (6) assisted the development of professional public health training in eight schools and institutes in seven countries and in twelve field training stations in the United States and abroad ; (7) gave aid to fifteen nurse training schools in ten countries ; (8) helped Brazil combat a new attack of yellow fever ; (9) continued studies of that disease on the West Coast of Africa ; (10) took part in malaria control demonstrations or surveys in six American states and eighteen foreign countries ; (11) continued contributions toward the emergency budgets of eighty-five county health organizations in seven states of the Mississippi flood area ; (12) aided the governments of twenty-one countries in fighting hookworm disease ; (13) gave funds to organized rural health service in 191 counties in the United States and toward state supervision of such service in fourteen states of that country ; (14) aided in the establishment or maintenance of certain essential divisions in the national health services of twenty-three foreign countries and in the state health departments of eighteen American states ; (15) provided directly or indirectly fellowships for 802 men and women from forty-six different countries, paid the traveling expenses of sixty-one officials or professors making study visits in the United States or abroad and provided similar opportunities for 128 nurses and other public health workers ; (16) contributed to the work of the Health Organization of the League of Nations through the support of international interchanges of public health personnel and the development of a world-wide service of epidemiological intelligence and public health statistics ; (17) lent staff members as consultants to many foreign governments ; (18) made surveys of health conditions or of medical or nursing education in five countries ; (19) collaborated with the Rockefeller Institute for Medical Research in field studies of respiratory diseases and verruga peruna ; (20) assisted in mental hygiene projects in the United States and Canada, in demonstrations in dispensary development, research, and teaching in hospitals and clinics in New York City and in numerous other undertakings in public health, medical education and allied fields.'

Thus thousands, and probably millions of people can say "God bless the Rockefeller Foundation." It is impossible to underestimate its work in anti-hookworm campaigns, malaria control, yellow fever elimination, or its contributions to Johns Hopkins and other universities. Before 1928 this work was split amongst a number of boards. The first was the Rockefeller Sanitary Commission established in 1909 for the control of hookworm, which was reorganized as the International Health Board. Later the China Medical Board was set up, and before the reorganization of the Rockefeller Foundation to unify these activities, the General Education Board, the Laura Spelman Memorial, and the International Education Board were all making contributions to public health. Dr Vincent declares that these boards not only distributed all their incomes but appropriated $225,000,000 of capital funds, which is a little difficult to understand since even they did not have that amount in capital funds, although, of course, their combined income and capital funds has, over the years, amounted to much more than that. In order to promote public health, the Rockefeller Foundation found that it had to help build up medical schools. As Dr Vincent remarks : "Only of late have a few schools, notably in Great Britain and the United States, shown a determination to prepare the doctor to take his place in a rapidly changing social order."

Diseases such as typhoid, once a source of profit, have almost disappeared. Health centers rob physicians of their practise. However, greater interest in personal hygiene, school health, maternal and child welfare may send more patients to the private practitioners. Public health staffs may become agents for doctors. The foundations are faced with a ticklish problem : they can support public health without criticism and with general popular acclaim up to a point : but if they go beyond that point they tread on dangerous ground. The point, of course, is the no man's land of "socialized medicine," a phrase which has as many meanings as there are medical societies. If foundations appear to advocate and encourage that, then they incur the hostility of a large section of organized medicine. It is therefore interesting to note how warily they have walked. In one instance, as we shall see, when a foundation stepped courageously into the problem it took it, figuratively, on the chin. They wish to do great public good, but it is difficult for them to carry their programs to logical or practical conclusions without running afoul the one thing they dread most : criticism from respectable, vested interests.

Thus the Rockefeller Foundation has attacked the problem from what might be called an oblique angle. It has concentrated on the task of training and educating public health workers. In order to avoid being caught in the midst of a quarrel amongst doctors, health officers, and the public, the Foundation has restricted its direct aid to official government agencies, leaving the pioneering and voluntary health programs to others. Throughout the world the Foundation has supported the training of doctors and health officers, trying to get medical students to devote themselves to public health, establishing and supporting important schools or institutes of hygiene, such as the Harvard School of Public Health ; the Institute of Hygiene, São

Paulo, Brazil ; the London School of Hygiene and Tropical Medicine ; the State Institute of Public Health, Prague ; and the State Hygienic Institute, Budapest. Field stations for training and investigation were assisted in Alabama, Mississippi, North Carolina, Ohio, Spain, Corsica, Italy, Poland (3), Hungary, and Czechoslovakia.

The Foundation's battle against yellow fever has been told so many times it need not be repeated here. In 1927 there was hope that the fight had been won even in the back-country of Brazil. But, as the Foundation's reports graphically describe it, the jungle struck back in Rio de Janeiro in 1928 and in Colombia in 1929. Most people know the work of Hideyo Noguchi, W. A. Young, and Adrian Stokes who gave their lives in 1927 in this struggle. Almost as well known is the work in anti-malaria measures, and extremely well publicized have been the hookworm campaigns. Such work is beyond praise. It is, perhaps, invidious, but none the less it is important that the economic value of this work be pointed out : the tropics have been made more habitable for the white race, for American agents of great industrial organizations such as, let us say, the Standard Oil companies. It cannot be said that the great humanitarian work in Central and South America of the Foundation bears any relation to American commercial imperialism in that region. It was, of course, no part of the thought of the Rockefeller benefactors that their efforts should be followed by such investors as the Chase National Bank. American philanthropy abroad is, in part, at least an outgrowth of Baptist and Presbyterian desires to convert the heathen, to send out missionaries to uplift mankind, and its inspiration has no taint of such commercial considerations as the enhancement of Rockefeller prestige in those countries where Standard Oil salesmen were to follow later. But it is nonetheless true that the work of the International Health Division is as world-wide in its organization as the almost countless Standard Oil subsidiaries. It might also be pointed out that few American young men would be enthusiastic about selling oil for the lamps of China if they thought they would be treated by local, native, Chinese doctors.

The Foundation's aid to county or local health organizations expanded until, in 1928, it included 263 projects in twenty-four countries, of which 191 were in the United States. The average budget of these was about $10,000 of which the Foundation contributed approximately 15%. When the League of Nations set up a Health Section the Foundation immediately assumed a substantial part of its budget, and has aided in the publication of its reports. Thus the Rockefeller Foundation has avoided being involved in controversial matters. Its main emphasis has been on the control of specific diseases by means of field investigations, practical demonstrations, and laboratory research. The laboratories of the Rockefeller Institute of Medical Research enable it to do this. Those in charge of the Foundation have never lost sight of their conception of the Foundation's role ; they say it can "serve only to initiate and to exemplify modern methods of health promotion, and tasks of carrying on this work to fulfillment belongs properly to government authorities with their powers to tax, and to enact and enforce appropriate legislation." Reaching a peak of $3,-561,891 in 1929, the expenditures of the International Health Division have declined : $2,644,132 in 1930, $3,247,384 in 1931, $2,488,142 in 1932, $3,044,318 in 1933, $2,433,535 in 1934,* $2,731,194 in 1935, and $1,934,217 in 1936.†

Considerable appropriations were also made in fields related to public health, such as the medical sciences, mental hygiene, experimental biology, nursing service. Some projects, such as that connected with the League of Nations, formerly included in the International Health Division appropriations, are now separate grants made by the Foundation itself, although the Division carries on the major portion of its public health pro-

* 1934 report.
† 1936 report.

gram. "Advances," it states frankly in its 1934 report, "cannot be safeguarded at a level very far above the general level of government standards." The need for central leadership in rural health was recognized and the Foundation gave "assistance for the promotion of such leadership" in twenty states. In North America 109 local health services received aid in 1934, 95 of these in the United States, nine in Canada, five in Mexico, to the extent of $109,504, or 15.4% of their total budgets. In 1936 the Division contributed $6844 to seven public health administration projects in the United States and two in Mexico, representing 29% of their total budgets, and its aid to all local health services amounted to $78,149, its portion varying from $25,000 or 100% in the case of a project in the Eastern Health District of Baltimore in conjunction with the School of Hygiene and Public Health of Johns Hopkins to $571 or 6% in the case of a foothills unit in Alberta, Canada — a total average of 34%. In addition to this emergency grants were made to many existing public health organizations to tide them over until Federal funds were available under Social Security Act appropriations. These amounted to $28,756 or an average of 24% of the total budget.

At the same time generous contributions were made abroad : $2,000 for a survey of public health administration in Hungary ; malaria control work was advanced in Cuba and Venezuela ; technical direction was given in Nicaragua on water supply plans ; consulting service was furnished on sewerage systems in other Central American countries ; latrines were installed in Costa Rica. In Greece aid was given in a study of water supply and excreta disposal, where the Division had a share in forty-eight sanitary engineering projects ; a course in sanitary engineering was given in the School of Hygiene in Ankara, Turkey. In India cooperative sanitary work included the improvement of wells and installation of urinals, latrines, bathing platforms, and manure pits. A survey of the marshes in Cyprus was made and a demonstration of soil pollution made. Help was given

Poland from 1929 to 1935 for the establishment of a Bureau of Public Health Nursing. Since 1929 the Division participated in public health work in Albania and Hungary. Six thousand dollars was provided for a health center in Istanbul, and demonstrations were carried on in Rumania. Diphtheria was studied in Austria ; a rural health unit supported in Poonamallee, India, and at Bangalore District in Mysore State. A demonstration health unit was aided for a five year period at Poerwokerto, Java. "Of the twenty-five countries in Europe, excluding the British Isles and Russia, fourteen are equipped with national institutes or schools of hygiene. In ten of the fourteen the International Health Division has cooperated in creating these institutions." In Italy it contributed $939,500 toward the building and equipment of the institute and in Rumania $110,000.

Up to 1936 the Division expended a total of $185,042 for public health administration. $85,080 of this was spent in the United States, and $99,961 in foreign countries. For "other state health services" $50,691 was spent in the United States and $133,890 in foreign countries. For the control of malaria $724,363 was expended in the United States and $917,275 in foreign countries. For investigations and surveys $197,260 was spent in the United States and $828,504 in foreign countries. On the control and investigation of tuberculosis $276,-594 has been spent in the United States and $2,535,545 in foreign countries, chiefly in France where a war-time organization to fight tuberculosis was turned over to the French Government. For schools and institutes of hygiene and public health $10,623,372 was paid in the United States and $7,290,844 abroad. For schools of nursing $1,500,000 was spent in the United States and $1,478,102 in foreign countries. Of the $15,715,119 expended for the control and investigation of diseases the greatest portion went to yellow fever : $5,947,023 ; the next greatest to hookworm, $3,834,727 ; while $2,684,596 was spent on malaria ; $2,812,139 on tuberculosis (see above) and $89,795 on yaws and syphilis (all in Jamaica). Only $8521 is reported by the Division to have been spent on cancer. Infantile paralysis is not listed in the index.

The next largest foundation devoted to public health is the Commonwealth Fund, established in 1919, by Mrs E. S. Harkness by an original gift of securities worth $9,956,111 at market value and an additional gift of $6,379,929 later. The first gifts of the fund were : $50,000 to the United War Work Fund ; $50,000 to Syrian Relief ; $10,000 to the National Committee of Mental Hygiene ; $6000 to the Committee on After Care of Infantile Paralysis ; $10,000 to the National Research Council ; $15,000 to Johns Hopkins Medical School. On June 17, 1919 $750,000 was appropriated for the work of the American Red Cross in the Balkans, but the Red Cross was able to finance this work without this gift, so $500,000 was used for food drafts through the American Relief Administration in 1920 ; 40% in Vienna, 35% in Warsaw, 12½% each to Budapest and Prague. Educational and legal research began in 1920. It was then that the Fund turned its major interest toward public health, giving $45,000 for Eskimo Hospital at Barrow, Alaska, $30,000 for a survey of leprosy in South America ; and $25,000 for a survey of hospitals in New York City by the New York Academy of Medicine. For the medical school of "Yale in China" $30,000 was appropriated and a generous gift of $75,000 was made for the aid of crippled children ; the Committee on After Care of Infantile Paralysis, $52,500 ; the Visiting Nurse Association of Brooklyn, $15,000 ; and Child Welfare League, $25,000 ; and Social Hygiene Association, $25,000.

The Fund's interest in juvenile delinquency and child health dates from 1922 when an appropriation of $527,200 was made for a study of the causes of juvenile delinquency and for a psychiatric study. At the same time fifteen fellowships were granted at the New York School of Social Work. The following year those in charge of the Fund decided to finance a public health demonstration at Fargo, N.D. Aware of the inevitability of criticism and hostility of a part of the medical profession it stated : "it has no expectation of reforming the world . . . it has no desire to interfere with the practice of private physicians ; on the contrary, their cooperation has been sought and freely offered . . . an educational and preventive program of this character far from decreasing the need for physicians should increase it."

Mrs Harkness died in 1926. By reason of her bequests and the appreciation in the value of the securities held, the assets in 1926 amounted to $40,099,365 at market value. The Fund's activities expanded. The year previous the fellowships for twenty British graduate students to spend two years in the United States were started. In 1927, through help from the Fund, the Bureau of Children's Guidance became the Institute for Child Guidance and thirty seven students were in training there under the directorship of Lawson G. Lowrey for psychiatric social work.

Other foundations, chiefly local in scope, also established child guidance clinics about this time : the Amherst H. Wilder Charity in St Paul, the Michigan Children's Fund in Detroit and Grand Rapids, the Martha Beeman Foundation in Niagara Falls, the Bemis-Taylor Foundation in Colorado Springs, and the Buhl Foundation in Pittsburgh. Psychiatric social workers were supplied by the Commonwealth Fund to Liverpool and Birmingham. In 1932, however, the Fund began to feel the effects of diminished income on its securities and in scaling its appropriations downward, curtailed the work of the Institute for Child Guidance and closed it June 30, 1933. The Fund did not give up its interest and support of projects for child welfare, however. It simply felt that the training of psychiatric social workers could be done by the clinics themselves or by medical schools in conjunction with schools of social work.

Meanwhile the Division of Rural Hospitals helped to establish six hospitals in Tennessee, Massachusetts, Mississippi, and Virginia. The Fund contributed roughly about two-thirds of the cost of the hospital building, while the cost of the site and one-third of the anticipated cost of the building were raised locally. The local residents retained full property rights and responsibility for the cost of operation. The report noted that it was difficult to make many business men understand that a good hospital, if it is to be of real service to the community, must always have a deficit. The rural hospital, it declared, must be a "community asset not merely a workshop for physicians or a luxury for the well-to-do." The task of building a hospital is easy, it was found, compared with the task of building the hospital into the life of the countryside. The Fund also commented : "A large part of the medical profession does not yet recognize the value of preventive health work and is probably suspicious of those who advocate it are proponents of some socialistic scheme of state medicine." Fellowships were offered for post graduate study for members of the hospital staff, to help the local physicians to observe the best current practices. In 1931 the report remarked that no inclusive formula had been found for the Fund's public health activities, but they rely on "the interplay of selected social factors to accomplish ends which the exclusive use of a single approach would be less likely to attain." The three factors were : (1) the small general hospital, (2) the rural public health unit, (3) the rural physician. In 1934 the report said of the rural physician : "He defends his pocketbook as quickly and as shortsightedly as his neighbors do when threatened." However, "a basic reality is that rural medicine, by and large, is not good enough" and "so far as the Fund is aware no one has found any sure way to make it better, at least not in the present generation."

Many other projects were aided, such as a study of maternity death in New York ; pneumonia sera research in Massachusetts ; trachoma research in Washington University. $100,000 was granted to the Provident Hospital for education of Negro physicians in the medical school of the University of Chicago. In 1928 a Division of Publications was started with *The Problem Child At Home* as its major publication. The health work in Austria was completed that year, $663,429 having been spent on it. A child guidance clinic was opened in London. In 1926 a grant was made to Yale of $50,000 annually for mental hygiene instruction, lectures, and consultation. The legal research division explored "the new borderline between administrative and judicial processes which is traced by the growth of such innovations in government as the Interstate Commerce Commission and the Federal Trade Commission." Important also, taking 13.1% of its total appropriations in 1936, have been the Commonwealth Fund Fellowships for British students, the number having been raised to thirty in 1928 when Eric Linklater was brought over, among others. The report remarked in 1932 : "Traveling by auto and averaging 14,000 miles apiece they met many interesting Americans" . . . another year it said the Fund was "exposing young Britons to an unfamiliar educational setting in the hope it will be fruitful of a new type of international understanding." Of those so exposed, it was found, 40% became teachers.

The Fund has declared its policy was to finance, in public health, only such projects as can "in due time be fully supported locally." The gift that "primes the pump of local spending for socially valuable purposes accomplishes far more than the gift which merely meets the cost of a proprietary program." The report declared in 1933 that the Fund believed that rural health should be organized on a county-wide basis with a full-time health officer who is a physician, with clinical service, and one public health nurse to each 6000 people, and two sanitary inspectors. Of medical research it commented that projects might be successful in four or five years or they might be unsuccessful after a whole lifetime. Yet endowments, it noted, must guard against immobility and "creeping paralysis" and "tend to avoid longtime commitments which may handicap them in the future." Hence grants are usually made one year at a time and rarely for more than three years at a time.

In 1936, 69.5% of the appropriations were for the promotion of public health, which included a conditional grant of $250,-000 to Columbia University for new facilities for graduate medical education. "From whatever point of view one approaches the question of better health," it said, "it is soon evident that a fundamental need is for well-trained personnel – in health departments and in the centers of research and teaching, in medical practice generally." The Fund, it declared, has tried to show that public health service of increasingly good quality can be provided in rural and small city communities "when intelligent local leadership and understanding cooperation between the private and public practitioners of medicine are coupled with sound technical advice." It has therefore supported demonstrations, provided educational facilities for the local physicians, and attempted to win over the taxpayer to the desirability of supporting health programs.

Among other things, it noted : in two Massachusetts districts toxoid has been experimentally offered to school children as a protection against scarlet fever. In the last four years the services in Southern counties have been developed for the control of venereal disease. Federal funds are now becoming available, and in Lauderdale County, Mississippi, such funds have been used to employ an additional nurse and clerk. In Gibson County Tennessee, the Fund sponsored two inquiries ; one on venereal disease control, and the other on maternity hygiene. Syphilis was indicated in about 1½% of the whites and 4½% of the Negroes. That would indicate that there were approximately 700 cases of syphilis in the county in addition to those already being treated. A tuberculosis control unit consisting of a medical director, a nurse, and a clerk was organized for Berkshire County, Massachusetts, where the nurse did a careful teaching job in each family where tuberculosis was found. "In a state which, like Massachusetts, is well supplied with beds for tuberculosis and where there is no large Negro population to complicate the picture, such an effort to find and to bring under adequate supervision every case of tuberculosis in a rural community has real promise. . ."

The reports do not mention directly the organized opposition of medical associations to health demonstrations and a greater state participation in the problem of preventive medicine, but the 1936 report touched on the subject indirectly : "Except for those physicians who profess to believe that all is well in medicine so long as the doctor's vested interest in his patients is left undisturbed, there is general agreement that medical practice lags behind medical knowledge." To professional education, declares the Fund, one must look to diminish this lag. Preventive medicine is taught at Vanderbilt, Tufts, and Tulane through the Fund's subsidies. "The student in physical diagnosis is at the threshold of clinical medicine, . . . he is perhaps more impressionable than he will ever be again. It is a good time to sensitize him to the possibilities of prevention." Preventive medicine, it adds, is the habit and technique of treating people as "if they were people and not symptom pictures. It is a point of view, not a clinical entity. . . To the layman who has thought at all about medicine it seems incredible that there should be any novelty about such a point of view. But the layman is not often aware of the parochialism of medical education — of the extent to which the human body and its ailments are parceled out between different departments of instruction which are keenly aware of their independence even in a well-integrated school and may not be on speaking terms in a poorly organized one."

According to its balance sheet of September 30, 1937, the Commonwealth Fund's assets amount to $51,832,691. During the year Edward S. Harkness made it two gifts : $3,000,000 for support of the hospital program, and $5,000,000 to provide increased income for grants to medical research and to "certain

phases of medical education." Seventy-four per cent of the
$1,838,059 appropriated in the year was earmarked for health,
12% of this for mental, and 62% for general health.

The Milbank Fund is the foundation which tried to attack
this problem directly.   From 1905 until her death in 1921,
Elizabeth Milbank Anderson, a genuine, sincere philanthropist
if there ever was one, conducted the larger part of her public
benefactions through the agency of the Memorial Fund Association.   After her death this was reorganized and incorporated as the Milbank Memorial Fund with assets of a little
less than ten million dollars in securities.   Edward W. Sheldon
was the original president, Albert G. Milbank was treasurer,
and the board of directors consisted of Thomas Cochran, John
G. Milburn, George L. Nichols, Elihu Root, and Dr Charles M.
Cauldwell.   It was advised by a technical board which included
the late Dr Hermann M. Biggs ; Bailey B. Burritt, director of
the AICP ; Livingston Farrand, president of Cornell ; Homer
Folks, State Charities Aid Association ; James Alexander Miller,
Dr William H. Welch, ex-officio, of Johns Hopkins ; and Dr
Lindsley R. Williams.   John A. Kingsbury, who had been
Mayor Mitchell's Commissioner of Charities, was secretary of
the Fund.

Courageously, the Fund set out in 1922 to inquire : What
are the major elements in an effective community health program, what would it cost, and can normal American communities assume that cost ?   With adequate resources can tuberculosis be practically reduced ?   In pursuance of these objectives the Fund set up three health demonstrations in New York
State ; one in Cattaraugus County, one in urban Syracuse, and
one in the New York Belleville-Yorkville district.   Each community undertook to provide quarters for the clinic, to give
whole-hearted cooperation, and to promise eventual community support.   It was estimated that these three demonstrations
would cost, in all, from $300,000 to $400,000 yearly.   Syracuse

was chosen not because it needed a health demonstration but because the city assured the Fund full cooperation. It was a demonstration *by* Syracuse, not *on* Syracuse. The same considerations led to the selection of the other places for the demonstrations, yet they all aroused hostile criticisms from sections of the medical profession who feared that people would get free service who could afford to pay regular practitioners. In Cattaraugus County, of sixty-eight physicians, seventeen were more or less antagonistic and eight actively hostile. In addition to these demonstrations help was also given the Home Hospital at 315 East 158th Street, where the practicality of family care for tuberculosis was demonstrated. The more far-sighted physicians approved this program and Dr Biggs declared : "Public health is purchasable. Within natural limitations, any community can determine its own death rate."

They amply proved themselves. Of the Cattaraugus demonstration Dr C-E. A. Winslow of Yale declared it "was one of the most effective and inspiring contributions made to the care of rural public health anywhere in the world." Yet, after it was completed, he noted : of 3000 counties in the United States, 2500 are rural, and only 500 have full time health services. Of these 500, less than fifty have health budgets and health personnels that can be considered adequate. Only Cattaraugus County and perhaps a dozen others have health machinery "comparable to that essential in an urban community." From 1912 to 1922 Syracuse had a health organization better than average ; before the demonstrations started $1 per capita was spent on health. The Milbank Fund brought this up to $2.08 per capita and the city voted to take on the increase. New York City continued the Yorkville-Belleville health services and recently opened a new clinic.

Meanwhile the Milbank Fund made grants to a number of other projects, such as the Diphtheria Prevention Commission of New York City for toxin-anti-toxin immunization of children. Contributions were made to the program of St Luke's

International Hospital in Tokio, Japan. A Division of Research was established in 1928 which published a study, *Measurement of Results of Public Health Activities.* An epidemological study of tuberculosis was financed. The Survey Associates were aided. Up to 1929 the Fund gave a total of $449,-638 to the Milbank Memorial Choir at Princeton ; * $160,000 to Phillips Academy ; $135,000 to the Serbian Child Welfare Association ; $40,000 to the American School in Japan. Its largest annual appropriation was in 1930, $1,436,425, which cut into its capital, when $500,000 was appropriated for the State Charities Aid Association ; $250,000 for the Emergency Relief Committee ; and $20,000 was pledged to the Chinese National Association of the Mass Education Movement for China's first medical department of public health at Ting Hsien. A pledge of $30,000, or $10,000 a year for three years, was made to Syracuse University for a course in public health nursing.

The chief project, however, after the New York health demonstrations, was the support of the Committee on the Costs of Medical Care organized in 1927, headed by Ray Lyman Wilbur. Other agencies collaborating were the U. S. Public Health Service, the National Tuberculosis Association, the American Dental Association, the National Institute of Public Administration, the Society for Control of Cancer, the National Bureau of Economic Research, the American Medical Association, the Metropolitan Life Insurance Co., and the Rosenwald Fund. Up to 1930 the Milbank Fund gave $132,-499 for this research, 39% of the Committee's income. To complete the twenty-eight volumes of studies the Committee obtained further support from the Carnegie Corporation, the Josiah Macy Jr Foundation, the New York Foundation, the Rockefeller Foundation, the Russell Sage Foundation, the

---

* Albert G. Milbank was A.B. Princeton 1896, is chairman of the Princeton Fund, trustee of Princeton, was decorated, Order of St Sava by Kingdom of Serbs, Croats, and Slovenes.

Twentieth Century Fund, and the Social Science Research Council. In 1931 the Committee revealed that it had discovered that "the great majority of people — not the indigent only — cannot under the present system make adequate payment for medical care." The following year it exposed, by publication of its research, the extent to which the people of the United States are unable to purchase medical care while physicians fail to receive even reasonably adequate compensation.

It was clear that within the Committee there was a passionate difference of opinion. The dominant group in the American Medical Association led by Dr Morris Fishbein was definitely hostile to the work of the Committee, suspicious of its findings, and ready to attack its conclusions. John A. Kingsbury was suspected as the evil genius who instigated the Committee. Physicians who feared that the public health movement would lead to "socialized medicine" prepared to discredit the Committee's findings. Finally, in 1932, the majority report was published, together with a minority report and several independent dissenting opinions. The majority report declared that the costs of medical care "fall very unevenly upon different families in the same income and population groups." Most communities, it said, "have already taken the position that no human being should be allowed to suffer, on account of poverty, from remediable illness or distress," and concluded that the costs should be taken care of "on group payment basis or through the use of insurance, through the use of taxation, or through the use of both." Medical service, it recommended, should be organized by groups of physicians, dentists, nurses, around a hospital, all basic public health services should be extended so that they will be available to the population according to its needs. It also declared that the medical service functions of the state should be studied, and that training in health and prevention should be extended.

Nobody seemed to be satisfied with these conclusions. The dominant group in the American Medical Association felt that they were revolutionary, socialistic, and threatening to their interests. Others were disappointed that the final report of the Committee did not give any comprehensive program or show any practical way to solve the basic problems. John A. Kingsbury, writing the Milbank report for 1932 said : "in all fairness it should be said much of the fault lay with obstructionist tactics on the part of certain groups of physicians who control medical organizations and habitually use the great prestige of these organizations to prevent, rather than promote the delivery of adequate medical services to all the people." He added : "The personal relation between patient and physician should be emphasized as the essential element in safeguarding the quality of medical service, but the private business relation is not necessary."

It was obvious that Mr Kingsbury was leading with his chin, challenging the most conservative, strongly entrenched, and powerful group within the American Medical Association. What happened to Mr Kingsbury has been graphically described by James Rorty in the *Nation*, June 24, 1936. Mr Kingsbury wanted to have the work of the Committee on the Costs of Medical Care carried on. He said : "The President and the Congress should have placed before them a real plan of public health." Already he had instigated the studies on health in Europe by Sir Arthur Newsholme, he had gone with Sir Arthur to Russia in 1932, and had written a book on *Red Medicine*. But Dr Fishbein and his group had enough counts against him. Mr Kingsbury had made the fatal error of thinking straight on a question that threatened vested interests. He was largely responsible for the direct attack upon the kernel of the problem of public health. Other foundations did important and constructive work in health demonstrations and training of personnel, in medical research and eradication of plagues. But while Mr Kingsbury was secretary of the Milbank Fund he sought to find out what the trouble was : why, in the United States, we do not have adequate public health service. In his

1933 report he said : "The Milbank Fund may be classified as a foundation that seeks a solution rather than the alleviation of a situation." He saw the solution, and he saw what stood in the way, but the Dr Fishbein group saw the problem just as clearly from their point of view. Mr Kingsbury had to be eliminated.

The story of how that was done is as dramatic as any in the history of American medicine, although it is not one that the medical profession should be proud of. It was done by means of a boycott against the products of the Borden Company. A large part of the income of the Milbank Fund comes from investments in the Borden Company or its subsidiaries. Albert G. Milbank, president of the Fund, is financially interested in the Borden Company and is chairman of its board and affiliated companies. He is a member of the law firm of Milbank, Tweed, Hope, and Webb, and counsel for the Chase National Bank. He is director in the Oceanic Investing Company and trustee of the Title Guarantee Trust Company. Pressure was brought to bear upon him. The medical press warned physicians of the "social experiments" of the Milbank Fund. "If you do not approve of the policies of these foundations make certain you are not contributing directly to their campaign funds." Mr Milbank was put on the spot to get rid of Mr Kingsbury. It is not clear that the boycott went very far, but threat of boycott was sufficient. When it came to a crisis it was demonstrated that foundations are in no financial position to show genuine independence in the face of powerful economic pressure. On March 28, 1935, Mr Milbank, at a meeting of the board of counsel of the Milbank Fund, repudiated his former advocacy of health insurance. Three days later he told Mr Kingsbury that he had had to choose between the Borden Company and the Fund. He then informed the press that John A. Kingsbury "had brought to a close his official connection" with the Fund.

No other statement was forthcoming except that there had been a difference of opinion on policy. Those who feared lest the Milbank Fund further the cause of "socialized medicine" rejoiced. When Mr Kingsbury declared that pressure from the American Medical Association had kept health insurance out of the Social Security Act, Dr Fishbein was asked about that. "Mr Kingsbury," he said, "talks like a disappointed man who has lost his job." In the 1936 report Mr Milbank points with pride to the Fund's principal contributions in "financial support and technical assistance. . . It continued its support of the public health experiment in Ting Hsien, China, carried on by the Chinese National Association of the Mass Education Movement. . . It cooperated with the League of Nations in the development of health indices which would be applicable internationally. It contributed to the advancement of health center development in New York City. It assisted a number of organizations seeking the solution of specific public health problems, such as the control of venereal diseases, tuberculosis, maternal and infant mortality. Through its technical staff, it continued its studies in health administration, in the appraisal of public health procedures, in population, in the relation of economic status to public health, and in various other subjects within its fields of interest." No one can criticise that, least of all Dr Fishbein.

There are many other foundations throughout the country, chiefly local, engaged in various phases of public health. Notable among these are those in Michigan, and best known is the Children's Fund established in 1929 by the late Senator James Couzens with ten million dollars to be spent in twenty-five years. In 1934 he added $2,100,000 more, stating that constructive helpfulness to children was more in the nature of justice than in the nature of charity. As of April 1937, the total assets of the Fund were $10,132,792. Disbursements for the year, May 1, 1936 to April 30, 1937, totaled $720,151, serving directly or indirectly 375,000 children. Fifty-nine counties in Michigan, mainly in the northern part of the state, are served by the Child Health Division. When the Fund was founded there were only four county health departments in the state.

Four demonstrations of united-county or district health departments of four counties each were organized and one single county unit in sparsely settled northern Michigan. The Fund reports : "Michigan now has a total of 53 counties out of 83 that enjoy organized public health work." $109,970 was spent during the year on this type of work. Maternal and child death rates have been appreciably reduced. Thirty-three public health nurses have been supplied. Dental programs have been emphasized, special clinics organized and aided, eye treatment and vision correction conducted, and a child guidance clinic is conducted for Detroit children who are in trouble with parents, teachers, the neighborhood, or themselves. Psychiatrists, psychologists, and psychiatric social workers diagnose the reasons for a child's behavior. Boarding homes have been maintained as a part of the treatment. Teachers are acquainted with the ways of understanding personality difficulties. A medical research laboratory is being used for the study of metabolism and growth, integrating a number of studies. A grant was made to Dr Joseph A. Johnston to carry on his study of childhood tuberculosis, and a number of summer camps are helped. Frank Couzens is chairman of the board of the Fund and Dr Hugo A. Freund is president.

Following this lead the W. K. Kellogg Foundation founded in 1930 with $40,000,000 has been doing similar work, concentrating on southwestern Michigan, with seven counties participating in the Michigan Community Health Project, which includes a broad educational program on public health. Postgraduate courses in medical schools or children's hospitals have been made available to local physicians, and in cooperation with the county medical associations speakers are obtained who keep the doctors abreast of research findings and newer procedures in medical practice. The same has been done for dentists, and the first postgraduate course in children's dentistry was arranged by Northwestern University at the request of the Kellogg Foundation. Rural teachers have been assisted in health education. Two camp schools are owned and operated by the Foundation near Battle Creek where, in September, adult groups meet for lectures and discussions. These camps are open all year and underprivileged children in groups of fifty remain for three month terms.

The Foundation discovered that in southwestern Michigan the rural population had schools, physicians, dentists, health, and educational services but lacked any coordinating agency to create a genuine public health program. Several thousand school children had any number of physical defects but neither they nor their parents or teachers had knowledge of or interest in the use of preventive medical services. Rather than have the parents and children rely on the school nurse or physicians, the Foundation has made it a policy to encourage children and parents to consult the family physician about health matters. It has tried to have physical examinations held in doctors' and dentists' offices instead of in the schools. This placates these professions and elicits their cooperation. Dr George B. Darling of the Foundation touched on this tender subject in an address to school superintendents and principals.

"Health officers have been accused of being the advanced guard of state medicine," he said. "In the Michigan Community Health Project all conflict of this nature is avoided by changing the function of the director. . . Faced with the same responsibilities as the average health officers, he must achieve the same results ; but he must arrange to do this through the cooperation of physicians and dentists in the county. So it is that all school examinations, immunizations and so on are made by the family physician, and emergency remedial work is handled in the same way. The health officer has funds available to him through the Foundation for payment of these services. . . The problem is not one of providing services to an impoverished area. The challenge is to see whether group leadership can be produced under democratic methods that will be able to coordinate the program, find new possibilities for service in it and advance the cause of child health and welfare over many fronts. The Foundation has made a start along this line possible and to a certain extent has initiated some of its phases, but this is as far as the Foundation can go." About forty to fifty thousand dollars annually is spent in each of the seven counties by the health departments and the Community Health Project.

Thus the progress toward more adequate public health has been achieved, as the Foundation speakers are fond of saying, "over many fronts." Sometimes this progress is peaceful ; frequently cooperation is obtained by foundations with the medical associations, sometimes it breaks into a sharp skirmish or an open battle. The foundations, always sensitive to criticism of any sort, want no unpleasantness. Inevitably, however, if they set out to advance the cause of public health materially, or even if they merely try to discover the facts about the problem, they find themselves involved in the conflict now raging within the American Medical Association. The American Foundation of Philadelphia became embroiled in this warfare when it discontinued the American Peace Award, which had been established in 1921 "to further peace through justice" and to "foster international relations" and began active research work in the "Science of Government." This Foundation, established in 1925 by the late Edward W. Bok with $2,000,000, has developed the Mountain Lake Sanctuary in Florida ; established the Citizen's Award of Philadelphia ; the Philadelphia Award ; the Harvard Advertising Award ; and maintained the Philadelphia Commission for eight years. On April 1, 1937, as a result of research sponsored by a special committee, a report was published entitled : *American Medicine, Expert Testimony Out of Court.*

This committee consisted of : Curtis Bok, chairman, president of the Foundation, Esther Everett Lape, member-in-charge, Hugh L. Cooper, Thomas W. Lamont, Robert A.

Millikan, James D. Mooney, Roscoe Pound, Mrs Ogden Reid, William Scarlett, Truman G. Schnabel, M.D., Mrs F. A. Vanderlip, John G. Winant, and Elizabeth F. Read, director of research. It proposed "a study of the legitimate functions of Government as related to such subjects as Public Defence, Finance, Taxation, Health, etc.," Curtis Bok declared. The committee wondered, "If it were discoverable in measurable terms how far and in what manner a government's capacity for service to its citizens is conditioned by its form." In the introduction to the report Dr. Schnabel writes : "The study of the relation of government to health was begun with no assumption either that government should or that it should not, play a larger part than it now plays in the advancement of public health activities or, so far as the individual citizen is concerned, in the organization of medical care. . . The study was singled out because the situation seemed to us to be singularly in need of clarification."

Those in charge of the inquiry did not attempt to clarify the situation by means of a questionnaire. They believed that what was needed was to find out what the situation really was and they did not think that the story could be told entirely in figures. So they sent a letter of inquiry to selected groups of physicians, which led to a considerable correspondence. The two volumes of the report contain the answers from 2100 physicians, presented as impartially as possible. The inquiry asked, in effect : "Has your experience led you to believe that a radical reorganization of medical care in this country is indicated ? If so in what direction ? If you do not believe that radical reorganization is indicated, what, if any changes or revisions would you like to see made ? What evolutionary possibilities would you stress ?" One of the first difficulties encountered was the problem of defining the word "adequate." As one physician remarked, "the general population is without *adequate* anything, and this is lost sight of by those whose particular interest is in adequate medical care." However, he added :

"It certainly should not be beyond the power of civilization to make adequate medical care 'available' to all citizens."

One Fellow of the American College of Surgeons wrote : "It is a dangerous and horrifying thing for one class of human beings to depend for their livelihood upon the sickness of other human beings. The system of paying the doctor to get you well is just about the most illogical thing human beings practice." In answer to the question "Is medical care now generally available ?" the consensus of opinion was, "No." Medical care, the doctors insisted, was not a commodity. The organization of public health work was found to be "perhaps the most controversial aspect of the whole matter of medical care." There was a widespread feeling that a different system is needed for the distribution of medical care to make it more readily available to indigent and low income groups. Many physicians thought that the theory of insurance is applicable to health, but some did not. Most of them recognized that the evolutionary progress may be expected to continue. "This alone," commented the report, "points to the logic of a federal research, standardizing and stimulating authority in the shape of a Federal Department of Health."

This report split the medical profession wide open. The conflict simmering below the surface broke into heated argument at the American Medical Association convention at Atlantic City in June 1937, where the Fishbein group maintained their control. As a result, the Cabot-Osgood-Peters Committee was formed, presenting their "Principals and Proposals" which have since been the subject of wide discussion within the medical profession and in the newspapers. Dr Fishbein has fought the $750,000 appropriation by Congress for cancer research on the grounds that "granting of immense public funds quite definitely discourages private philanthropy." * This, in spite of the fact that there is not at present one fund spending as much as a million dollars a year exclusively on cancer research.

* The *New York Times*, November 7, 1937.

The *New York Times* declared that this flat disapproval "has shocked medical men as a class. . . No doubt they resent the callous opposition of *The Journal* to government support of medical research in cancer or any other disease." *

Dr Milton C. Winternitz, in a letter to the *Times* * compared the American Foundation report with Dr Abraham Flexner's survey of medical education. "The inquiry furnished a fair sample," he said, "of medical opinion and revealed that complacence is not the state of mind of the majority of the group that responded. . . The public is growing increasingly conscious of the questions involved. Vituperative argument will amuse it temporarily, but in the end constructive modification of the existing order must be forthcoming."

Slight modification has begun. Under the Social Security Act $8,000,000 may be and has been appropriated by Congress annually in aid to the states through the U.S. Public Health Service. $2,000,000 of this is for research and personnel. $3,800,000 has been granted by Congress to the Federal Children's Bureau. Dr Parran warns, however: "Do not hope for too much from the health measures which can be carried out under the present Social Security Act. They are only the first feeble steps of a people who at last are beginning to realize what they need. In public health work we stand today just about where we were in public education in the middle of the last century."

The role of the American philanthropic foundations in advancing public health has been great, but it can be overestimated. There are numerous other organizations and individuals not connected with the foundations who have done much to arouse the nation to its public health needs. The public is coming to realize that what has been done so far is only a beginning. We cannot leave the job to the philanthropic foundations, for private philanthropy has very severe limits: its resources, great as they are, cannot cope with the problem. Pri-

* The *New York Times*, November 7, 1937.

vate philanthropy is usually cautious, it is often diffuse, it frequently spreads its energies and contributions over a very wide field, it avoids "controversial" issues that are sometimes the heart of the problem. Important and difficult problems are left to others. What we really need is a Federal Department of Health with a budget comparable to that of the navy. What we must aim at is an era when every individual gets adequate health and medical care as a matter of right, whether he can afford it or not.

CHAPTER XII

WHERE THE MONEY COMES FROM

THE FINANCIAL POLICIES OF THE BIG FOUNDATIONS

Alexander D. Noyes, financial editor of the *New York Times*, closed his Monday column, November 1, 1937, with these words : "After all, a glance at the investment schedules of the Rockefeller and Carnegie Foundations will throw some light on the judgment of experienced investors." In answer to an inquiry on how such a glance might be obtained, the *Times* replied, a few days later, that the schedules could be found in the Annual Reports, which are given to the public at the offices of the foundations in New York.

Mr Noyes' remark implies that investors might learn something from a study of these reports. Many small investors imagine that if they could get an insight into what the Rockefellers are doing, or have done, in the management of large funds, they might get some valuable hints on how to manage their own modest fortunes. The popular notion is that big philanthropic funds are invested once and for all, and that the money spent by the big foundations comes from fixed income securities which are rarely, if ever, changed. The ordinary observer does not realize that in order to keep large funds intact it is necessary to shift investments constantly. It may be something of a surprise to learn, therefore, that to safeguard their funds the big foundations operate very much like investment trusts. By glancing at the Treasurer's report of the Carnegie Corporation dated October 28, 1937, for example, the small investor will discover on page 81 that a net profit was made for the year ended September 30, 1937, of $6,302,773 on securities redeemed or sold, and a careful study of the accompanying pages will disclose exactly how it was done.

A glance at the Rockefeller Foundation reports, however, is not so enlightening. If the Foundation made a profit for the year it is impossible to find out how much or by what means it was achieved. Many pages are devoted to appropriation figures which present many difficulties to the patient investigator. If they seem confusing, however, they become child's play in comparison with those on the investment side of the picture. A schedule of securities held is given in the latest available report as of December 30, 1936. Here are listed alphabetically the bonds and stocks owned by the Foundation. For instance, "Burlington, Cedar Rapids and Northern Ry. Consolidated First Mortgage Gold," is listed in the first column ; the "interest rate per cent," 5%, in the second column ; the date of maturity, April 1934, in the third column ; the "amount" $64,000.00 in the fourth column ; "Foundation's ledger value per cent," 101.5625, in the fifth column ; and in the last column, "Foundation's total ledger value," $65,000.

The only thing likely to strike the ordinary investor as strange about that is the long past date of maturity, April 1934. He would be likely to pass over without reflection the phrases about "ledger value," for he might very well assume that the Rockefellers are both smart and conservative and would therefore place a conservative valuation upon securities held by the Foundation. Supposing, however, he bought a copy of the *Annalist*, a "journal of finance, commerce and economics" published by the *New York Times*, for January 22, 1937, which gives a review of bond and stock prices for the year 1936. On page 168 he will find this same bond listed. Its last price in 1936 was 27 and during the year it had sunk as low as 19. A few asterisks and other marks indicate that this security is in default of interest, that its negotiability has been impaired by maturity, that the company is in receivership or being reorganized.

But, the small investor may say, the Rockefeller Foundation carries this security among its assets as bearing 5% interest, as being valued, in "ledger value" at 101.5625, having a total "ledger value" of $65,000. What then, does ledger value mean ? Does it mean the price paid for the security ? The Foundation does not tell you. Glancing at the list of stocks you read "Chehalis and Pacific Land Co. Capital, 220 shares, Foundation's Total Ledger Value, $1.00." If you look up the report for 1922 you will find this security carried at 24 * in the column entitled "Foundation's Ledger Value per share" and worth $5,324.75 in the "Foundation's Total Ledger Value." Evidently this particular security has been "written down" to approximately its market value. It is also evident that other securities have also been written down. But it is just as clear that the Burlington, Cedar Rapids, and Northern bonds have not been written down.

The Carnegie Corporation follows the accepted accounting practice of listing its securities at their market value, at their par value, and at their cost to the Corporation. The Rockefeller Foundation does not give the market value of its securities. In the early reports of the Foundation a footnote declared : "All securities valued at the price at which they were purchased or at the value assigned to them when they were donated." This footnote has been omitted since 1917. "The ledger value" is apparently the price paid for some of the securities, but not for all of them, because some corrections have been made. In an effort to decide what the term means the small investor might conclude that "ledger value" means the opinion those in charge of the investment portfolio have of the value of the securities. But he could not accept that definition without losing respect for their opinion.

The investigator is even further confused when he compares the ledger values of the same securities as listed on the General Education Board schedule. Evidently the finance committee of the G.E.B. is not of the same opinion as those who judge the Rockefeller Foundation's securities. And neither opinion is

* In 1915 it was carried at 49.4545.

concurred in by those who buy and sell these securities on the market. Let us glance at a list of bonds held by the Rockefeller Foundation and compare these values:

Name of Security	*Interest*	*Date of Maturity*	*Amount held*	*Foundation's Ledger Value*	
Chicago & Alton RR Refunding Mortgage	3%	Oct. 1949	$551,000	65	$358,150
(Last sale in 1936 was 55, low 41, high 61. Carried by G.E.B. at 59.)					
Chicago, Milwaukee St Paul & Pacific 50 year Mortgage Series "A"	5%	Feb. 1975	$446,300	95	$423,985
(These are in default. Last sale, 1936, 33½, low 17⅛, high 33½. Also carried by G.E.B. at 95.)					
Chicago, Milwaukee St Paul & Pacific Convertible Adjustment Mortgage Series "A"	5%	Jan. 2000	$1,785,200	62.5	$1,115,750
(In default. Last sale 10⅝, low 6, high 10⅝. G.E.B.'s value also 62.5.)					
Chicago & Northwestern General Mortgage	5%	Nov. 1987	$201,000	98.097	$197,175
(In default, last sale 52, law 38½, high 57¾. Carried by G.E.B. at 105.625.)					
Chicago Rys 1st Mortgage Gold (25% paid Certificates of deposit)	5%	Feb. 1927	$375,000	96	$360,000
(In default. Last sale 82, low 70, high 82½. Not on G.E.B. list.)					
Chicago, Rock Island & Pacific Ry. 1st Refunding Mortgage Gold	4%	Apr. 1934	$3,345,000	81.45	$2,724,776.93
(In default. Last sale 20⅝, low 15, high 23. Carried by G.E.B. at 60.46678.)					
Denver & Rio Grande RR 1st Consolidated Mortgage Gold	4%	Jan. 1936	$810,000	96.42	$781,033.15
(In default. Last sale 34½, low 29⅛, high 38. Carried by G.E.B. at 92.68218.)					
Denver & Rio Grande Western RR General Mortgage	5%	Aug. 1955	$574,000	59	$338,660
(In default. Last sale 19⅜, low 13⅛, high 20¼. Also carried by G.E.B. at 59.)					

Name of Security	Inter-est	Date of Maturity	Amount held	Foundation's Ledger Value
Kansas City, Fort Scott & Memphis Ry Refunding Mortgage Gold	4%	Oct. 1936	$274,000	95.75	$262,370.64

(In default. Last sale 62½, low 40¼, high 63. Carried by G.E.B. at 96.5393.)

| New Orleans, Texas & Mexico Ry Non-cumulative income Gold series "A" Certificates of Deposit | 5% | Oct. 1935 | $75,000 | 99.05 | $74,287.52 |

(In default. Last sale 45¼, low 24⅞, high 49⅜. Not on G.E.B. list.)

| Philadelphia & Reading Coal & Iron Co. Refunding Mortgage Sinking Fund | 5% | Jan. 1973 | $167,000 | 94.25 | $157,401.42 |

(Last sale 47⅜, low 37, high 55. Not on G.E.B. list.)

| St Louis, Southwestern Ry General & Refunding Mortgage Gold series "A" | 5% | July 1990 | $1,918,500 | 66.79 | $1,281,418.80 |

(In default. Last sale 53, low 28⅛, high 56¼. Carried by G.E.B. at 86.80567.)

| St Louis, San Francisco Ry. Prior Lien Gold series "A" | 4% | July 1950 | $1,500,000 | 72.75 | $1,091,250 |

(In default. Last sale 35, low 15¾, high 35⅝. Not listed by G.E.B.)

| Western Pacific RR 1st Mortgage Gold Series "A" (Assenting) | 5% | Mar. 1946 | $200,800 | 83 | $166,664 |

(In default. Last sale 37¼, low 32⅛, high 42¾. Not listed by G.E.B.)

The above is only a selected list.* It indicates some of the losses the Rockefeller Foundation has apparently suffered on its bond investments. There are also a number of other Chicago, Milwaukee, and St. Paul, Chicago, Rock Island, and Pacific, and other bonds in default which are not listed in the *Annalist* as dealt in during the year 1936. Of course, a number of the bonds held have appreciated in value, but it does not seem that their appreciation could balance these losses. The total "ledger value" of the investment of the Rockefeller Foundation

* All these are carried in the 1937 report at the same ledger values.

is given at \$172,546,008.71.   What the market value may be it
is impossible to discover because it is impossible to find out
what some of the securities are actually worth, since they have
not been traded in, i.e. are "inactive." By comparing the
market values with the ledger values of the fourteen bonds
listed above it is easy to see that the total "ledger value" given
by the Foundation bears little correspondence to market values.
The General Education Board uses the same method of listing.
Its fiscal year ends on June 30th, but that does not account for
the divergence in ledger values, particularly since they bear so
little relation to market values.   It gives its total "ledger value"
of securities as \$49,059,399.87.   What the market value may be
can only be guessed.

What would you think of an industrial corporation which
listed its assets in such a way ?   Would you want to invest in it ?
Yet it is in these foundations that the Rockefellers want you to
invest your confidence and good-will.   To paraphrase Mr
Noyes, this throws some light upon the judgment of experienced investors.   It is not clear in the reports whether the
specific bond issues noted above were purchased by the Foundation or whether they were a part of one of the large donations
made by the senior Rockefeller.   Whatever the Rockefellers
do, they do deliberately ; whatever they omit doing, you may be
sure the omission is intentional.   Why then do they persist in
the "ledger value" practice ?   If the Carnegie Corporation can
be candid about its profits and losses, why cannot the Rockefeller Foundation ?

Let us glance at its financial history.   The Rockefeller Foundation was chartered May 14, 1913 with the following trustees :
John D. Sr, John D. Jr, Frederick T. Gates, Henry Pratt Judson, Simon Flexner, Starr J. Murphy, Jerome D. Greene, Wickliffe Rose, and Charles O. Heydt.*   All were Rockefeller employees except Dr Judson who was president of the University
of Chicago.   On May 29, 1913 John D. Sr transferred to the

* John D. Jr's private secretary.

Foundation securities whose value was $3,200,000 ; on June 4, 1913 securities whose market value was $21,052,028 ; and on June 27, 1913 securities whose market value was $10,178,402. To this Mrs Rockefeller Sr added securities whose par value was $48,000 to start the special Spelman Fund.

On March 6, 1914 Mr Rockefeller Sr transferred to the Foundation securities whose market value * was $65,569,569, making a neat total of exactly $100,000,000. During 1914 the Foundation "sold or redeemed" $215,505 worth of securities at a profit of $170,901 ; it bought $4,051,169 worth, and it had in its portfolio at the end of the year $35,803,606 in bonds, $49,-503,458 in oil stocks, and $17,708,256 in miscellaneous stocks. These figures represent the prices at which the securities were purchased or "the value assigned to them when they were donated."

Already, in 1914, when the Foundation was a little more than a year old, there were losses on the sale of securities :

		Sold at	Carried at
50 shares of American Ship-building Pref.	Loss: $257.69	(79)	(85)
145 shares Borne, Scrysmer Co.	" 275.92	(293)	(295)
787 shares Crescent Pipe Line	" 1,925.57	(57)	(60)
65 shares Eureka Pipe Line	" 1,538.10	(337)	(361)
30 shares New York Transit Co.	" 669.97	(277)	(?)
695 shares South West Penn Pipe Lines	" 7,671.00	(148)	(160)
13,700 shares Wabash Railway Common	" 13,968.75	(98)	(not given)
15,600 shares Wabash Railway Pref.	" 18,296.50	(48)	(not given)
Loss on sales in 1914:	$44,603.50		

This loss was made up by the profit on other securities sold. During 1915 trouble came. H. B. Claflin and Co. failed, so that four hundred and fifty-one shares valued at seventy-nine and

* With accrued interest.

carried at $35,719, a part of John D. Sr's original gift to the Foundation, became worthless.   The Chicago, Milwaukee and St Paul railroad exchanged $500,000 par value debenture 4s carried at 91.0625 for Refunding 4½s at 89.   The report stated that the higher interest rate offset the difference in market price.   On February 1st the International Mercantile Marine failed to meet the interest on $1,305,000 par value 5% bonds of the International Navigation Co. carried at 75, and it also defaulted on $3,692,000 par value of its own 4¼% bonds carried at 55.*   This income of $231,390 was therefore cut off.   A "protective committee" was formed.   On March 1st the Western Pacific Railroad "failed to meet interest due" on its 1st Mortgage 5% bonds — $4,039,000 par, $2,786,910, market — which the Foundation carried at 69.   This curtailed the income by $201,950 annually.   The Sunday Creek Co. defaulted on July 1st on its 5% bonds, $81,000 par value, carried at 78. A "protective committee" was formed.   On September 1st, 1915, the Missouri Pacific defaulted on its 40-year Collateral, $2,198,000 par value carried at 60, curtailing the income by $87,920.

There were also other losses that year.   The Pope Manufacturing Co. capital stock was written off : $4,200 loss.   A number of stocks were sold at a loss :

		Loss:
16,603 shares of International Mercantile Common		
mon		$24,495.84
5,832 shares of International Mercantile Pref.	"	29,282.06
2,000 shares of Missouri Pacific Common	"	29,605
6,000 shares of St Louis & San Fran. RR 2nd		
Pref.	"	7,265
388 shares of Swan and Finch (oil stock)	"	28,125
Total loss on stock sales 1915:		$118,923.57

However, enough other securities were traded in to show a net gain of $1,004,497.   At the end of the year the bond assets were listed at $40,893,315, the oil stocks at $49,425,858, and the

*December 1914 high was 32.

miscellaneous stocks at $14,610,000, a total of $104,929,729.
The Foundation purchased $6,337,998 of securities in the open
market. The ledger value fiction had already started, however, so there was even then a discrepancy between the market
value of the assets and the value at which the Foundation carried
them.

In 1916 there were further losses, although total security
transactions showed a net profit of $432,970. In the sales,
$350 were lost on Pittsburgh, Cincinnati, Chicago and St Louis
railway stock ; $18,875 on St Louis and San Francisco Railway
refunding bonds ; $176,400 on St Louis and San Francisco,
(New Orleans, Texas, and Mexico Division) 1st Mortgage
bonds ; $1,446,466 on Western Pacific stock ; and $32,409 on
Swan and Finch, a total loss of $1,674,900 happily covered by
other transactions. The assets based on ledger values were :
$42,623,843 in bonds, $47,679,704 in oil stocks, $15,652,438 in
miscellaneous stocks, a total of $105,955,986. Discrepancies
between the market value and the value at which the securities
were carried was even more noticeable : Chicago and Eastern
Illinois 5s, 1955, for example, carried at 63 never got higher than
36 in the market, and Missouri, Kansas and Texas Sinking Fund
4½ carried at 84 closed at 49 that year.

In 1917 the Foundation was unable to cover its losses in secu-
rity transactions. Previously enough securities had been sold at
a profit to more than balance the losses, but that year it admitted
a loss on securities "exchanged, sold or redeemed" of $554,501.
The losses were : Atlantic Coast Line Railway, Consolidated
Mortgage bonds $64,019 ; Chicago, Burlington, and Quincy,
General Mortgage bonds, $143,410 ; Denver, Rio Grande 1st
Consolidated Mortgage bonds $210 ; Kansas City Southern 1st
Mortgage bonds $29,873 ; Lake Shore and Michigan Southern
Railway Debentures $101,870 ; Missouri Pacific Railway Col-
lateral Trust 4%, $98,910 ; Northern Pacific General Lien,
$25,000 ; Union Pacific R.R. Refunding Mortgage bonds
$158,413 ; Galena Signal Oil Co. $13,856 ; H. H. Kohlsaat Co.,

(in bankruptcy) $95,000 ; Swan and Finch stock $5520 ; Long Island Refunding Mortgage bonds $15 ; total loss : $735,696.85 on transactions of $6,084,734.   The total bonds carried in portfolio were at $36,165,382, stocks $98,118,408 or $126,283,-791 in all.   Beginning in 1917 the oil stocks and the miscellaneous stocks were no longer separated, but were listed together as "stocks."   Note, however, a new asset, which first appeared in 1916 when it was called "cash loaned on call," $530,000 and in 1917 "moneys loaned," $9,675,000.   The Foundation was in the call money market.   This additional asset brought the "grand total" up to $134,692,441.

The only loss reported in 1918 was $89.88 on 1st Liberty Loan.   A gain of $42,123 was made on transactions of $11,456,-259.   The bonds and stocks were listed at what was called "cash price" : $35,883,791 for the bonds and $90,110,384 for the stocks.   This was simply another name for "ledger value" ; it was not market value.   The footnote about the valuation was omitted, never to reappear.   Notice the rise in income during the war years : in 1915 it was $4,183,084, in 1916, $6,-226,709, in 1917, $7,153,851, in 1918 $7,609,710.   The increase between 1915 and 1916 was explained in 1916 as "due to a change in the method of reporting and additions of securities formerly in default."

On Christmas Day 1919 Mr John D. Rockefeller Sr announced a gift of $50,000,000 to the Foundation.   This was all in oil stocks.   "The executive committee noted that this gift should be merged, as to principal, investments and income at a valuation of $50,438,768," the market value at the time they were transferred.   This brought the "cash price" value of the bonds to $36,279,437 and the stocks to $139,335,097.   The additional asset, "money loaned," brought the "Grand Total" up to $183,776,432.   No losses were reported on any of the security transactions of the year and a profit of $1,454,634 was made on $5,235,406 "sold or redeemed." $2,962,363 worth of securities were purchased, chiefly 4¼% 2nd Liberty Loan.

The income was piling up faster than it was disbursed. The balance of income from the previous year was $5,212,643, leaving $12,303,626 on hand for disbursement. But only $7,760,-355 was disbursed.

The income continued to rise in 1920, amounting to $8,727,-730 and making $13,282,172 available for disbursement, of which only a little more than $7,000,000 was disbursed. The Foundation reported $174,432,713 invested and $1,450,000 loaned. A strange item, $1,800,000 borrowed, appears. The explanation given is that "moneys loaned were to be disbursed shortly after the close of the year, and it was deemed better to keep them in liquid form until needed rather than repay the loans and negotiate others later." The "Grand Total" was given at $188,222,068. A loss of $50,000 was suffered on the sale of Consolidated Gas Co. Convertible Debentures, but on the total proceeds of $3,571,578 from securities sold, a profit of $398,617 was shown. The amount "purchased or received through exchange" was $6,838,230. The total bonds listed : $34,161,148, and stocks : $145,118,658, a noteworthy increase in the common stock portfolio.

The following year, 1921, the income was still more than $8,000,000, making nearly $15,000,000 available for disbursements while actually $7,630,358 was disbursed. Gains were reported on securities "sold, redeemed or exchanged" of $63,-169 and a profit on the sale of land in China belonging to the Foundation was $16,075. Only $800,000 was in "moneys loaned" but the "Grand Total" came to the imposing sum of $206,403,026. This was evidently a little more than the Rockefellers could look upon without uneasiness. Perhaps somebody in the Foundation questioned its size : it looked too big. Securities were then carried at "book value," which had as little relation to market value as "cash price" or "ledger value." The fiction was being stretched a little too far ; it represented a pretense which even the Rockefeller philanthropic agents could not be complacent about.

It is clear that the trustees were not fooling themselves ; they must have realized what a pretense this "Grand Total" was. Perhaps they doubted the wisdom of leading people to suppose that the Foundation was much wealthier than it actually was. At any rate, in 1922 it reported : "The Foundation has heretofor carried its investments at their purchased price or at an appraised value based upon their market value when the gifts were received. As securities have been redeemed or sold from time to time any difference between the price received and the ledger value has been debited or credited, as the case happened to be, to a reserve fund." With a few exceptions no change was made in the valuation of other securities that have depreciated. "The Finance committee came to believe that recovery in the case of a number of issues was more or less uncertain and so recommended to the Trustees the adoption of the long established commercial and fiduciary practice of readjustment, from time to time, the valuations of the depreciated securities. . . The Trustees directed that the net sum received from the sale and redemption together with the balance to the credit of the reserve fund be used to reduce the ledger valuations. . . These instructions have been carried out."

All along, it appears, the trustees knew that they should be listing the securities at market value. The report admits that such is the accepted practice. It confessed it should have done so. That was in 1922. But in 1936 the Foundation still carried securities at a fictitious "ledger value." The readjustments recommended by the Finance Committee, which consisted of John D. Rockefeller Jr, Raymond B. Fosdick and Frederick Strauss, were made in 1922. But with a few exceptions they have not been made since. The reserve fund of $3,190,533 was wiped out. The Grand Total shrank from $206,403,026 to $194,204,924, the General Fund schedule of securities dropped from $177,694,930 to $161,573,215 between December 31, 1921 and December 31, 1922. Approximately sixteen million dollars disappeared. Where did it go ? Well, six million dollars' worth of securities, presumably at market value, were given to Johns Hopkins out of the principal. What these securities were and at what price they were transferred we are not told. They simply disappeared from the list. This leaves ten million dollars to be accounted for. It was not lost on market speculations and it cannot be accounted for in disbursements, since there was $16,202,270 of undisbursed income and refunds on hand and only $9,990,408 disbursed. The ten million dollars was not thrown out the window or down the sewer ; nobody put it in his pocket and made off with it. It was not lost overnight. The truth is that it was not there, and it had not been there for some time. It had been lost over the years since 1914. The Foundation merely got around to admitting it.

This sum represented inflated, fictional valuations. What happened in 1922 was that some of the "water" was wrung out of this great philanthropic trust. It is true that there was a gain in the capital assets during those eight years since 1914. This gain did not occur, however, as might be expected, by appreciation in market value. The market value fluctuated, while the "ledger value" remained in most cases stationary. The gain came from additional gifts, and by piling up surplus undistributed income, to which was added a reserve fund of profits on the sale of securities. It is illuminating, therefore, to discover that when the correction was made, it was a correction *downward*, at a time when security values were, in general, on the upgrade.

Some light is thus thrown on the character and quality of the securities the senior Rockefeller gave to his greatest philanthropic enterprise. The amazing accumulated depreciation in eight years, which, added to the loss on securities sold, is evidence not of mismanagement by experienced investors, but is rather a reflection on the type of bonds transferred by John D. Sr. He did not give the Foundation worthless securities ; many were extremely valuable. But many others became worthless or depreciated radically in a surprisingly short time. It is unjustifiable to say that Mr Rockefeller knew that this would happen. He may well have expected the reverse. Even a Rockefeller may sometimes buy bonds that default. Few men, however, can pass them off on a philanthropy amid the cheers of a populace that has been stimulated by shrewd publicity. It is possible that Mr Rockefeller had an idea that many of these bonds were not quite as valuable as others he presumably held or transferred directly to his son. That is certainly not beyond the bounds of reason, nor considering the record, beyond the bounds of plausibility. Remember, this was before the time when capital losses could be used to offset capital gains on income tax reports. Indeed, it was before there was such a thing as a Federal Income Tax.

After 1922 the transactions of the Foundation became veiled in secrecy. We are not told what was sold, bought, or transferred to other Rockefeller philanthropies. When a security disappears from the list we have no idea what has happened to it. It is merely missing. Thus we can only guess at gains or losses. If a security is listed which has not been listed before we may assume that it was purchased at the "ledger value per cent." The practice has continued to this day. We know that the present ledger values do not correspond to market values, and since it is impossible to discover the market values of all the securities held, many of them seldom traded, or the value of which is open to debate, we cannot know the actual market value, whether it is more or less than the present Rockefeller estimates.

Some of the Foundation's financial operations, however, are fairly clear. Most noticeable is the "secured demand loan" item. In 1922 $3,631,409 was carried in the "investment asset" column in demand loans and $1,368,590 in the "income asset" in demand loans. The loans were thus split into two items, evidently because the "income asset" figure was the amount of the income invested in such loans, and the "investment asset" figure was the amount of the principal put into demand loans instead of stocks or bonds. From 1923 to 1928 they were :

	Investment assets	Income assets
1923	$392,426.50	$2,207,573.73
1924	$2,781,281.49	$1,268,718.51
1925	$12,490,000.00	$1,100,000.00
1926	$10,200,000.00	$1,050,000.00
1927	$19,186,866.67	$3,363,433.33
1928	$22,689,463.09	$4,298,631.10

These were the years when the rate for call money on Wall Street was rising. The Foundation cannot pretend that these loans were made for philanthropic purposes. They were made as investments, to make money. Instead of speculating in common stocks like the small investor, the Foundation sold its common stocks and lent the money out in secured demand loans to those who were speculating. Thus it did its part in stimulating the boom. If brokers and investors were foolish enough to speculate, and to pay high interest rates for cash with which to speculate, why should not the Foundation lend its funds for such a purpose ? Is this consistent with the ideals of the stewardship of great wealth ? Should a philanthropic foundation go into this kind of money-lending ? In 1929 these call loans reached their peak : $37,650,000. Add to this the $16,575,-169 * which General Education Board loaned on call and you will see that the Rockefeller philanthropies in the year of the great boom and crash had more than $53,000,000 in the call money market.

A small investor, studying the Rockefeller Foundation's investment schedule for the period from 1922 to 1929, would learn little that would be useful to him. The portfolio of common stocks shrank from $121,943,271 in 1922 to $112,364,997 in 1929. Some of this was given away, it may be assumed,

* And $1,500,000 Spelman Fund invested in "secured demand loans."

when securities amounting to $8,962,154 were disbursed in 1925 for land and building in China and when $12,000,000 was transferred in 1928 out of principal to the China Medical Board ; but it is also probable that some common stocks were sold and the proceeds loaned "on demand." In the gifts to China there may have been some bonds also, but the bond total rose between 1922 and 1929 from $39,629,937 to $64,442,906. But this does not necessarily mean that the Foundation was buying bonds in those years, because in 1929 the Laura Spelman Memorial was merged with the Rockefeller Foundation, adding $53,006,078 in "ledger value" securities and $5,750,000 in securities earmarked for disbursement. In the middle nineteen-twenties, furthermore, the Foundation began to dig into the principal, and in nearly every later year a sum was set aside out of the general funds and placed in the funds "available for disbursement." In this bewildering shifting of funds it is impossible to draw any conclusions about the investment policy. While nearly everybody was speculating in common stocks the Foundation appeared not to, but in fact, did so at second-hand, by lending money to the gamblers, thus indirectly using philanthropic funds for speculative purposes.

We read in the 1928 Report with slight surprise that the Rockefeller Foundation has gone out of existence, but in the next sentence we are relieved to discover that it was succeeded by another corporation of the same name, which was consolidated with the Laura Spelman Memorial. This led to a number of bookkeeping transfers, but when all was said and done, the "ledger value" of the securities was placed at $176,807,903. The secured demand loans dropped thereafter so that in 1930 they were reported to be $13,100,000. It is apparent that when the loans were repaid $5,000,000 was put into Chase National Bank "certificates of deposit," a kind of savings account for large funds, and nearly $20,000,000 was invested in bonds. The secured demand loan item dropped in 1931 to $8,625,000 and in 1932 it disappeared altogether. However, the "certifi-

cates of deposit" rose to $14,000,000, indicating that the invest-
ment officers kept the proceeds from the loans in cash as the
depression deepened. The total amount of securities decreased
in these years because the Foundation exceeded its income and
spent part of its principal. However, in 1933, the bonds increased by $4,000,000 while the stock portfolio remained un-
changed. After that the principal shrank again as disbursements exceeded income.

There is recorded in the Foundation reports for 1926–27 a
highly curious transaction which may, or may not, be significant from a legal standpoint. The sum of $10,000 in the Laura
Spelman Rockefeller fund was returned in 1926 by the trustees
of the Foundation to the executors of her estate. This was
part of a sum given by her to the Foundation in 1913. In 1927
the Foundation reported that the executors refused to accept its
return and sent it back to the Foundation with interest. Possibly this was merely a bookkeeping transaction often necessary
in the settlement of large estates. If so, why was the sum returned one year and sent back the next? The legal question
this raises is : have the trustees of a foundation the power to
transfer back to the donor, funds he or she has given outright?
If they have not that power, then why did they do it? If they
have the power to transfer back to an estate, why cannot they
also transfer everything back to the original donor? If they
can do that, then foundations may become the most astounding
tax-evading scheme ever invented. Perhaps the Rockefeller
lawyers saw some of the possibilities and therefore advised the
executors of Mrs Rockefeller's estate to establish a precedent.

Thus we come to the latest available report, 1936, and glance
at the assets. Here is Exhibit A, Balance sheet — December 31,
1936, Assets :

Investments
  Securities (ledger valuation)................ $172,546,008.71
Current Assets
  Cash on deposit $8,868,087.07

Foreign currencies purchased to meet specific appropriation payable in foreign exchange of at least the same dollar amount (Exhibit F)	2,083,635.16	
Advances and deferred charges under appropriations and sundry accounts receivable	1,601,629.22	12,553,351.45
Building and Equipment		
In New York	55,378.71	
In Paris	63,889.29	119,268.00
		$185,218,628.16

We have seen the first item, the "ledger valuation" is a partly fictional figure. To this imaginary estimate is added "current assets," cash in the bank and foreign currencies which may be said to be very real and tangible. The third item, "Advances and deferred charges, etc." is not explained. "Sundry accounts receivable" usually means money owed to the corporation, not money on hand. The building and equipment is certainly a tangible asset. This is added up to get the "grand total," although it is no longer called that. To a skeptical investor this looks as if apples were added to pears to get — oranges.

It is the popular notion that the Rockefeller philanthropies own oil stocks that are extremely valuable. That is true, but they also own oil stocks which have no ascertainable value, not having been traded in on any exchange, and oil stocks whose market value is less than the "ledger value." The General Education Board, for example, carries Ohio Oil common, 326,-920 shares at 28.919119 per share, but the high for 1936 was 18, and for 1935 it was 14¼. The Board also owns 315,414 shares of the South Penn Oil Company whose capital stock is not listed on either the "big board" or the Curb. The Rockefeller Foundation carries its Ohio Oil common at 35.375 per share, and it also owns a number of oil stocks which are not listed. The Buckeye Pipe Line, of which the Foundation owns 49,693 shares, is carried at 76 while its high in 1936 was 50. The

Foundation lists its total stocks in 1936 at $108,855,150 and its bonds at $63,690,857. The G.E.B. lists its stocks at $31,175,148 and its bonds at $17,884,251.

The Rockefeller philanthropies have probably engaged in fairly large security transactions, but it is impossible, since 1922, to find out what they were. No Interstate Commerce Commission nor insurance or banking laws interfere, control, or regulate the investments of these foundations. Although operating on the exchange they do not have to report to the Securities and Exchange Commission. In a sense they are beyond the law. The Rockefeller philanthropies tell us only what they choose, somewhat capriciously, to tell.

On July 29, 1938 in a publicity release to the press coincident with the publication of the 1937 Report, the Rockefeller Foundation revealed some, but not all, of its security transactions in 1937. It announced that it had purchased $5,-000,000 in U. S. Treasury notes, series "A," dated June 15, 1937, $726,000 par value of Bethlehem Steel Consolidated sinking fund, series "E," bonds, and $150,400 of Phelps-Dodge Corporation convertible debentures. During the year the Foundation sold $838,000 of Armour and Company real estate first mortgage bonds, $178,000 of Delaware and Hudson 15-year gold notes, $168,000 of New York Central miscellaneous equipment bonds and $500,000 of Pacific Telephone and Telegraph Company first and collateral mortgage bonds. It also sold 19,944 shares of Atchison, Topeka and Santa Fe common and 49,635 shares of New York Central capital stock. Whether these securities were sold at a profit or a loss was not revealed. Other than listing the securities acquired and not listing the securities sold, no reference is made to these or any other transactions in the 1937 Report. However, the statement shows an even better cash position than in 1936: $9,462,275 in cash on hand as of December 31, 1937 as compared with $8,868,087 as of December 31, 1936.

Proudly it pointed out that its holdings in Standard Oil of New Jersey capital stock, carried at $36,962,526, had a market value on July 28, 1938, of $61,260,004. No mention was made of the railway bonds whose value had depreciated, but they are carried at the same "ledger value" as in the 1936 Report.

After studying their reports it is a relief to look at the Carnegie Corporation's statements. No such whimsicalities are to be found there, for those in charge of the Carnegie Corporation make very complete reports of all transactions : what was bought, sold, redeemed, exchanged, with prices received and paid. One wonders why the Rockefeller philanthropies do not do likewise.

What is surprising about the Carnegie Corporation is the size of its annual transactions. For several years prior to 1928 the Corporation had been selling or redeeming the steel bonds which were the bulk of its assets. When the U. S. Steel Corporation redeemed the remainder, the Carnegie Corporation showed a profit on them of nearly $16,000,000. In the difficult years since then the investment officers have tried to find equally good investments, not always with success, as we have seen in Chapter IV. During the fiscal year 1934–35 they sold $44,950,015 worth of securities of the main endowment fund for a loss of $541,478 for the year. A loss was also incurred in sales from the "British Dominions and Colonies Fund," so that, in all, the loss for the year was $612,165 on security transactions of $47,998,027. During the fiscal year 1935–36 the investment officers sold $49,208,401 in securities at a profit of $528,-929 and purchased $52,024,680 in the open market. A cash balance in the banks as of October 1, 1935 of $5,173,123 made possible this excess of purchases over sales. Notice that the security turnover represented nearly one-third of the Corporation's assets. It also represented a rather nice commission for the brokers handling these transactions. They probably made almost as much in commissions as the Corporation did in profits.*

In 1936–37 from the main endowment fund $46,377,115 worth of securities were sold, redeemed, or exchanged, at a profit of $6,302,773. This compares favorably with the total profits from the previous years which stood on February 29, 1936, after losses had been deducted, at $7,900,000. Securities purchased, transferred or exchanged for the main endowment fund amounted to $48,218,706. This turnover must also have been pleasing to the brokers. The British Dominions and Colonies Fund broke even, selling $2,771,906 in securities at no profit or loss and purchasing $2,650,203. Since the purchases for the main endowment fund again exceeded the sales, another dent was made in the cash balance, reducing it to $342,159. Compare this cash position with that of the Rockefeller philanthropies : the G.E.B. with more than $11,000,000 in cash and the Foundation with more than $8,000,000. The Carnegie Corporation apparently prefers to keep its cash in government bonds. There is no unanimity about what constitutes good investments among the foundations, even among those in the Carnegie orbit. It even happens sometimes that one foundation is selling the same security another foundation is buying.

Let us see what the Carnegie Corporation sold and what it bought. Few losses were suffered on the sale of bonds. The largest bond loss was incurred in redeeming the Cumberland Telephone and Telegraph Company 1st and General 5s which were sold at their face value but for which the Corporation paid $7441 more than "par" on a $100,000 lot. Gains were made on the sale of Northern States Power Company 1st and re-funding 5s, 1941, and refunding 4½s, 1916 ; Atchison, Topeka and Sante Fe Gen 4s 1996 ; Bell Telephone Company of Pennsylvania 1st and refunding 5s, Series "C," 1960 ; Chicago, Burlington, and Quincy R.R. Gen 4s, 1958 ; New England

---

* The Corporation's financial agent and advisor is J. P. Morgan and Co.

Telephone and Telegraph 1st 4½ Series "B," 1961 ; and a number of others.   The largest profit, $378,036, was made on the Sante Fe bonds.

While the Rockefeller Foundation held and traded in common stocks from the time it was established, the Carnegie Corporation did not purchase common stocks in any considerable amount until 1933, at a time when the Rockefeller Foundation was buying bonds.   The Carnegie Corporation has been quite successful in its common stock dealings, however, and profits on sales of common stocks have cut down in bad years the losses suffered on bonds.   During 1936–37 profits were shown on nearly every sale from Air Reduction to Westinghouse Electric.   Notable profits were :

Stocks:	Shares	Cost	Sold for	Profit
Allis-Chalmers	3,000	$134,158.33	$234,725.24	$100,466.91
General Electric	3,400	97,649.00	198,220.00	100,571.00
International Harvester	1,400	65,477.45	146,508.55	81,031.10
Johns-Manville	2,000	108,721.96	297,251.46	88,529.50
Westinghouse Air Brake	8,100	231,160.00	351,761.85	120,591.85

The total profit on bonds amounted to $4,676,112, and the total profit on stocks amounted to $1,583,743.   The total amount of bonds redeemed, sold or exchanged was $39,274,749.   The only exchange made was in converting the Allis-Chalmers Debenture 4s, 1945 into common stock.   A profit was also made on the sale of seven preferred stocks, $433,068.18 worth sold at a profit of $42,918.   The total amount of stocks sold was $6,669,280. Rights were sold in Allis-Chalmers, Johns-Manville, Montgomery Ward, Sears, Roebuck, and Texas Corporation. Rights were exercised in American Brake Shoe, Inland Steel, Johns-Manville, Phelps Dodge, and Texas Corporation.

The bond purchases during 1936–37 were chiefly in public utilities and governments.   The public utilities were :

	par	*amount paid*
American Telephone & Telegraph Co.,		
3½ Deb. Oct 1, 1961	$925,000	$935,468.85
3½ Deb. Dec 1, 1966	855,000	872,100.00
Buffalo Niagra Electric Corp.		
Deb. 2s Ser. A June 1, 1938–40	204,000	205,195.20
Consolidated Gas Co. of N.Y.		
Deb. 4½s June 1, 1951	50,000	53,625.00
Detroit Edison Co.		
Gen. & Ref. 5s Ser. E. Oct 1, 1952	50,000	53,437.50
Iowa Light & Power Co.		
1st 4½s Ser A., March 1, 1958	15,000	15,806.25
Nebraska Power Co.		
1st 4½s June 1, 1981	100,000	107,301.25
Philadelphia Electric Co.		
1st & Ref. 3½s March 1, 1967	900,000	922,500.00
Union Electric Co. of Missouri		
Notes 3s July 1, 1942	500,000	502,500.00
Total amount of public utilities bought:		$3,667,934.05

More than forty million dollars' of government bonds were purchased. These are considered by the Corporation as a temporary investment made because of a lack of good investments available for large sums.

The following common stocks were purchased : (1,000 shares or more).

	Shares	*Amount paid:*
Air Reduction	1400	$102,997.50
Bethlehem Steel	2000	191,825.00
Caterpillar Tractor	1000	95,625.00
Dow Chemical	1000	149,975.00
Gulf Oil	3300	197,731.00
International Nickel	2800	202,565.00
Johns-Manville	1526	173,975.00
Kennecott Copper	3000	200,225.00
Monsanto Chemical	2000	192,685.00
Montgomery Ward	4800	299,627.50
National Lead	2500	80,562.50
N. J. Zinc	1100	101,557.50

Pullman, Inc.	5500	347,500.00
St. Joseph Lead	5200	301,260.00
Sears, Roebuck	2200	200,577.50
Standard Oil of Cal.	4300	202,182.50
Standard Oil of N. J.	2600	194,395.00
Texas Corp.	5866	281,530.00
Timken Roller Bearing	1700	96,297.50
U. S. Gypsum	2200	271,975.00
U. S. Steel	6000	681,825.00
F. W. Woolworth	3500	149,225.00

Although all these industries are fundamental to a modern economy, many of these might be classified as "war babies." The steels, oils, chemicals, lead, zinc, copper, and nickel all belong in that category. Although supplementing the annual endowment of the Carnegie Endowment for International Peace, the Carnegie Corporation is in a good position to profit if war should come. Common stocks purchased in 1936–37 amounted to $5,448,892.

These purchases are a fair example of the securities already owned by the Corporation. In addition to the utilities already mentioned the Corporation own bonds worth a half a million or more in each of the following : Central Hudson Gas & Electric, Cleveland Electric Illuminating Co., Commonwealth Edison, Duquesne Light Co., and New York Telephone Co. It also owns more than a million dollars worth of bonds in General Motors Acceptance Corporation, Socony-Vacuum, and in the Dominion of Canada.

The small investor may get some valuable tips from a study of these schedules. However, he should also be aware that even the more experienced investors differ sharply among themselves. Recently a number of financial experts have worried publicly about university endowments, fearing lest Roosevelt inflation would wipe out these and the big philanthropic funds because they are invested chiefly in "fixed income" securities. They might much better worry about the insurance companies and savings banks upon whom restrictions are placed in regard to investments. There is nothing to prevent the endowments or foundations from investing in anything they choose ; their restrictions are entirely of their own making. Unlike the savings banks and the insurance companies they can invest in common stocks as much as they like. The Rockefeller philanthropies have not invested in real estate mortgages at all while the Carnegie Corporation owns two : one on the Lotos Club, 110 West 57th Street, New York, for $275,000 and one on the North West Corner of Broadway and 42nd Street, underlying the *New York Times* building, for $50,000.

In addition to the "main endowment fund" from whose schedule all the foregoing figures have been taken, the Carnegie Corporation also administers the British Dominion and Colonies Fund, amounting to $12,920,303.39, for expenditure in those portions of the globe under the Union Jack. These parallel very closely those in the "main endowment fund," in many cases the same securities. The British fund owns no common stocks, however. Bonds of the Dominion of Canada, of the city of Ottawa, of the provinces of Ontario and Quebec, in the Argentine government and £48,300 or $255,-626.81 * worth of the United Kingdom of Great Britain and Northern Ireland War Loan 3½s of 1932 are held. As in the "main endowment fund" only the income can be spent ; the principal must remain intact in perpetuity for future generations, although it is conceivable that the principal might be lost by unwise investment or a complete collapse of the economic system.

The names and titles of the securities have been given in the foregoing pages in partial answer to the question at the head of this chapter : Where does the money come from ? It came originally from the donors, from the senior Rockefeller's oil profits and Mr Carnegie's steel. The cry of "tainted money" has been forgotten, although recently it has been raised in another form, by those who declare that these profits have come

* Cost.

from exploitation of the working class. In any case, the money has been made, and it has been set aside for philanthropic expenditure. Although dedicated, supposedly, for such uses, there is no governmental supervising authority to watch how these funds are spent or how they are invested. Foundations may be made the repository of dubious securities. They may give to the public financial reports which place purely arbitrary and fictitious values on the securities they hold. What is told here is only what they admit in their published reports ; what yet remains to be discovered only a Congressional investigation could unearth.

Some of these philanthropic funds may come from speculation. There is nothing to stop them from speculating as much as they like. It cannot be proved that the foundations play any part in "running the market up" or "running the market down" ; it is not probable that the investment officers use the funds to take part in any "pools," although it is possible. The foundations do not "control" the stock market because nobody, not even the Roosevelt administration, can "control" the market. But whether they wish to do so or not, they influence it in a greater or less degree. Those who have speculated only a little know how sensitive Wall Street is to rumors. The whisper that the Carnegie Corporation or the Rockefeller Foundation is buying or selling a certain security might very easily effect its market price. When the Carnegie Corporation sells nearly $50,000,000 worth of securities in a year and buys more than $50,000,000 that same year, it cannot deny that such operations are without effect. Even though they do not take part in "pools" or whatever it is the Securities and Exchange Commission may still permit, if the investment officers know their business, as they seem to, they know as much as any "insider" what is going on. The same may be said for the Rockefeller financial agents.

The profits are set aside as a "reserve against possible depreciation," that is, against the possibility that the investment officers might guess wrong next year. If and when this reserve gets sufficiently large it may be used, or a part of it, for philanthropic purposes. So, eventually, if not lost, the profits go into qualified philanthropic channels. This is one source of income. But a more direct one is from the dividends on stocks and bonds. This is where most of the money comes from. We have seen in what railroads, corporations, and public utilities some of these dividends are derived. Eventually, however, they come out of the pocket of the American consumer. When you ride on these railroads, buy the products of these corporations, purchase oil or gas, pay your electric bills, you are helping to pay, in a small way, of course, the dividends of these corporations. The General Education Board, for example, is one of the ten largest stockholders in the Pennsylvania Railroad. The Rockefeller Foundation owns large blocks of Standard Oil stocks, the Carnegie Corporation, as we have seen, is a heavy investor in public utilities.

These supply the income to the foundations. The profits of these corporations make possible the large philanthropies. But who makes possible the profits? Good management? Yes, but more than good management, good patronage, good expenditure by the ultimate consumer. Who, then, pays for these philanthropies? The American people, the middle class, the working class, as well as the wealthy. We pay, very indirectly, it is true, and after a number of people have taken a part of each dollar we expend, but nevertheless we pay, in the ultimate analysis, for all these philanthropies. It is to our interest to know whether they are wisely and efficiently managed. It should be a part of the duty of the Federal government to see that they are. Since it is our money, coming from the American consumer and the American worker, we should insist that they submit to closer public scrutiny and control. After all, it is our money which is being spent, managed — and withheld — in the name of the Carnegie Corporation and the Rockefeller Foundation.

CHAPTER XIII

WHO'S WHO IN THE FOUNDATIONS

Who are the men who run American philanthropic foundations? Who are the trustees, the executives, the presidents and secretaries of these philanthropic trusts? Supposing you, for God knows what reason, aspired to become a trustee or a president of a foundation, how would you go about it?

The answer, to anybody who inspects the list of trustees and foundation officers, is plain. Their names are not, with a few exceptions, those of America's "sixty families." They are not, with those few exceptions, the men who actually "own" or "run" America. But they come very close to that inner circle. They are men who have learned in a very special and thorough manner the meaning of that magic American word *service*. They have found early in life the opportunity to be of service, and they have had the intelligence or the astigmatism to call it the service of humanity, or the promotion of education, or the advancement of some socially recognized and acceptable cause. To have done their serving so well, and not to have made mistakes, it would appear that they must have known from the beginning very well indeed whom they really served.

They are, in a word, employees, the top employees, the very best employees, highly paid, and worth every cent they draw. They belong to a very select club, a club whose members run American business, the American economic system, and the American educational system. They are, in short, the finest flowers of our American culture, and being rather self-conscious about what they are, and particularly self-conscious about the God-given opportunities and blessings of private initiative, they have considered it their duty to perpetuate the culture which has conditioned them. Their ideas, prejudices, and economic interests have, in turn, conditioned and are now

275

conditioning the pattern of American culture. Editorial writers and popular apologists are inclined to point out how wonderful it is that these important men, so busy running the world, have found the time and the social consciousness to devote a part of their thought and energy to humanitarian, philanthropic work. It just shows, they have said, how noble, how disinterested, how eager they are to help their fellow men. What an admirable economic system it is that can develop such beneficent institutions as philanthropic foundations! Here, they cry, is a complete, thorough, unanswerable justification for all the evils of a capitalist system which does, unfortunately, sometimes make mistakes.

Of course that is true. It is, to put it mildly, very decent of them to spend money they cannot use on themselves or invest profitably, money which the government, unless they are very careful, might collect in taxes. But the popular apologists do not seem to realize that these philanthropic interests are all part and parcel of the job these gentlemen have undertaken of running the economic system. It is all a very necessary part of the world these gentlemen are so busy managing. Consciously or unconsciously, they are playing a role, they are functioning as important cogs in a system which is, however out of gear it may be at times, all of a piece. Philanthropic and business interests are not merely complementary, they are identical. Just as you can't run a steel mill without machine guns, so you can't run a capitalist democracy without a pretense of philanthropy. If you tried it, the results might not be happy. Either you would have to abandon the pretense that this is a democracy or the pretense that we can still have capitalism. The Rockefeller Foundation at present is vitally interested in seeing that governmental machinery runs smoothly. If it doesn't run smoothly, those in charge of the Foundation have the foresight to see, there might not be any Foundation, and worse than that, there might not be any Standard Oil Company or Chase National

Bank. A certain amount of charity is necessary, as the Roosevelt administration has demonstrated ; there is necessary work to be done in medical research, education, public health, and the promotion of "right" economic and social ideas. American business needs a halo and the American people need a certain amount of "social service." Hence the interest of those who run our economic system in philanthropic foundations.

Eduard C. Lindeman has made a study of four hundred trustees to find out what sort of men they are. He has inquired into their age, their professions, their social connections. He has concluded that the typical foundation trustee is a man well past middle age,* "more often than not a man of considerable affluence, or one whose economic security ranks high ; his social position is that of a person who belongs to the higher income receiving class of the population ; he is presumably 'respectable' and 'conventional' and belongs to the best clubs and churches and he associates with men of prestige, power, and affluence. His training has been largely in the arts and humanities, and he possesses only a slight background in the sciences and technologies. He resides in the Northeastern section of the United States and has attended one of the private colleges in that region. His 'intelligence' is ranked high by various institutions of higher learning from which he has received signal honors. He receives his income primarily from profits and fees. In short, he is a member of that successful and conservative class which came into power in the latter part of the nineteenth century." Out of 402 trustees the average age was 56.7 years, Dr Lindeman found, the youngest was 35 and the oldest 85 ; 15% were Harvard graduates, 13% Yale, 8% Princeton, and 5% Columbia, the rest scattered. Out of 400 trustees 15% were lawyers, 10% corporation executives, 9% bankers, 9% university or college administrators, 6% physicians, the rest scattered among many professions. Out of 161

* *Wealth and Culture*, Harcourt, Brace and Co., 1936.

trustees 34% were Episcopalians, 20% Presbyterians, 15% Jewish, 9% Methodist, 7% Baptist, the remainder scattered in religious affiliation.

Let us, in this chapter, take up these gentlemen by name, and by referring to "Who's Who" and the "Directory of Directors" discover what sort of men run, today, the Rockefeller, Carnegie, and a few of the other large foundations. As members of a very select club by virtue of being trustees, it is interesting to see to what other clubs they belong. It is also interesting to note the colleges and universities from which some of them obtained honorary degrees. But more important is it to see the vast interlocking directorates, binding together in one group the men who run the railroads, steel companies, corporations, banks, insurance companies, philanthropies, charity organizations, colleges and universities. Each group is represented in the directorship of every other group. Nicholas Murray Butler is a director in the billion-dollar New York Life Insurance Company. Morgan partners are to be found on both Rockefeller and Carnegie boards. Let us see :

ALDRICH, Winthrop W., represents the Rockefeller money power in nearly all its varied manifestations. He is the son of the late stand-pat Old Guard Republican Senator Nelson W. Aldrich of Rhode Island, brother-in-law of John D. Rockefeller Jr, and chairman of the board of the Chase National Bank. He is a trustee of the Rockefeller Foundation, on its finance committee, and is a member of the General Education Board. A.B. Harvard, 1907, LL.B. in 1910, he was in the Rockefeller family law firm, president of the Equitable Trust Co., and then president of the Chase Safe Deposit Company. Now he is director of the American Telephone and Telegraph Co., Westinghouse Electric and Manufacturing Co., the Discount Corporation of New York and Rockefeller Center, Inc. He succeeded Thomas I. Parkinson as president of the New York State Chamber of Commerce in 1936. His philanthropic connections include Tuskegee University, Welfare Council, Greater New York Fund, the Girl Scout Federation, the Shanghai American School, American Association for the Control of Cancer, Nassau Hospital, Association of Legal Aid

Societies; he is a trustee of Barnard College, Riverside Church, United Hospital Fund of New York, New York Community Trust; he is president of the board of managers of the State Charities Aid Association, a member of the American Bar Association, 250 Associates of the Harvard Business School, Academy of Political Science, New York County Lawyers Association, American Bankers Association, American Institute of Banking, Harvard Fund Council, Society of Naval Architects and Marine Engineers, American Commission of the International Chamber of Commerce, the Navy League and the Japan Society. His clubs are: Harvard, Knickerbocker, Grolier, Bond, Broad Street, Down Town, River, Racquet and Tennis, Piping Rock, National Golf, The Brook, Century, Links, The Creek, Meadowbrook, Seawanhaka-Corinthian, New York Yacht of New York; the University, Harvard, Eastern Yacht of Boston; the Hope, of Providence; the Tarantine of Dark Harbor, Maine; the Spee of Cambridge; the Faculty Club of Harvard, the Rookery, Beaver Dam, Jekyl Island, and The Hangar.

DAVIS, John W., is best known as chief legal counsel for J. P. Morgan, but it may be recalled that he ran for President of the United States on the Democratic ticket in 1924. He is on the board of the Rockefeller Foundation and a trustee and vice president (1938) of the Carnegie Endowment for International Peace. He was one of the founders of the Liberty League in 1934 and proud of it. He is a director in the Mutual Life Insurance Co., United States Rubber Company, (general counsel), Guaranty Trust Company, American Telephone and Telegraph Company, and head of the law firm of Davis, Polk, Wardwell, Gardner and Reed. A.B., Washington and Lee, 1892, he collected honorary degrees not only from his alma mater but also from the University of West Virginia, University of Birmingham, England (when he was U.S. Ambassador), University of Glasgow, Union College, Yale, Dartmouth, Brown, and Princeton. His clubs include the Metropolitan, University, National Press, Chevy Chase, Lawyers, in Washington; and the Century, University, Recess, Piping Rock and The Creek in New York.

DODDS, Harold W., the president of Princeton University since 1933, is not only on the Rockefeller Foundation Board but is also a trustee of the Carnegie Foundation for the Advancement of Teaching. A.B., Grove City College, Pennsylvania, 1909, he got an A.M. from Princeton in 1914 and an honorary LL.D. from

Yale, Dickinson, American University, Rutgers, New York University, Harvard, Williams, Cincinnati, and an Litt. D. from Columbia. He was secretary of the National Municipal League from 1920 to 1928 and went to Princeton in 1927 as professor of politics. His clubs are the Century, University, and Princeton of New York ; the Nassau and Princeton of Princeton.

DOUGLAS, Lewis W., recently a manufacturing executive, before that Director of the Budget, now president of McGill University at Montreal, is on the board of the Rockefeller Foundation and the American Cyanamid Company. A.B. Amherst, he taught history there, engaged in citrus ranching and mining in Arizona, became Congressman in 1927. In the 1936–37 *Who's Who* he gives his home address as R.F.D. 2, Phoenix, Arizona and his business address as 30 Rockefeller Plaza, office of the American Cyanamid.

DULLES, John Foster, is a partner in the law firm of Sullivan and Cromwell, on the board of the Rockefeller Foundation, (a member of the executive committee), director in American Agricultural Chemical Co., International Nickel, North American Co., American Bank Note Co., Babcock and Wilcox, Detroit Edison, Gold Dust, Standard Investing Co. A graduate of Princeton, 1908, he has been busy attending financial and debt conferences in all parts of the world. He was a member of the Reparations Commission and the Supreme Economic Council in 1919 and he has since been honored by the Order of the Crown, Belgium ; Legion of Honor, France ; Order of Polonia Restituta, Poland. His clubs include the University, The Rookery, Piping Rock, Down Town, New York ; the Metropolitan in Washington.

FOSDICK, Raymond B., was drawn into the Rockefeller orbit with his brother, when Frederick T. Gates, chief of the Rockefeller philanthropic brain trust, discovered Harry Emerson Fosdick preaching in the First Baptist Church of Montclair N.J., where Gates, the two Fosdicks, and Starr J. Murphy, Rockefeller lawyer, were fellow-townsmen. B.A. Princeton, 1905, M.A., 1906, LL.B. New York Law School, 1908, he became assistant corporation counsel of New York City and distinguished himself as commissioner of accounts in charge of investigating city departments. His first Rockefeller job was in 1913 when he was sent to Europe to study police organizations and write a book about them. Later he was special representative of the Secretary of War, Newton D. Baker, on the Mexican border, chairman of Training Camp

Activities of the War and Navy Departments and under-secretary of the League of Nations. Gifted with exceptional personal charm he is now the chief mouthpiece for the Rockefeller philanthropic interests, president of the Rockefeller Foundation, chairman of the executive committee, member of the General Education Board, trustee of the Rockefeller Institute of Medical Research, the China Medical Board, National Institute of Public Administration, Princeton University, Sarah Lawrence College ; his clubs include the Broad Street and Century in New York and the Union Interalliée in Paris.

FREEMAN, Douglas S., editor of the Richmond *News-Leader*, Pulitzer Prize biographer of Robert E. Lee, is a trustee of the Rockefeller Foundation, president of the board of the University of Richmond, the Confederate Memorial Institute, president of the Edgar Allan Poe Foundation, chairman of the Rhodes Scholarship Committee for Virginia, member of the National Economic Council, Southern Interracial Commission, Alumni Council of Johns Hopkins, National Boy Scouts of America; he is also a trustee of the Carnegie Endowment for International Peace. A.B. Richmond College, 1904, he received a Ph.D. at Johns Hopkins in 1908 and honorary degrees since from Washington and Lee, William and Mary, University of Richmond, Wake Forest and Dartmouth.

GASSER, Herbert S., director of the Rockefeller Institute for Medical Research since 1935, is a trustee of the Rockefeller Foundation. A.B. University of Wisconsin, 1910, M.D. Johns Hopkins 1915, he taught at Wisconsin and at the Cornell Medical School before succeeding Dr Simon Flexner. He is the lone representative of science on the General Education Board.

GIFFORD, Walter S., president of the American Telephone and Telegraph Company since 1925, is on the executive committee of the Rockefeller Foundation, and director of the United States Steel Corporation, the First National Bank of New York. A member of the General Education Board, he is a trustee of the Carnegie Institution in Washington, Cooper Union in New York, the Bank for Savings in New York, president of the New York Charity Organization Society, member of the board of overseers of Harvard. A.B. Harvard, 1905, he became assistant secretary and treasurer of the Western Electric in Chicago, chief statistician 1911–1916, and vice president 1919–1925. Williams, Colgate and

Oberlin have given him honorary degrees ; his clubs are the University, Harvard, India House and National Arts.

GREENE, Jerome D., retired banker and former Rockefeller employee is on the executive committee of the Rockefeller Foundation, has been associated with the Rockefeller philanthropic interests from the time the Rockefeller Foundation was organized, when he served as its first secretary, having begun his apprenticeship as assistant to the general manager of the Harvard University Press and secretary to President Charles W. Eliot of Harvard. He is now secretary of the Corporation of Harvard University. He was general manager of the Rockefeller Institute, 1910–12, and has been a trustee of it ever since, as well as trustee of the International Health Commission, a member of the General Education Board and for a time, overseer of Harvard. He is now a trustee of the Brookings Institution of Washington, vice president of the Japan Society, treasurer of the American Social Hygiene Association and the American Council of the Institute of Pacific Relations, president of the American-Asiatic Society, director of the Manhattan Railway Co. In spite of all of that he has found time to be a member of the banking firm of Lee, Higginson, 1919–32. He has been made a Grand Officer of St Sava (Kingdom of Serbs, Croats and Slovenes) and Chevalier of the Legion of Honor of France.

HOPKINS, Ernest M., has been president of Dartmouth since 1916 ; he is a trustee of the Rockefeller Foundation and a member of the General Education Board, director of the Boston and Maine Railway, Phillips Andover Academy, Newton Theological Institute, and the National Life Insurance Company of Montpelier, Vermont. A.B. Dartmouth, 1901, he served as secretary of the college, engaged in organization work for industrial concerns in Chicago, Boston, and Philadelphia. Amherst, Colby, Rutgers, Brown, University of Pennsylvania, University of New Hampshire, McGill, Yale, Williams, Harvard, St John's and Wabash have bestowed honorary degrees upon him. He is a Baptist, a D.K.E., a Phi Beta Kappa, and a Republican. His clubs are the Century and Town Hall in New York, the University and Tavern in Boston, and the University in Washington, D.C.

PARKINSON, Thomas I., while president of the Equitable Life Assurance Society, director of the Chase National Bank, Consolidated Coal, Western Electric, the Borden Company, Continental Insurance Company, is a trustee of the Rockefeller Foundation, on its executive committee ; he is a member of the General Education

Board, and is on the board of Sailors' Snug Harbor, New York. His clubs are the Century, Lawyers, City, Cosmos and Pennsylvania.

RICHARDS, Alfred N., professor of pharmacology at the University of Pennsylvania since 1910, is the only scientist on the Rockefeller Foundation board who is not a Rockefeller employee or connected with any other Rockefeller philanthropy. B.A., Yale 1897, Ph.D. Columbia 1901, he belongs to many scientific societies.

ROCKEFELLER, John D. Jr, never directly in the oil business, has devoted his life to his own and his father's philanthropic interests ever since he graduated from Brown in 1897 and married the sister of Winthrop W. Aldrich of Providence. He was the first president of the Rockefeller Foundation, is now chairman of the finance committee, has been on all the Rockefeller boards, always active in the direction of the formation of the policies of all of them, particularly the General Education Board, the Rockefeller Institute, the Bureau of Social Hygiene, the International Health Board, the China Medical Board. His own private philanthropies have been considerable, particularly at Williamsburg, Va., and Versailles, France. Although presumably a large stockholder in Standard Oil companies his name does not appear as director in any of them. He has always been prominent in big charity drives in New York City, particularly during the war, and is now one of the chairmen of the Greater New York Fund. Incidentally, he built Rockefeller Center.

ROCKEFELLER, John D. 3rd, with his brother Nelson, is taking on some of his father's burdens; already he is on the Rockefeller Foundation executive committee, the General Education Board, the board of the Rockefeller Institute, The Spelman Fund, the Davison Fund, Colonial Williamsburg, Inc., Industrial Relations Counselors, China Medical Board, American Museum of Natural History, the Dunbar National Bank, Rockefeller Center, Inc., and Riverside Church. B.S., Princeton, 1929, his clubs include the University, Knickerbocker, Princeton, and Broad Street.

STEWART, Walter, W., economist, chairman of the board of Case, Pomeroy and Co., (investment bankers), is on the boards of the Rockefeller Foundation (both executive and finance committees), the General Education Board, the Institute for Advanced Study at Princeton, and Bennington College. A.B., University of Missouri, 1909, he taught economics there and at Amherst before

joining Case, Pomeroy. He was economic advisor to the Bank
of England, 1928–1930.

SWIFT, Harold H., Chicago packer, is vice chairman of the board
of directors of Swift and Company, and on the boards of the
Rockefeller Foundation, the General Education Board, Union
Stock Yards, Libby, McNeil, and Libby, as well as president of the
board of the University of Chicago, director of the Harris Trust
and Savings Bank, trustee of the Museum of Science and Industry,
on the board of the United Charities of Chicago. Ph. D. of the
University of Chicago, 1907, his clubs include the University and
Bankers of New York, University, Chicago Literary, Quadrangle,
City, Onwentsia, Midlothian Country, and Union League of
Chicago.

WHIPPLE, George H., pathologist, on the board of the scientific
directors of the Rockefeller Institute, has been a member of the
Rockefeller Foundation board since 1927 and is now on the executive committee. A Nobel Prize winner in 1934, he has an A.B.
from Yale, 1900 ; M.D. Johns Hopkins, 1905 ; he was pathologist
at the Bay View Hospital at Baltimore, later professor at Johns
Hopkins ; he directed the Hooper Foundation for Medical Research at the University of California and was dean of the medical
school there ; later dean of the medical school at the University of
Rochester. He is the third scientist on the Foundation's board.

WILBUR, Ray Lyman, also holds an M.D. degree but he is best
known as president of Leland Stanford, Jr University since 1916
and as Secretary of the Interior in Hoover's cabinet. He has been
on the board of the Rockefeller Foundation since 1923 and been
a member of the General Education Board since 1930. Honorary
degrees have been conferred on him by the universities of California, Arizona, Pittsburgh, New Mexico, Pennsylvania, Duke, Maryland, Rochester, Chicago, Southern California, Puerto Rico, Princeton, Yale, Dartmouth, Illinois, Wesleyan, Syracuse, Western
Reserve, and the University of the State of New York. He was
chairman of the Federal Oil Conservation Board 1928–29 and of
the Committee on the Costs of Medical Care. His clubs include
the University, Commonwealth, Bohemian, Pacific Union and
Family of San Francisco, and the Century in New York.

YOUNG, Owen D., chairman of the board and director of General
Electric, director of the National Broadcasting Co. (advisory
board), American and Foreign Power, General Motors, Allgemeine
Elktricitate Gesellschaft, Société Financière pour le Developpe-

ment de l'Electricité, is on both the Rockefeller Foundation and the General Education Board ; he is a member of the National Industrial Conference Board (councillor), National Electric Manufacturers Association, Osram Corporation, National Bureau of Economic Research, International Education Board, Leonard Wood Memorial Foundation, League of Nations Association, trustee of St Lawrence University where he got an A.B. in 1896, chairman of the Federal Reserve Bank, formerly chairman of the board of the Radio Corporation (until 1929). He has collected honorary degrees from Boston University, Union, Tufts, Harvard, Dartmouth, Johns Hopkins, Colgate, Yale, Columbia, Rutgers, Princeton, Lehigh, Wesleyan, Brown, Notre Dame, Queen's University, (Kingston, Ontario) University of Nebraska, Marietta College, Rollins College. After winning a suit against the General Electric he came from Boston to New York as counsel for the General Electric, was made vice president and became chairman of the board in 1922. His clubs include Bankers, Century, Harvard, India House, Exchange (honorary), Engineers (honorary) of New York, Tavern, Union, and Club of Odd Volumes in Boston, the Mohawk and Mohawk Golf in Schenectady. He is also Regent of the University of the State of New York.

Thirteen out of these twenty are also members of the General Education Board, which includes four gentlemen who are not at present on the Rockefeller Foundation board. Of these Trevor Arnett was formerly a trustee of the Foundation and Max Mason was formerly president of it.

ARNETT, Trevor, British born, got an A.B. at the University of Chicago in 1898, was a post graduate fellow, auditor, and trustee. He became secretary of the General Education Board in 1920 and was vice president and business manager of the University of Chicago 1924–26; trustee of the Rockefeller Institute, International Education Board, Institute of Social and Religious Research (treasurer) and is recognized as an authority on college finance.

MASON, Max, was president of the University of Chicago 1925–28 but resigned to become director of the natural sciences of the Rockefeller Foundation. A graduate of the University of Wisconsin where he also got a Ph D., he studied at Göttingen, instructed mathematics at the Massachusetts Institute of Technology, was assistant professor at Yale, on the committee of the National

Research Council 1917–19 and invented submarine detector devices. His clubs include the University, Union League, Chicago, City, Quadrangle, Cliff Dwellers.

The other two members of the General Education Board who are not trustees of the Foundation are Harry Woodburn Chase and Edwin Mims.

CHASE, Harry Woodburn, an educator who started his career as director of a clinic for subnormal children, is now Chancellor of New York University. A.B. Dartmouth, 1904, A.M. 1908, Ph.D. Clark, 1910, he has been professor of education, president of the University of North Carolina 1919–1930, President of the University of Illinois 1930–33; he is now a trustee of the Phelps-Stokes Fund, the Russell Sage Foundation, League for Political Education, and was a trustee of the Rosenwald Fund 1928–33. He is a member of Trinity Church vestry and his clubs include the University, Century, Lotos, Town Hall.

MIMS, Edwin, head of the English Department at Vanderbilt University since 1912, is also on the General Education Board. He has been a member of the Joint Hymn Book Commission of the Methodist Episcopal Church. A.B. Vanderbilt, 1892, he is a Phi Beta Kappa and D.K.E.

Other important Rockefeller trustees are those on The Spelman Fund.

DODGE, Cleveland E., financier, graduated from Princeton in 1909 and went into the Phelps-Dodge Corporation, becoming vice president in 1924. He is also vice president of the Old Dominion Company, director of the City Bank Farmers Trust Co., the Y.M.C.A. of New York, Southern Pacific Co., trustee of the Atlantic Mutual Life Insurance Co., Bank of New York and Trust Co., chairman of the board of Teachers College, president of the Near East Foundation. His name is usually to be found on the sponsors of important charity drives in New York. He is a Democrat, a Presbyterian, and a member of the University, and the Racquet and Tennis Clubs.

GARDINER, William Tudor, ex-governor of Maine, 1929–33, is chairman of the Pacific Coast Co., Incorporated Investors and is a practising lawyer in Boston. A.B. Harvard, 1914. He is a thirty-second degree Mason.

LAMONT, Thomas W., the Morgan partner who acts as a sort of public relations counselor for the Morgan interests graduated from Harvard in 1892, became secretary and treasurer of the Bankers Trust Co. in 1903, vice president in 1909, joined J. P. Morgan in 1911. He is director in the United States Steel Corporation ; Guaranty Trust Co. ; American Telephone and Telegraph Co. ; Atchison, Topeka, and Santa Fe ; Lamont, Corliss and Co., among others. He was overseer of Harvard 1912–25 ; his clubs are Harvard, University, Union League, Metropolitan, City, Piping Rock, Down Town, Links, and Englewood Country. In addition to being a trustee of the Spelman Fund he is chairman of the board of trustees of the Carnegie Foundation for the Advancement of Teaching [1937].

MERRIAM, Charles E. is head of the department of political science at the University of Chicago and member of the Social Science Research Council of which he was president 1924–25.

RUML, Beardsley, has already been partially described in this book. He hails from Cedar Rapids, Iowa, got his B.S. at Dartmouth in 1915, his Ph.D. at the University of Chicago. After working for the Scott Company in Chicago he came to New York as secretary to the Carnegie Corporation for one year. Then he directed the Laura Spelman Memorial from 1922 to 1929 where he disbursed millions for the social sciences. In 1928 he became a trustee of the Rosenwald Fund and was dean of the social sciences at the University of Chicago, 1931–33, when he was made treasurer of R.H. Macy in New York. Since then he succeeded Owen D. Young as deputy chairman of the Federal Reserve Bank of New York. He is still a member of the Social Science Research Council, committee on problems and policy, and one of the directors of the National Bureau of Economic Research. Wherever the Rockefeller interests have made contributions in the social sciences, Beardsley Ruml's name is usually to be found. He is generally conceded, by all who have had contact with him, to be a very brilliant man.

WOODS, Arthur, ex-police commissioner of New York City, 1914–18, is now chairman of the Spelman Fund. A.B. Harvard, 1892, he was a schoolmaster at Groton ; reporter ; in the lumber business in Mexico and the cotton-converting business in Boston. His clubs are the Racquet, Harvard, Coffee House, Dutch Treat in New York, Harvard, Boston, the Chevy Chase, National Press in Washington and the Union Interalliée in Paris. He wrote *Crime Prevention*, 1918, and *Dangerous Drugs*, 1931.

Among the administrative officers of the Rockefeller Foundation are two vice presidents.

APPLEGET, Thomas B., Baptist go-getter, who graduated from Baptist Peddie Institute in his native Hightstown, N.J., went to Baptist Brown, became executive secretary of Brown University and assistant to the president. In 1926 John D. Rockefeller Jr appointed him his executive secretary and in 1928 he became an officer of the Foundation.

GUNN, Selskar M., British born bacteriologist, came to the United States in 1900, got a S.B. at Massachusetts Institute of Technology in 1905, was editor of the American Journal of Public Health and became director of the Rockefeller division of hygiene in 1915. He directed the Paris office of the International Health Board from 1922 to 1927, and he is a Grand Officer in the Order of St Sava (Croats, Serbs, and Slovenes) ; Officer of the Order of the White Lion of Czechoslovakia ; "Merituel Sanitar" of Roumania ; Commander of the Royal Order of St Olaf, Norway ; the Order of Danneborg, Denmark ; and Legion of Honor of France.

DASHIELL, Lefferts M., who had been treasurer of the Rockefeller Foundation and five other philanthropic organizations died in February 1938. A graduate of Brown in 1897, he was in the brokerage business in New York until 1914 when he joined the Foundation as assistant treasurer, becoming treasurer in 1932. He was also treasurer of the General Education Board ; the Rockefeller Institute ; the China Medical Board ; the Spelman Fund ; the Davison Fund ; and the New York State Colonization Society. He was also president of the Tilden Mining Co., and a trustee of the New York Produce Exchange Safe Deposit and Storage Company.

Five of the trustees of the Carnegie Corporation are heads of Carnegie institutions.

ARBUTHNOT, Thomas S., has been president of the Carnegie Hero Fund since 1933. A graduate of Yale, 1894, he got his M.D. at Columbia College of Physicians and Surgeons, was dean of the Medical School of the University of Pittsburgh from 1909 to 1918.

BAKER, Newton D., was first and foremost a corporation lawyer although since his death his associates have tried to immortalize him as a statesman, since he served with distinction as Secretary of War in Woodrow Wilson's cabinet while professing to be a pacifist. In addition to being a trustee of the Carnegie Corporation, practising law in Cleveland, he was a former president of the Woodrow Wilson Foundation ; a director of the Cleveland Trust Co. ; the Baltimore and Ohio Railroad ; the Radio Corporation of America ; and the Goodyear Tire and Rubber Co. B.A. Johns Hopkins, he got his LL.B. at Washington and Lee, was mayor of Cleveland before becoming Secretary of War. His clubs included the Union, University, City, Chamber of Commerce of Cleveland ; Army and Navy and Cosmos of Washington ; and the Century in New York City. At this writing no one has as yet been elected to take his place on the Carnegie Corporation board.

BUTLER, Nicholas Murray, president of the Carnegie Endowment for International Peace and of Columbia University ; trustee of the Carnegie Foundation for the Advancement of Teaching is still on the board of the Carnegie Corporation although it is rumored he was so miffed at not getting additional funds for his peace endowment he refused to attend meetings. He has a most imposing list of degrees and decorations. A.B. Columbia, 1883, Ph.D. 1884, he has received honorary degrees from Syracuse, Tulane, Johns Hopkins, Princeton, Yale, St Andrews, Manchester, Cambridge, Brown, Toronto, Wesleyan, Chicago, Pennsylvania, Glasgow, Oxford, Breslau, Strassbourg, Nancy, Paris, Louvain, Prague, Kings College (New South Wales), and Rome. He has been president of Columbia since 1902 and of Barnard College since 1912 ; he is proud of having run for vice president on the Republican ticket in 1912 and of getting 69½ votes in the Republican convention in 1920 which nominated Harding. He is a director in the New York Life Insurance Company ; a trustee of the Cathedral of St John the Divine, the Columbia University Press, Kahn Foundation for the Advancement of Teaching, Philharmonic Society of New York. His honors include the Legion of Honor of France ; Grand Commander of the Royal Order of the Redeemer, First Class, of Greece; Order of St Sava (Serbs, Croats, and Slovenes); Grand Cordon, Order of Leopold of Belgium; Grand Officer, Order of Polonia Restituta; Commander of the Order of Saints Mauritius and Lazarus of Italy ; Grand Cordon, Order of the Crown of Italy ; and Commander of the Red Eagle of Prussia (with star).

His clubs include the Union, Century, Church, Metropolitan, University, Union League, Republican, and Lotos.

CHURCH, Samuel Harden, is president of the Carnegie Institute of Pittsburgh. Litt. D., Western University of Pennsylvania, he got an A.M. at Bethany and Yale, and an LL.D. at Pittsburgh. He suppressed riots in Cincinnati in 1884 as colonel on the staff of Governor Hoadley of Ohio, and has been an active Republican campaign speaker. For many years he was vice president of the Pennsylvania railroad lines west of Pittsburgh and he has written a corporate history of that division of the road in fifteen volumes.

COFFMAN, Lotus Delta, president of the University of Minnesota since 1920, is also secretary of the board for the Carnegie Foundation for the Advancement of Teaching. A.B. Indiana State, 1906, A.M. 1910, he got a Ph D. at Columbia in 1911, was superintendent of schools in Indiana ; professor of education at the University of Illinois ; dean of the college of education at Minnesota. Honored by Columbia, Indiana, Carleton, Michigan, Northwestern and George Washington universities, he was representative of the Carnegie Corporation to the universities and scientific societies of New Zealand and Australia in 1931. He is a member of the board of curators of St Stephens College and of the board of overseers of Chevy Chase College, on the advisory council of Yenching Union College at Peiping, China, a member of the educational committee of the Boy Scouts, a Republican, a Baptist, a brother in Phi Delta Kappa, Sigma Xi, Phi Beta Kappa, and Kappa Delta Pi.

JAMES, Henry, is the son of William James, nephew of the novelist, a member of the board of trustees of the Rockefeller Institute of which he was business manager for a time. A.B. Harvard, 1899, LL.B., 1904, he practiced law in Boston, was a member of the War Relief Committee of the Rockefeller Foundation, overseer of Harvard 1922–28, he is now chairman and president of the Teachers Insurance and Annuity Association. Hamilton and Williams colleges have honored him ; he is Pulitzer Prize biographer of Charles W. Eliot, editor of the letters of William James and is a member of the Knickerbocker, the Century clubs of New York and the Union of Boston.

JESSUP, Walter A., president of the Carnegie Foundation for the Advancement of Teaching got his A.B. at Earlham College in 1903, an M.A. at Hanover, Ph. D. at Columbia and has been honored by Wisconsin, Indiana, Missouri, Columbia and Iowa. He was once a superintendent of schools, then dean of the School of Education at Iowa State, later president of the University. He is a Methodist and an overseer of Chevy Chase College. Recently he was elected a director in the Johns-Manville Corporation.

KEPPEL, Frederick P., has been president of the Carnegie Corporation since 1923, written books and made speeches on the subject of foundations. A.B. Columbia, 1899, he became secretary of the college, dean, Assistant Secretary of War, and secretary of the New York Regional Plan before joining the Carnegie Corporation. He is a director in the Equitable Life Assurance Society and the Guaranty Trust Co. of New York, has been honored by the universities of Pittsburgh, Michigan, Toronto, Melbourne, and Hamilton and Union colleges. He is a Chevalier of the Legion of Honor of France. In addition to being a Psi U., a Phi Beta Kappa, and a Democrat, he is a member of the Cosmos Club of Washington and the Century and University of New York.

KELLEY, Nicholas, counsel for the Chrysler Corporation, is a Quaker and the son of a well-known social worker. A.B. Harvard, 1905; he was with Cravath, Henderson and de Gersdorf from 1909 to 1915 ; now he is a partner in Larkin, Rathbone, and Perry. After serving as assistant secretary of the Treasury, 1920–21, he headed a financial mission to Peru, and for one year, 1934–35, he was on the Automobile Labor Board. He is a trustee of the Henry Street Settlement, the American Museum of Natural History, the American Geographic Society, and treasurer of the Association for Social Security. An Officer, Order of the Crown, of Italy, a Phi Beta Kappa, he belongs to the Harvard, Century, City, Midday, Down Town, University clubs of New York, the Cosmos and Metropolitan in Washington and the Detroit in Detroit.

MERRIAM, John C., paleontologist and educator, has been head of the Carnegie Institution of Washington since 1920. After getting his B.S. at Lenox College in Iowa, 1887, he obtained a Ph. D. at Munich in 1893, was an instructor and professor of paleontology and historical geology at the University of California and dean of faculties in 1920, when he was also chairman of the National Research Council. Author of many books on paleontology and geology, he is a member of many learned and scientific societies. He is not a clubman.

ROOT, Elihu Jr, succeeded his father to the board. Like his father, he is a corporation lawyer. A. B. Hamilton, 1903, LL.B.

Harvard, 1906, he joined the firm of Root, Clark, Buckner and Ballantine in 1909. He is on the executive committee of the Teachers' Insurance and Annuity Association, is a trustee of Hamilton College, Cooper Union, and the Oceanographic Institute. He has been a member of the committee to visit Harvard Law School since 1922. His clubs include the University, Harvard, Century, Knickerbocker, City, Midday, and Seawanhaka-Corinthian.

The other member of the Carnegie Corporation's board is Mr Carnegie's daughter, Margaret Carnegie Miller.

The group of business men, corporation lawyers, and educators who compose the board of the Carnegie Endowment for International Peace are described in the chapter on "An Endowment for War," and the collection of college presidents who constitute the board of the Carnegie Foundation for the Advancement of Teaching were discussed in the chapter on "Pensions and Educational Standards." It would need a whole volume to list all the trustees and officers of the leading foundations and to discuss the financial, social, philanthropic connections of the boards of Russell Sage, Duke, Commonwealth, Milbank, Rosenwald funds and the others. A few individuals, however, as members of several boards, appear to effect a liaison between foundations or between philanthropic agencies and big business. Among those who might be mentioned are :

DELANO, Frederic A., A.B. Harvard, 1885, ex-receiver for the Supreme Court in the Red River Boundary case. For many years he was with the Chicago, Burlington, and Quincy Railway, then he was president of the Wheeling and Lake Erie Railway and the Wabash-Pittsburgh Railroad. He was first vice president of the Wabash and later one of the receivers. He was a member of the Federal Reserve Board but resigned to enter the army where he became a colonel in the Transportation Corps. In addition to being on the board of the Carnegie Endowment for International Peace, he is a trustee of the Russell Sage Foundation, a Regent of the Smithsonian, a trustee of the Carnegie Institution in Washington, of which he is secretary and on the executive committee. For a time he was chairman of the board of Brookings. He was chairman of the international committee of the League of Nations inquiry into the production of opium in Persia and chairman of the Regional Plan of New York City. His clubs include the University, Chicago Literary, Metropolitan, Chevy Chase, and the Cosmos of Washington.

KINGSLEY, William M., president of the U.S. Trust Company, is treasurer of the Commonwealth Fund, president of the board of directors of the Union Theological Seminary since 1913, treasurer of New York University (A.B. 1883) since 1905 (resigned 1938), president and treasurer of the Syrian Protestant College, chairman of the New York State and president of the New York City Y.M.C.A. He was with Brown Brothers, bankers, 1883–91, and a broker with Kingsley, Mabon, 1891–1906. His clubs include the University, Down Town, and Psi Upsilon.

KIRKBRIDE, Franklin B., gives his profession as "trustee." He serves in this capacity the Milbank Fund, Stevens Institute of Technology, the New York Association for Improving the Condition of the Poor. He was chairman of the Empire Cream Separator, 1911–22, and is a member of the New York Chamber of Commerce. A.B. Haverford, 1889, he belongs to the Century, Republican, University, Down Town Clubs, the Adirondack League, and is the author, with H. Parker Willis and J. E. Starrett, of *The Modern Trust Company*.

MURRAY, George Welwood, Scotchman, formerly on the board of the Laura Spelman Memorial, is now on the Commonwealth Board. He has been general counsel for the Equitable Trust as well as a director. He is a director of the Mortgage Bond Company of New York, the Montclair Trust Co., the Albany and Susquehanna railroad, the American Linseed Co., member of the advisory board and counsel for the National Surety Company. He graduated from Columbia in 1876. His clubs include the Century, Midday, Broad Street, Montclair, Golf, Colonial, and the Cosmos in Washington.

MORRIS, Roland S., trustee of the Carnegie Endowment for International Peace, the Brookings Institution and the Milbank Fund, has been a member of the law firm of Duane, Morris, and Hecksher of Philadelphia since 1904. He was ambassador to Japan 1917–1921 ; is a member of the Asiatic Society, the Japan Society, the Oriental Society, and the American Philosophical Society. A.B. Princeton 1896, LL.B. University of Pennsylvania, he belongs to the Philadelphia, Princeton, Contemporary, University Barge clubs of Philadelphia, the Racquet of Washington and the Century of New York.

These are the trustees who are responsible for the broad policies of the foundations ; they determine the general direction and point of view. The real power, of course, is usually in a small group, particularly in the Rockefeller philanthropies. The execution of the policies, their oral and tangible expression, resides in the administrative staff : the presidents and secretaries. Here are a few of them:

EMBREE, Edwin R., president of the Rosenwald Fund since 1928, got his B.A. at Yale in 1906, M.A. in 1914. Successively he was alumni editor of the Yale *Alumni Weekly*, organizer and director of the Class Secretaries' Bureau at Yale, alumni registrar, secretary to the Bureau of Appointments. In 1917 he became director of the bureau of studies of the Rockefeller Foundation and in 1927 vice president. He has specialized in the study of races and education in primitive cultures, also Negro education and the relations of Negroes and whites. His clubs include the Graduate of New Haven, Yale of New York, Quadrangle, Cliff Dwellers, Tavern of Chicago. Author of a number of books, he contributes frequently to magazines.

LESTER, Robert M., secretary of the Carnegie Corporation since 1934, received his A.B. at Birmingham-Southern College in 1908, where he taught Greek for a year, studied at Vanderbilt and Nashville universities and was Buhl Fellow at the University of Michigan. A.M. Columbia 1917, he joined the University library staff, and after a brief absence when he was superintendent of schools in Mayfield Ky., and Covington, Tenn., he returned to Columbia to the Department of English in Extension where he was for a year administrative officer of men undergraduates. In 1926 he went to the Carnegie Corporation as assistant to the president.

SANDS, Alexander, secretary and trustee for the Duke Endowment began as a banker in Virginia, became connected with J. B. Duke. He is now a trustee of the Doris Duke Trust, secretary of the Angier B. Duke Memorial, treasurer and director of the Durham Holding Corporation, Pearson Investment Corporation, Linden Investment Corporation, Newton Investment Corporation and director of the Duke Power Company. He lives in Montclair, N.J.

SAVAGE, Howard J., secretary since 1931 of the Carnegie Foundation for the Advancement of Teaching, obtained his A.B. at Tufts College in 1907. A.M.Harvard 1909, Ph D. 1915, he was an instructor in English at Tufts, Harvard, and Radcliffe, associate professor at Bryn Mawr, staff member of the Carnegie Foundation in 1923 in charge of the studies of college athletics. He is a member of the American Dialect Society, Modern Language Association, the Harvard, Dutch Treat, Salmagundi, Scarsdale Golf clubs, a Phi Beta Kappa, author of *American College Athletics*, 1929, and contributor to the Encyclopedia Britannica.

SMITH, Barry C., director of the Commonwealth Fund since 1921, got his B.A. at Yale in 1899, graduated from the New York School of Social Work in 1914. He taught in private schools in New York City, became financial secretary of the New York Charity Organization Society in 1915, organized and directed the National Information Bureau 1918–21. He is a Phi Beta Kappa, Beta Theta Pi, honorary member of the American Psychiatric Association, Chevalier of the Legion of Honor, France, Das Grosse Ehrenseichen (Austria) and the Yale, University, Old Country clubs.

STEVENS, David H., has been vice president of the General Education Board since 1931. A.B. Lawrence College, Appleton, Wis., 1906, A.M., 1910, A.M. Harvard, 1912, Ph.D. University of Chicago 1914, he taught Latin and English in Wisconsin, became registrar at Northwestern University in 1910, instructor, and then assistant professor of English and later dean. At the University of Chicago he was made associate professor, dean, assistant to the president, associate dean before going to the Rockefeller Foundation where he became director of the "division of humanities." He is a member of the Modern Language Association, Quadrangle Club of Chicago, the Congregational Church, is a Phi Beta Kappa and a Phi Delta Theta. He also lives in Montclair, N.J.

It must be repeated that these trustees and administrators are public spirited gentlemen. They must be given credit for what professional social workers call "social consciousness." When a man, having achieved a certain position in society, a

certain economic security, devotes time, thought, energy to the
work of educational and philanthropic institutions as a member
of the board of trustees, he should not be criticised or held up
to ridicule.   He is fulfilling his function in society, he may say,
and it is only as he fulfills that function he can be of real "service."   That is precisely the point of this chapter : to show the
function, the role these gentlemen play in our economic society.
Many of them probably believe that their philanthropic and
business interests are separate.   The Rockefellers, however,
draw no sharp line of distinction, and it is very doubtful if the
trustees of the Duke Endowment imagine that their power
interests are separate from the educational and philanthropic
interests of the Endowment.   The connection was made crys-
tal clear by Mr Duke himself.   The other philanthropic trusts
are less direct.   But it would be very stupid to imagine that the
money, the power, the influence of the foundations could be
used for anything except the safeguarding, promotion, and enhancement of the group in society which the trustees serve and
to which they belong.

No less public spirited and anxious to serve are those in administrative positions.   They are usually drawn from the universities.   Some of them, such as Dr George E. Vincent and
Dr Henry S. Pritchett, were college presidents before they became foundation presidents.   Others, like Dr James R. Angell *
and Dr Edmund C. Day, became university presidents after
serving the foundations.   It might be said that the foundations
have a deciding voice in choosing university presidents, but
that is too involved a digression to be pursued here.   At any
rate, such is the type of man who is usually chosen to head the
big philanthropic trusts.   Raymond B. Fosdick and Frederick
P. Keppel, both high-minded, broad-visioned gentlemen, would
make excellent university presidents.

Very much the same type, not yet quite ready for lofty positions are those in the lower administrative jobs.   They have

* Now "educational counselor" for the National Broadcasting Company.

usually served their apprenticeship, either in teaching, as Mr Lester, or in administration, as Mr Appleget, in the colleges. A satirical portrait of what purported to be a foundation executive was published in February, 1927, in the *New Republic*, entitled "The Fat Boy." This anonymous article described, perhaps a little unjustly, these gentlemen as being "all alike . . . young, confident, busy, they seem to know everything although in reality they only know *about* everything. . . They had their ears to the ground and knew what was going on, rather than what that something was, which seemed to interest them." Once promising young men, but "A few years of promise when lo ! a Foundation happens along looking for a bright young man to act as its executive. No wonder they achieved the same outward personality, that irritating blend of ignorance and omniscience."

That neglects to describe how pleasant they are, how charming they can be in giving information or explaining the purpose of endowments. It is true, however, that they have stopped expressing themselves and have become spokesmen for the foundations. They will often admit, quite frankly, that they do not know whether foundations have "proved themselves." They maintain that endowments have done a lot of good, although they concede that they have, unfortunately, sometimes made mistakes. Naturally they resent a hostile or unfavorable interpretation of their role. They are trained in spending other people's money ; the millions are there, and it is no business of theirs how they were amassed. Their job is to see that the money is spent wisely, and in such a manner as will do as little harm as possible, while at the same time earning the approval of the trustees and the general public. They have served faithfully and selflessly ; they have not offended against any of the taboos of the rich and respectable ; they have shown brilliance without independence, cleverness without self-seeking, sincerity without awareness of hypocrisy. They can talk in terms of high idealism and make speeches which sound disarmingly frank.   They get along with the rich and influential smoothly ; pleasing, amusing, stimulating, but never frightening them or permitting them to feel uneasy.   They have achieved names which look well in the showcase, on the board of trustees. They are the gentlemen who, in cooperation with the trustees, run the philanthropic foundations.

CHAPTER XIV

THE FUNCTION OF FOUNDATIONS

Since the word "foundation" has an impressive, nobby sound, suggestive of noble purposes, many purely commercial organizations call themselves "foundations" rather than "bureaus" or "institutes." Of course they must be ruled out of any discussion of philanthropic foundations. Family trusts, organized to keep an estate together and to pay dividends to a number of heirs must also be ignored, although the chief difference between them and the big benevolent trusts is that the income goes to friends and relatives instead of to strangers. Charitable organizations whose capital was furnished by a number of donors and which depend upon regular contributions often call themselves "foundations" with some justification, but they cannot be classed with the Carnegie and Rockefeller benevolent trusts. The American Foundation for the Blind is one of these doing splendid work in its specific field. Founded in 1921, a part of its income is derived from an endowment raised by Helen Keller. Recently an increasing number of wealthy donors have set up funds to be used for a definite purpose, each at one university. The Mayo Foundation connected with the University of Minnesota is one of these. Another is the George F. Baker Foundation which furnished the original endowment for the Harvard Graduate School of Business Administration. Usually, however, such funds are for scholarships.

One of these attracted publicity because it was a project to send newspapermen to Harvard. The *New Yorker* pointed out some of the drawbacks : "For one thing, newspapermen don't get leaves of absence. They either get fired or they take sick and die. . . Obviously the people who could use a spell at Harvard are the publishers of papers, not the employees. Go into any newspaper office and you'll find it teeming with Harvard men most of whom need, not another term at Cambridge, but a dollar and a half to get their shirts back from the laundry. . . It is publishers who hold back a newspaper, not people like J. Otis Swift, Eleanor Roosevelt, and Westbrook Pegler. Why ? Because publishers want to make a lot of money so that their widows can leave a million dollars to send somebody back to Harvard. Hearst went to Harvard, and he couldn't elevate a standard if it was rigged with pulleys."

More difficult to ignore are the local foundations whose activities are restricted to a comparatively small area. The largest of these is the Buhl Foundation of Pittsburgh, (assets $13,344,466.26) which supports projects to find "factual bases for social work and regional economic effort in the Pittsburgh area," to promote health demonstrations, to stimulate higher education, and to advance housing standards. In 1932 this foundation built Chatham Village as a business project for the middle class, which now has two hundred homes renting from $50 to $86 a month, representing an investment of $1,600,000. This is not a charitable project but a "sound long-term investment yielding moderate returns with a regularity that suggests an approach to depression-proof use for large funds," declared C. V. Starett, the Associate Director, in the *Survey Graphic*.* "Chatham Village," he said, "is the type of planned neighborhood that offers guaranty against social and economic deterioration. It has created a fine neighborhood, but of greater importance is the fact that because of control by long-term investment management, it will remain a fine neighborhood."

In considering the function of foundations notice should also be given to those whose purpose is the promotion of better understanding between the United States and foreign countries by means of fellowships, exchange lecturers, and books. The Netherland-American and the Scandinavian-American Foundations are examples of these. One of the best known is the

* January 1938, reprinted in April *Readers Digest*.

Carl Schurz Memorial Foundation (assets $52,952.55) with which the Oberlaender Trust (assets $955,388.21) has become associated. Anti-Nazi feeling has aroused anti-German sentiment, making difficult the task of fostering better appreciation of German art and literature and the furtherance of cultural relations with German-speaking peoples. However, the Foundation has persisted. Among other things a lumberman's tour of Germany, Austria, and Czechoslovakia was arranged in 1936 and the party attended the International Forestry Conference at Budapest ; a German art exhibition was held in 1937 ; a number of students and scholars were aided. Less known but larger, with assets of nearly three million, is the Commission for Relief of Belgium Foundation, of which Herbert Hoover is chairman of the board. It maintains fellowships for Belgian university graduates to study in the United States and for advanced American students to study in Belgium, arranges for the exchange of scholars, and makes a number of grants designed to promote closer relations and "the exchange of intellectual ideas between Belgium and America."

There are a number of foundations in the field of music, such as the Curtis Institute and the Presser Foundation in Philadelphia. Biggest and best known is the Juilliard Musical Foundation in New York with resources of approximately $14,000,-000 which in 1924 organized the Juilliard School of Music and in 1926 took over the Institute of Musical Art, a conservatory which had been established by Frank Damrosch in 1905. A new building costing several millions was opened at Broadway and 122nd Street in 1930 to house these schools. When the Metropolitan Opera Company got into financial difficulties in 1933 efforts were made to get help from the Juilliard Foundation since Augustus D. Juilliard had suggested such help in his will. The whole story has not been told publicly but apparently John Erskine, president of the Foundation, made specific stipulations regarding changes in the Metropolitan's policies as a condition. $50,000 was contributed by the Juil-

liard toward the $300,000 fund ; the public got the impression
that the Foundation was assuming the opera company's deficit,
and considerable confusion resulted.   Professor Erskine then
went on the money-raising committee, $150,000 was subscribed
by the Foundation for the following season, and to the board of
directors of the Metropolitan were added John Erskine, Ernest
Hutcheson, and John M. Perry, representing the Juilliard.   At
present the Foundation contributes about $250,000 a year
toward the opera's support.   After ten years as president of
the Juilliard, Professor Erskine resigned ; Ernest Hutcheson
succeeded him.

Also in New York City are several foundations associated
with banking firms, which make annual contributions to such
charitable causes as hospitals, public health projects, and medical research.   The New York Foundation, with about nine million dollars, managed by members of Kuhn, Loeb, and the
smaller Brez Foundation with only a million, managed by partners in Coudert Brothers, are examples of these.   Similar and
larger, with more than twelve million dollars in resources, is the
John and Mary R. Markle Foundation, of which J. P. Morgan
is president and Thomas W. Lamont and Seward Prosser are
directors.   Archie S. Woods is administrative officer. Its
contributions are to medical sciences through hospitals and
medical schools, to the Henry Street Settlement, the Seeing
Eye, Inc., the Citizens Family Welfare Committee, and the
John Markle Eye, Ear, Nose, and Throat Clinic of the Seamen's
Church Institute of New York.   It was organized in 1927.

Frequently calling themselves "foundations" are the numer-
ous community trusts to be found now in nearly every large
American city.   This movement was started by Judge Fred-
erick A. Goff of Cleveland, who was then president of the
Cleveland Trust Company, when he organized the Cleveland
Foundation * in 1914.   He defined it as an attempt to gather

_____

* The Cleveland Foundation created a reputation for itself by financing
and publishing a number of surveys in education.

into a foundation the surplus wealth of the community "for community purposes," thus eliminating the "dead hand" from philanthropies.   Wealthy donors were urged to bequeath their money to this Foundation to apply to specific objects or to purposes selected by a distribution committee.   It was also pointed out in pamphlets advertising the Foundation that people with moderate means can help endow a chair in a university by a number of small bequests.   Judge Goff's idea was that the Cleveland Trust Company would be custodian and administrator of the property received for foundation purposes.   A committee was appointed for five years : one member by the Mayor, one by the probate judge, one by the judge of the U.S. District Court, and two by the Cleveland Trust Company. "After income becomes available from gifts made or bequeathed such income less proper charges and expenses," Judge Goff explained, "shall be annually available for assisting charitable and educational institutions."   The "proper charges and expenses" collected by the Cleveland Trust Company for this service was set at 5% of the gross income of the fund, which is the customary charge for administering estates.

Other commercial trust companies throughout the country immediately saw what a fine idea this was.   Pamphlets were issued advertising the advantages of community trusts.   Big foundations and perpetuities were criticised as being too narrow in scope.   "I would fear the result in remote years in the operation of a foundation by a self-perpetuating board of trustees," Judge Goff testified before the U.S. Industrial Relations Commission in 1915, "fearing it would not be responsive either to the needs of the community and that the zeal and purposes of the founders might not be continued."   The community trust idea was therefore preferable, he thought.   "I would personally prefer more democracy rather than less upon boards having charge of the distribution of income, however secured, whether by appointment of governmental officers or otherwise."

Banks and trust companies did not think it right that one

trust company should have the exclusive privilege, so as the movement spread banks and trust companies shared in the administration, and donors were permitted to select which bank or trust company should have the custody of the funds given to the Foundation.　No charge is made for legal services in advising prospective donors, and a model form of bequest is included in the pamphlets.　As for the powers of the trustee, the Cleveland Foundation declares that it "may invest and reinvest irrespective of statutes or rules or practices of Chancery Courts now or hereafter in force limiting the investments of trust companies or trustees generally. . . The Trustee save for its own gross neglect or wilful default shall not be liable for any loss or damage and in no event be held liable for any neglect, omission, or wrong doing."　It also has the power to "determine whether money or property coming into its possession shall be treated as principal or income and charge or apportion any expenses or losses to principal or income as it may deem right and equitable."

In New York City there are more than forty such separate funds.　Each trustee is responsible for the investment of the funds held by it.　Outpayments are made on the periodical authorization of a central Distribution Committee named by the trustees and the presidents of the Bar Association, the Academy of Medicine, and the Chamber of Commerce.　Included in the New York Community Trust is the Westchester Welfare Foundation.　Winthrop W. Aldrich is chairman of the trustees of the New York Community Trust and Cleveland E. Dodge is on the distribution committee.　It is not strange that bankers should be enthusiastic about this type of foundation.　Some say they prefer it to the independent foundation which has its own administrative staff.　In 1936 the value of the funds in the New York Community Trust reached $8,764,712 ; it disbursed $200,794.　Although the total capital in the hands of Community Trusts in the United States is now more than $45,-000,000 it is said that trust companies are disappointed in the movement. A pamphlet issued by the New York Community Trust advertises these advantages : "It encourages gifts to charity, builds up a community fund for community needs, and enables the poor as well as the rich to add to this fund. Its largest advantage is its adaptability to the needs of each year, decade, and generation. Charity is made timely and the substitution of up-to-date charities for obsolete benefactions is easily accomplished without court action. The danger that antiquated and moribund charities may lie unnoticed for years and a great social waste occur is obviated."

Not to be overlooked in any study of foundations is the Fund established in 1889 with $10,000,000 by Baron de Hirsch for the colonization and Americanization of Jewish immigrants to the United States then coming here in a veritable tidal wave. During its history the Fund has had experience in nearly every variety of relief since tried by the Roosevelt administration from temporary aid to suburban resettlement at Woodbine, N.J., including trade schools, agricultural training, and general education. It established the first secondary agricultural school in the United States, it initiated the first credit unions and anticipated the Ickes program of subsistence-homesteading. Its history is worth studying from a sociological point of view as an example of a brilliant handling of a difficult problem and as a specialized philanthropic function. In comparison with other foundations, however, the Baron de Hirsch Fund is an example of a notable experiment in paternalistic and agricultural training rather than a broad-scoped foundation.

Completely different in point of view and general approach from any of the other funds mentioned in this book is the American Fund for Public Service, established by Charles Garland of Massachusetts in 1922 when he inherited approximately a million dollars and did not think he should have it. "With the crying needs there are in the world today," he wrote, "I do not believe it is possible to hold money unless human compassion is pretty well smothered in theories." He thought it could be spent in five years. No rigid rules were set up, but experimental movements in the field of education and industrial organization such as are not ordinarily aided by philanthropic funds were favored, with a tendency to help radical and left-wing groups. Roger N. Baldwin, assisted by Lewis Gannett and Scott Nearing, tried to spend the money as rapidly as possible ; they disbursed $79,000 and loaned $103,000 the first year. But they found it extremely difficult to do good and avoid doing harm, to decide what to keep alive and to whom to refuse help. At first estimated as being worth $850,000, the securities, the bulk of which were in First National Bank stock, appreciated rapidly in the boom years. Such agencies as the League for Industrial Democracy, the Rand School, the Federated Press, the Teachers' Union, and the Mooney committee were helped. A small sum was loaned to the *New Masses*, larger sums were loaned to the New York *Call* and the Brookwood Labor College, both of which went out of existence. The Vanguard Press with a $45,000 loan was financed to distribute radical books at a low price. A large loan (over $100,000) was made to the International Ladies' Garment Workers and a smaller one to the Furriers' Union ($45,000), not yet repaid in full. Many loans had to be cancelled or transferred to the "gift" column. A $10,000 bail bond for Fred Beal was forfeited. The Fund has been unable to wind up its affairs, and may be able to make further disbursements, provided the amounts owing to it are paid.*

For anything like a thorough discussion of the function of foundations to be found outside the reports and writings of the officers of the big philanthropic trusts, one must go back to the investigation made by the U.S. Industrial Relations Commission in 1915, headed by Frank P. Walsh. An attempt was made then, spurred by the industrial unrest at that time, to find out the role of foundations as social institutions, to discover if they could be considered in any sense a menace to democracy, and

* $180,470.22 as of June 30, 1936.

to define their position in the economic system. The interest of the public was aroused by the strike in the plants of the Colorado Fuel and Iron Company, a Rockefeller corporation, and the proposal of the Rockefeller Foundation to have an investigation of industrial conditions made by W. L. MacKenzie King. To some people there seemed to be a relationship between these events ; it looked as if perhaps the Rockefeller Foundation was to be used to whitewash the crimes committed by the industrial corporation. If not that, then, it was thought possibly the workers in Colorado were to be placated by the knowledge that the philanthropic foundation was looking into their troubles and might make some comforting recommendations. It was also thought that by questioning a number of witnesses some light might be thrown on the power and influence of corporate philanthropy in influencing and moulding education and public opinion.

A committee headed by Basil M. Manly made recommendations which are startlingly pertinent today, recommendations completely ignored by Congress and the public. The criticism of the foundations made by the various witnesses in 1915 is still acute and applicable, even though all these things were said and written before the foundations achieved their present size, power, or numbers. The criticisms and the Manly report cannot be dismissed as out of date ; some of the witnesses foresaw the role the philanthropic trusts were to play ; the Manly report offers recommendations entitled to serious contemporary consideration. It must be remembered that in 1915 the Rockefeller Foundation and the Carnegie Corporation had only just obtained their charters ; the General Education Board, although in existence for thirteen years' had only just made public its first report. The Carnegie Foundation for the Advancement of Teaching was paying pensions but it was not yet making public the fact that it would have to turn to the Carnegie Corporation for more funds to make good on its promises. The 1915 investigation was before John D. Sr had made his $100,000,000

"Christmas gift" in 1919 ; the International Health Board was still concerned with hookworm ; it had not yet turned its attention to yellow fever. The Russell Sage Foundation had not yet become the great power in the new profession of social work, the Carnegie Corporation had not yet found it necessary to assume some of the characteristics of an investment trust. Few people realized then the power the General Education Board and the Carnegie Foundation for the Advancement of Teaching had, or were to have, over the educational system of the United States. For that matter, few people realize it today.

Samuel Untermeyer was one of the first witnesses called. Although part of his testimony was summarized in the first chapter, his understanding of the nature and power of philanthropic trusts makes it worth while to repeat it at greater length : "The tendency of state laws regulating corporations," he said, "has been steadily away from the lines of adequate responsibility. The manner of the organization of the Rockefeller, Carnegie, Sage, and other similar foundations is a fair illustration of the vice of the system. These foundations make no pretence of being limited in their activities by State lines. They are not only national but international in their scope of beneficence. The Rockefeller Foundation sought a federal charter but was not satisfied with the terms on which it was offered by Congress. It wanted our fundamental laws against perpetuities ignored and repealed so far as concerned its powers and limitations. It promptly secured from the New York State Legislature what Congress refused to grant. The Sage and Carnegie Foundations did the same. If New York had not given them what they wanted they would have passed along from State to State until they found a corporate habitation on their own terms, without in the least interfering with their operation wherever they chose. This ought not to be possible.

"I do not share the fear and distrust of these foundations," he promptly added. "I believe them to be prompted by the highest ideals of patriotism and unselfish public spirit. They

are magnificently managed * by the best intellect of the country — far better than would be possible with any public institution. The genius and resourcefulness to which their founders
owed their material success have been unselfishly expended by
these men on these foundations which are to be monuments to
future generations of their usefulness to society. They are doing incalculable public good and no harm. Happily their conduct does not to any appreciable extent reflect the devious
methods by which these fortunes were accumulated, nor the
views or policies of their founders on economic questions.

"In every case in which the hope of expectation of future
endowments may possibly be influencing the policies of the
institution the effect will be at most temporary. It will pass
away with the life of the founder if there is any such present
restraint. I can see great benefits and no appreciable danger
from the existence of these foundations except from the forms
of their organization, which should be altered as I suggest in
the following particulars :

"First, they should be organized under a uniform Federal law
instead of under special State charters.

"Second, they should not be given a perpetual charter. One
generation has no right to bind another. We may have an

---

* The myth that the foundations were and are "magnificently managed"
has persisted to the present day in the face of overwhelming evidence to the
contrary in the reports of the foundations themselves. The series of mistakes
which characterized the Carnegie Foundation for the Advance of Teaching's
history have been noted and criticized by educational authorities and in the
Nation. Apparently nobody reads the General Education Board reports
closely enough to note the chaos in its bookkeeping. Many people have
been aware of the fantastic management of the Carnegie Endowment for
International Peace, but it has been subjected to little criticism. A public
institution would have been thoroughly investigated and its management
changed had it been one half as inefficient as some of our charitable foundations. At the time Mr Untermeyer made this statement business men were
fond of saying that only business men have the ability to manage such things
as philanthropic trusts and that government officials are incapable of efficient
administration, but business has fought a losing battle against the encroach-
ments of government and now the wealthy are contributing money for
schools of public administration, which is a tacit admission that they see the
inevitability of governmental administration of semi-public institutions.

entirely different social structure in fifty years to which these institutions may be most repugnant.

"Third, there should be a limit to size.

"Fourth, they should not be permitted to accumulate income.

"Fifth, there should be governmental representation when the time comes for replacing the present trustees.

"We can never have effective corporate reform until we get a National corporation law applicable to corporations in interstate commerce for the reasons above stated and because the corporations are too strong for the States and especially here in the East."

Regarding the legal status of the foundations, George W. Kirchwey, former Dean of Columbia law school, declared: "I have very grave doubts as to the constitutionality of the acts incorporating these three great foundations — Carnegie, Russell Sage and Rockefeller." Nobody has since raised that question. The legislature, he admitted, has the power to alter, amend or suspend or repeal the charters, but the foundations can fight that and use their resources to block any such move.

George W. Perkins, Morgan partner and director in numerous corporations, however, had no doubts at all about the foundations. "You ask me whether the large resources of endowed foundations constitute a possible menace," he said, "In my judgment no concern whatever need be felt on that score, provided that all their transactions in the minutest detail be made public once or twice a year. I mean by that a statement showing in detail what their money is invested in, what their income is spent for. If under such a system the money is used for improper purposes it will not take public opinion long to correct such a condition. I am an absolute believer in the efficiency of public opinion ; I believe that nine times out of ten it is not only right but all-powerful.

"I believe you," he continued, speaking to Mr Walsh, "threw out the suggestion last Sunday evening that the government should take these foundation endowments and administer them.

This, of course, would mean for them the same kind of efficiency in administration that we have in other branches of the government, which would be a distinct loss to the people, for I take it that no one questions the high efficiency with which these foundation endowments are being managed any more than any one questions the low order of efficiency with which in many instances the public's money is managed by public servants in this country. The function of the government should not be to manage but to regulate and control management."

Following him Henry Ford said that he had not given sufficient consideration to the foundation problem to justify an expression of opinion.

John D. Rockefeller Jr, who was then president of the Rockefeller Foundation and already was in charge of his father's philanthropic interests, went upon the witness stand and promptly made one of the most revealing and illuminating statements concerning foundations that was made in the whole course of the investigation. Asked concerning his personal staff of secretaries and advisors, such as Jerome D. Greene and Ivy Lee, he said : "Our office staff is a sort of family affair. *We have not drawn sharp lines between our business and philanthropic interests.*"

"Do you see any danger," inquired Chairman Walsh, "in interlocking directorates on boards of foundations which are entirely independent of each other ?"

"I do not," Mr Rockefeller Jr replied. "I should think on the other hand there might be great strength in that."

"Does a foundation controlling one hundred million dollars exert any influence in the financial world ?" Walsh asked.

"Simply as a large investment," Mr Rockefeller answered. "I think that contributions to educational institutions, generally speaking, should be made without retaining any sense of control on the part of the giver."

He was followed by Dr Charles W. Eliot, president of Har-

vard, who at that time was on the boards of the General Education Board, the Rockefeller Foundation, the Carnegie Endowment for International Peace, and received a pension from Mr
Carnegie.   Asked about the interlocking directorates, he said
that it "contributes to the efficiency to have the same men
of experience on the boards."   When it was pointed out that
Mr Rockefeller had the same men on his personal staff, on the
executive committee, on the powerful financial committee, and
nominating committee of the Foundation, Dr Eliot, said :
"The Rockefeller Foundation is the largest and freest attempt
to do permanent good in the world that I have ever heard of."
When Mr Walsh inquired if he would advise wealthy men to
follow the example of Mr Rockefeller and Mr Carnegie, Dr
Eliot said : "I should not know of any better advice to give
them."

John R. Lawson of the United Mine Workers had a different
opinion.   "I sat in this room and heard Mr Rockefeller read the
list of activities that his foundations felt calculated to promote
the well-being of mankind," he said.   "A wave of horror swept
over me during that reading and I say to you that that same
wave is now rushing over the entire working class in the United
States.   Health for China, a refuge for birds, food for the
Belgians, pensions for New York widows, university training
for the elect and never a thought for the many thousands of
men, women, and children in Colorado, for the widows robbed
of husbands, children of their fathers by law-violating conditions in the mines or for the glaring illiteracy of the coal camps.
There are thousands of Mr Rockefeller's ex-employees in Colorado today who wish to God that they were in Belgium to be
fed or birds to be cared for tenderly.

"As if this were not enough labor is now being informed that
this foundation has appropriated $1,000,000 for the purpose
of doing what this Commission was appointed to do.   An industrial relations division has been formed to find out why we
are discontented. . . They ask the laboring class to believe

that what they feel as coal company directors they will not feel as directors of the foundation."

Jerome D. Greene, secretary of the Rockefeller Foundation, after paying eloquent tribute to the great personal qualities of Mr Rockefeller Sr, and then admitting that he had only met him a few times, said he could see no objection to the interlocking directorate except that which President Eliot had stated : the limitation of the time and health and strength of the men who must devote themselves to so many boards. He resigned as overseer of Harvard when he joined the G.E.B. "Nobody can exceed John D. Rockefeller," he added, "in the desire to avoid paternalism in giving. A committee of economists invited by the Rockefeller Foundation to advise it in regard to some sort of an organization reported that such a proposed institution of economics research should not *at the outset* * attempt work directly educational in character. Although it is recognized that there is a great need of popular education in economics, it is inadvisable that such work of propaganda be undertaken as the first or main task of an institution for scientific research. Proper means of publicity should be sought for the publicity of the results of its investigations ; but any systematic effort at influencing public opinion might, if at all, be better attempted by a separate organization. . . It is essential for the permanent standing of an institution of economic research that it should early establish its reputation as scientific, impartial and unprejudiced and its finding and presenting of facts as to economic and social conditions." (It may not be wholly irrelevant to mention here that Mr Greene at that time was objecting to the union label on stationary of one of the organizations [Bureau of Social Hygiene] † with which he was connected. It is also interesting to note that Mr Greene was among the first trustees of the Brookings Institution.)

Mr Greene pointed out the economic enrichment resulting

---

* Italics are the author's.
† The Bureau of Social Hygiene has been largely supported by John D. Jr.

from the work of the Sanitary Commission in hookworm. "How can it be called a corrupting or pauperizing service ?" he asked when it benefited so many people, enabling them to make more money.   Of the trustees of the Rockefeller Foundation, Mr Greene noted that two were not directly related to Mr Rockefeller in a business way.   These two were Dr Eliot of Harvard and A. Barton Hepburn, chairman of the board of the Chase National Bank.

The most eloquent defender of the philanthropic foundations was Andrew Carnegie himself who won rounds of applause from the audience by his spirited testimony.   He agreed with Miss Ida M. Tarbell, he said, that "sane publicity is the cure for most evils in American industrial life."   He was coaching in Scotland, he said, when the strikers were shot at Homestead.   He wanted to come home at once, he declared, but his partners told him it was not necessary.   He quoted from his *Gospel of Wealth* and offered to bring in the heads of his foundations to testify.   "We have nothing to conceal," he repeated. He could not imagine his funds being used for deleterious purposes.

"Has your attention ever been called to an apprehension on the part of individuals that these large foundations were a possible menace to American life and education in that they might influence perhaps not immorally but along the lines of the interests of the managements of these foundations education, publicity and the like ?" Mr Walsh inquired.   "If you have I would like to hear what you have to say about it."

"I have never heard that suggested," Mr Carnegie replied.

"Do you believe that the State or Federal government should exercise any supervisory control over great foundations ?" the Chairman pursued.

"Why, I would be delighted to welcome them," Mr Carnegie answered.   "I do not think the United States government or the state legislature would have any desire to do anything that would not be agreeable to me. I would restrict nothing of the kind."

Asked about publicity the little Scotchman rose to the situation. "Now, I believe in advertising. I would like more men, more people to get interested in my foundations." Concerning the suggestion that interlocking directorates might be undesirable, he said shortly, "Never had the slightest indication of anything of the sort."

Mr John D. Rockefeller Sr followed him to the chair. "The sole motive underlying the various foundations which I have established has been the desire to devote a portion of my fortune to the service of my fellow men," he stated. "I regard the right to amend or rescind the respective charters of the several foundations which inhere in the legislative bodies which granted them as an entirely sufficient guarantee against serious abuse of the funds. Furthermore, I have such confidence in democracy that I believe it can be better left to the people and their representatives to remedy the evils when there is some tangible reason for believing they are impending rather than to restrict the power for service in anticipation of purely hypothetical dangers."

"When you established your various foundations did it occur to you that they might under any conditions become a menace to the public, either through mismanagement or by exercising a great influence upon the public mind in any direction?" Mr Walsh inquired.

"No," said Mr Rockefeller, "I cannot say that I had any fears on that question."

"And from your experience, so far as you have advanced, have you felt any such tendency?"

"I have had no occasion for any anxiety in that respect."

"What precautions or safeguards did you consider as a means of preventing such an outcome, say, in the future?"

"Well, I think that I have relied upon the people who are

constantly to watch and to know what these foundations are doing with the fund, that is, to see what use they are making of it, and the legislators will be much interested. They cannot," he added, "be more interested than I am."

"Would you consider that serious wrongdoing on the part of any such foundation would endanger the existence and hamper the activities of all ?" Mr Walsh asked.

"I think that if there were on the part of any of those foundations something found to be wrong that that would be corrected. I should hope it would not result in harmful inferences to the other foundations."

Asked about the proposal that foundations be chartered by the Federal government, Mr Rockefeller answered : "I feel the interests of the public are well protected just as they are. What the future might develop would have to be for the future." As for publicity, "Reports should be made," but a definite system of public inspection did not seem to him desirable. "I have not had the occasion to contemplate anything of that kind up to the present time." Concerning undue influence in education, he said : "I have no fear whatever in that regard. There has been nothing in my observation that has led me to have any anxieties so far." No institution had to alter its principles in order to get gifts, he added. "I have never known anything of the kind ; never heard of anything of the kind, and cannot imagine any of our people desiring anything of the kind."

"Does not the greatest power these foundations can exercise arise out of their ability to withhold money ?" Mr Walsh suggested.

"It is a great power to give," Mr Rockefeller answered. "It may be equally virtuous and commendable to withhold. A great responsibility rests upon the men in that regard, the men administering, the board of trustees."

Mr Rockefeller admitted that he had not attended any of the

meetings of the board of trustees of his Foundation. Mr Walsh brought out that there had been cases of mismanagement of funds in the mutual insurance companies by men who stood high in public esteem, indicating that having men of impeccable reputations on the board was no guarantee that mismanagement might not occur. Mr Rockefeller replied that he did not know anything about the insurance scandals nor did he know, should the charters of the foundations be repealed, whether the funds would revert to the donors or their heirs. That was a legal question he could not judge.

Among those who were critical of the foundations were John Haynes Holmes, Amos Pinchot, and Morris Hillquit. "I am not impugning the motives of the founders," declared Dr Holmes, "or those who direct them." But, "It seems to me that this foundation, in its very character must be regarded as essentially repugnant to the whole idea of democratic society. . . The fund is produced," he pointed out, "or the income of the fund is being produced every day, by the labor of men hitched up to the support of a great permanent institution in the direction of which they have no voice whatsoever and from the benefactions of which perhaps they may receive no good, no profit whatsoever. In other words, in studying these foundations we must never forget the human relationship that is involved between the money as produced and used for any purpose, however beneficent, and the labor of men which goes into the production of money. . .

"We have here in the midst of a society supposed to be democratic that which is essentially an autocratic system of administration which represents power, which is, of course, simply stupendous and that relationship is, therefore, of the most serious character to mankind : the autocratic administration on the one hand and the democratic administration on the other." He agreed that it was technically correct that the people of the state could annul or modify the charters. "But a battle against a power representing $100,000,000 is not an easy one, the power to get back the powers granted in the charter would be a very long and very persistent and very difficult fight."

Amos Pinchot, brother of Gifford Pinchot, was even more emphatic. "Assuming that the Rockefeller Foundation as well as the General Education Board have to do with educational matters as well as investigations, I can see grave danger in the acceptance by universities, schools, and institutions of donations upon a large scale from such sources. Take, for example, the influence upon courses of economics in schools, colleges, and universities. Suppose a young instructor of economics were giving a course of lectures upon industrial production and the relations between capital and labor. It is natural in his lectures he would want to go into such subjects as price-fixing, monopolies, the recognition of unions, collective bargaining, etc. . ."

Here Mr Pinchot quoted the saying that gratitude is a lively sense of favors to come. . . "Now what I say is this : The gratitude which the faculty and trustees of a university ought to feel to an instructor who showed the students the utter unsoundness of production under a system of absolutism might seriously conflict with the gratitude which they could not help but feel toward those whose gifts were making the university prosperous and useful. I say that this instructor who treated with frankness and intelligence the economic system for which the directors of the educational board of the foundation stood would find himself in a peculiar position. He would gradually realize that, somehow or other, through nobody's fault, perhaps, there had arisen a feeling of strain, a lack of sympathy, between himself and the members of the faculty and trustees whose duty it was to care for the university's well-being. Sooner or later he would become convinced that full appreciation of his efforts in this particular college or university had been rendered exceedingly improbable. His chances of a Sabbatical year, the acceptance by the university of his lecture courses as textbooks, the probability that he would represent the university at important conferences — these and many other things would seem to have become remote because he had committed the error of preaching a doctrine hostile to the sources from which the university had drawn and probably would continue to draw large and necessary sources of money.

"Mr Chairman, I speak advisedly and after some inquiry when I say that the smaller colleges of this country are full of instructors and professors who have not been deliberately driven from larger universities on account of economic opinions unfriendly to benevolent exploiters in industry, but who nevertheless have found their chairs in the large universities untenable and have left them owing to influences which were irresistible but too subtle to complain of aloud.   I do not say that this has been anything in the nature of a conspiracy on the part of the interests who gave the millions, but the ever-present and powerful spirit of acquisition which is an integral part of the consciousness of our monopolistic combinations has moved instinctively along logical, self-protective lines.

"In 1815 when Metternich saddled Austria, Prussia, and Bavaria with a system of feudal absolutism his powerful weapon against the spread of what he called 'revolutionary ideas' was control of education by vigilant censorship of universities. The decree of the conference at Carlsbad provided that this censorship, and I now quote 'without directly interfering with scientific matters should give salutary direction to instruction, having in view the future attitude of the students.'   Thus Metternich guided the thought of the rising generation so that the young men who graduated from universities should be free from the taint of democracy.

"The Rockefeller Foundation and the educational board are doing today less openly but quite as effectively what Metternich did in 1815.   They are providing to the best of their ability, conscientiously if you will, but none the less effectively that our young men in the course of their education shall gain as little as possible knowledge of the problems of industrial democracy. Today, Mr Chairman, our universities are teaching practically nothing in the realm of uptodate economics. Today they choose to deal with issues which are dust-dry, which are dead, which have already passed into the region of history. But we need not go back to 1815 to find examples of the control of thought by influence exerted over our educational institutions." He cited German militarism. Perhaps today he might find other modern examples. "But when we read of the expenditure of $57,000,000 by the General Education Board, when we think of the annual expenditure of five million dollars by the Rockefeller Foundation, our minds irresistibly compare the probable results of this, in its relation to things industrial, with the known results of the activities of Metternich and of the German militarists in the field of things political."

Although Morris Hillquit was a well-known socialist his writings were generally read with respect in the pro-Roosevelt * *Metropolitan Magazine.* "I think," he said, "that large foundations like the Rockefeller, Russell Sage, and Carnegie Corporation represent a very significant phase in modern development and probably one that has not yet been fully appreciated by the people of the United States. I should say in brief that they represent in the domain of philanthropy just what trusts represent in the industrial field. . . The movement of philanthropic consolidation bears a very close analogy to the movement of industrial consolidation. Just as the first two American trusts were the Oil Trust and the Steel Trust, so the two great first American foundations were the Rockefeller and the Carnegie."

Mr Hillquit then gave a brief resumé of the history of charity in this country, from the small alms-giving which was all that was necessary to care for the needy in the early days of the colonies, to the constantly increasing need with the constantly

* Theodore, of course.

increasing unemployment following upon industrial expansion until charity had to become highly organized to cope with the ever-growing problem. Industrial development had reached a point, he said, where "It is no more sufficient to help the unemployed, the poor worker, over a certain short period. It is necessary to maintain and organize permanent machinery for his relief. Hence the Charity Organization Society. It seems to me," he continued, "it is perfectly apparent that under such conditions of unemployment ever-tremendous amounts of money available for philanthropic purposes cannot shelter, feed, and clothe all the needy workers of this country. And therefore philanthropy has abandoned the task altogether.

"It is a noteworthy characteristic of these modern foundations," he pointed out, "they do not pretend to be charitable institutions. . . These foundations, it seems to me, often get away with their philanthropy as far as possible from home ; at least where they attempt philanthropic work." Belgian relief was one example. "It cannot be criticised. But I cannot help noticing this fact that while these ships were being loaded with wheat and corn and other food supplies for the relief of the Belgian war sufferers there were probably here in the City of New York and within less than a mile of 26 Broadway tens of thousands of American workers suffering from lack of food just as much, perhaps even more than these Belgian war sufferers. . . I say in common with all broadminded American citizens I have no criticism to make of the International Health Board. I should rather see any Malayan free from hookworm, but here in this country unnumbered workingmen and workingwomen are dying annually from tuberculosis.

"American industries have reached an international stage, particularly the large trustified industries." He referred to the economic effects of the hookworm, citing the Rockefeller agents' boast of how the work of the Sanitary Commission had lifted the buying and earning power of the South. "What I say, Mr Chairman," he went on, "is that the foundations such as the Rockefeller and the Carnegie Corporation are not philanthropies at all. It is a mistake to designate them as such. What they are actually is sort of supplements, appendices, to the business enterprises of certain large capitalists." He then quoted John D. Rockefeller Jr's remark: "We have not drawn a sharp line between our business and philanthropic enterprises." Instead of granting relief, Mr Hillquit declared, the function of the foundation is "to switch the issue into a general abstract prolonged study with somewhat debatable and uncertain conclusions." There is no such thing as impartiality in the social sciences, he declared. Summing up his evaluation of foundations, he said: "I believe the influence is pernicious in every way: that it militates against democracy in every field of endeavor, industrial, political, intellectual. The foundation springs up because the government has neglected the most legitimate field of endeavor. 'The foundation' should be subject to supervision by the State as insurance companies, or banking corporations, or fraternal and benevolent societies. It should not be exempt from taxation," or "a means of saving income and inheritance taxes." He estimated that the foundations in New York State at the time would pay, if taxed, $2,000,000 annually which the people pay because the foundations are exempt. Hence, he argued, the public subsidized the foundations to that extent.

In the closing days of that part of the investigation of the Commission that related to the foundations William H. Allen was called. Considerable testimony had been introduced concerning the Bureau of Municipal Research of which he had been director, and from which he resigned in protest against the acceptance of a Rockefeller gift. Mr Allen declared that the Rockefellers demanded a change of policy.* This the Rocke-

---

* An important point that Mr Allen makes now is that the Rockefellers tried in this instance to determine not only where their own funds went and how they were to be expended, but how funds contributed by other donors were to be disbursed.

feller agents denied, but Mr Allen introduced evidence to support his contention. Concerning foundations in general Mr
Allen, a prominent social worker who had made a study of
philanthropic trusts for the Commission, suggested, first of all,
that the applications which the foundations rejected be made
public so that the public would know what the foundations
refused to do. It is more significant, Mr Allen maintained
then, and still maintains today, what the foundations do not do
than what they actually undertake. He has repeatedly demanded that the foundations should inform the public "what
goes into the wastebasket."

His chief recommendations were that foundations be compelled to take out national charters of incorporation, that no
charter be granted to fewer than seven incorporators, that
changes be made in the charters only after due notice to the
government, that a standard budget plan be adopted by all of
them, that income, cash, rates of investments be made known,
that interlocking directorates be prohibited, that there should
be a public examination and auditing of accounts, and that
twenty years be the limit of the charters, after which time the
foundation would be subject to analysis. "It is not Mr Carnegie
who is pensioning the teachers of the country," Mr Allen
added, "It is the teachers of the country who are pensioning
Mr Carnegie."

The United States Industrial Commission which held these
hearings was appointed by President Wilson. In addition to
the chairman its members were : Professor John R. Commons
of Wisconsin, Florence J. Harriman of New York, Richard H.
Aishton of Illinois, S. Thurston Ballard of Kentucky, James
O'Connell of the District of Columbia, John B. Lennon of Illinois, and Austin B. Garretson of Iowa. Frederic A. Delano
was also appointed but resigned, his place taken by Harris
Weinstock of California. Mr Walsh wrote : "The assembling
of facts and reports of investigations under the direction of

Basil M. Manly might well be taken in my opinion as a model of efficiency and scientific treatment by governmental departments."

Walsh, Lennon, O'Connell, and Garretson signed Mr Manly's report. The others signed two minority reports. In the portion relating to foundations Mr Manly wrote : "The domination by men in whose hands the final control of a large part of American industry rests is not limited to their employees but is being rapidly extended to control the education and 'social service' of the nation. This control is being extended largely through the creation of enormous privately managed funds for indefinite purposes hereinafter designated 'foundations,' by the endowment of colleges and universities, by the creation of funds for the pensioning of teachers, by contributions to private charities, as well as through controlling or influencing the public press.

"Two groups of the foundations, namely, the Rockefeller and Carnegie foundations, together have funds amounting to at least $250,000,000 yielding an annual revenue of at least $13,-500,000 which is at least twice as great as the appropriations of the Federal government for similar purposes, namely, education and social service. The funds of these foundations are exempt from taxation, yet during the lives of the founders are subject to their dictation for any purpose other than commercial profit. In the case of the Rockefeller group of foundations absolute control of the funds and of the activities of the institutions now and in perpetuity rests with Mr Rockefeller, his son, and whomsoever they may appoint as their successors. The control of these funds has been widely pulished as being in the hands of eminent educators and public-spirited citizens. In the case of the Rockefeller fund, however, not only is the control in the hands of Mr John D. Rockefeller Jr and two of the members of the personal staff of Mr John D. Rockefeller Sr, who constitute the finance committee, but the majority of the trustees of the funds are salaried employees of Mr Rockefeller or the foundations who are subject to personal dictation and may be removed at any moment.

"The funds of these foundations are largely invested in securities of corporations dominant in American industry, whose position has been analyzed under the early headings of this section. The policies of these foundations must inevitably be colored if not controlled to conform to the policies of such corporations. The funds of the foundations represent largely the results either of the exploitation of American workers or of the exploitation of the American public through the exaction of high prices. The funds, therefore, by every right belong to the American people.

"The powers of these foundations are practically unlimited, except that they may not directly engage in business for profit. In the words of President Schurman of Cornell, himself a trustee of the Carnegie Foundation : 'Under the terms of this broad charter there is scarcely anything which concerns the life and work of individuals or nations in which the Rockefeller foundations would not be authorized to participate. As the safety of the State is the supreme condition of national civilization the foundation might in time of war use its income or its entire principal for the defense of the Republic. In time of peace it might use its funds to effect economic and political reforms which the trustees deem essential to the vitality and efficiency of the Republic. The foundation might become the champion of free trade or protection, of trusts, or of the competing concerns out of which they grow, of socialism or individualism, of the program of the Republican Party or the program of the Democratic Party. It might endow the clergy of all religious denominations, or it might subsidize any existing or any new religious demonination. Tomorrow it might be the champion of the Christian religion and a hundred years hence furnish endowment for the introduction of Buddhism into the United States. It might build tenement houses for the poor in New York City or carry the results of science to enrich the exhausted soils of the East or the arid tracts of the West. It might set up an art gallery in every State of the United States or endow universities which would rival the great State institutions of the West. With the consent of the legislature it might relieve the state of the care of the insane, pauper and dependent classes, or construct roads for the benefit of farmers and motorists. These may not be likely objects for the application of funds of the Rockefeller Foundation. I am not, however, attempting to forecast its work but to understand its charter. And so far as I can see the proposed charter would authorize these and a multitude of other activities. If the object of the Rockefeller Foundation is to be co-extensive with human civilization, then it may do anything and everything which its trustees think likely to effect reform or improvement in the material, economic, intellectual, artistic, religious, moral, and political conditions of the American people or of mankind.' "

"The charters of these foundations," Mr Manly's report continues, "with their almost unlimited powers were granted under conditions of such laxity that it has been testified by an eminent legal authority who made an extensive investigation that those granted by New York State are legally defective and unconstitional. Furthermore, evidence developed by the hearings of the Commission showed that in increasing the number of trustees without complying with the requirements of the law governing corporations, the Rockefeller Foundation has already been guilty of a breach of law.

"These foundations are subject to no public control, and their powers can only be curbed by the difficult process of amending or revoking their charters. Past experience, as for example, in the case of insurance companies, indicates that the public can be aroused only when abuses have become so great as to constitute a scandal. The entrance of the foundations into the field of industrial relations through the creation of a special division by the Rockefeller Foundation constitutes a menace to the national welfare to which the attention not only of Congress but of the entire country should be directed. Backed by $100,000,000 of the Rockefeller Foundation this movement has the power to influence the entire country in the determination of its most vital policy. The documentary evidence in the possession of the Commission indicates (a) That the so-called 'investigation of industrial relations' has not as is claimed, either a scientific or a social basis, but was originated to promote the industrial interest of Mr Rockefeller. (b) That the investigation forms a part of what Mr Rockefeller in a letter to Mr Ivy L. Lee called the 'union educational campaign.' (c) That Mr Rockefeller planned to utilize this campaign literature. (d) That the investigation of industrial relations is not being made in good faith.

"The purpose of Mr Rockefeller to influence the public press is clearly shown by the employment of an experienced publicity expert as a member of the personal staff and is indicated by his evident interest in the ownership and control of a number of publications of which we have records dating from the inquiry of his secretary regarding the *Pueblo Star Journal* in May 1913, to the extensive conference regarding a loan of $125,000 to finance the *Nation's Business,* the organ of the National Chamber of Commerce which was established and given official status through instrumentalities of the Secretary of Commerce and Labor, with the sanction of the President of the United States.

"The extension of the possible influence of these foundations and private endowments of institutions for education and public service is shown by a large amount of evidence in the possession of the commission. The following examples may be cited : (a) The adoption of a definite line of policy by the Bureau of Municipal Research of New York to meet the conditions imposed by Mr Rockefeller in connection with proposed contributions. (b) The abandonment by several colleges and universities of sectarian affiliations and charter clauses relating to religion in order to secure endowments from the

Carnegie Corporation and pensions for professors from the Carnegie Foundation for the Advancement of Teaching. It would seem conclusive that if an institution will willingly abandon its religious affiliations through the influence of these foundations, it will even more easily conform to its will any part of its organization or teaching.

"Apart from these foundations, there is developing a degree of control over the teachings of professors in our colleges and universities which constitutes a most serious menace. In June of this year, two professors, known throughout their professions as men of great talent and high character, were dropped from the positions they had occupied and no valid reason for such action was made public. Both were witnesses before the Commission and made statements based on their own expert knowledge and experience which were given wide publicity. One was a professor of law in a State university who had acted as counsel for the strikers in Colorado ; the other a professor of economics who had not only been active in fights in behalf of child labor legislations and other progressive measures, but had recently published a work comparing the income for property ownership with the income paid for all classes of service. In the case of the State university we know that the coal operators in conjunction with other business interests had gained ascendancy and exercised a great degree of control over the former governor of the State, that the coal operators were bitterly opposed to the professor in question, and that the dismissal of the professor had been publicly urged by the operators upon numerous occasions, and we have the uncontroverted statement of the professor that he had been warned if he testified before the Commission he would not be reappointed. In the case of the professor in the other university (which, though privately endowed, receives large appropriations from the State) we know that its trustees are interested in corporations which have bitterly opposed progressive legislation and are men whose incomes are derived from property ownership and not from service.

"In the face of such an enormous problem one can only frankly confess inability to suggest measures which will protect the nation from the grave dangers described," Mr Manly summed up, "It is believed, however, that if Congress will enact the measures already recommended, providing for a heavy tax on inheritances with a rigid limitation on the total amount of the bequest, for the reclamation by the Federal government of all parts of the public domain (including mineral rights) which have been secured by fraud, and for a tax on non-productive land and natural resources, a great step in the right direction will have been taken.

"As regards the foundations created for unlimited general purposes and endowed with enormous resources, their ultimate possibilities are so grave a menace, not only as regards their own activities and influence but also the benumbing effect which they have on private citizens and public bodies, that if they could be clearly differentiated from other forms of voluntary altruistic effort it would be desirable to recommend their abolition. It is not possible, however, at this time to devise any clear-cut definition upon which they can be differentiated.

"As a basis for effective action, it is suggested that the Commission recommend :

"1. The enactment by Congress of a statute providing that all incorporated non-profit-making bodies whose present charter empower them to perform more than a single specific function and exceed $1,000,000 shall be required to secure a Federal charter. The Federal charter should contain the following provisions :

"(a) Definite limitation of the funds to be held by any organization, at least not to exceed the largest amount held by any at the time of the passage of the act.

"(b) Definite and exact specifications of the powers and

functions which the organization is empowered to exercise, with provision for heavy penalties if its corporate powers are exceeded.

"(c) Specific provision against the accumulation of funds by the compounding of unexpended income and against the expenditure in any one year of more than 10% of the principal.

"(d) Rigid inspection of finances as regards both investment and expenditure of funds.

"(e) Complete publicity through open reports to the proper Government officials.

"(f) Provision that no line which is not specifically and directly mentioned in the articles of incorporation shall be entered upon without the consent and approval of the board of trustees, nor unless Congress is directly informed of such intention through communication to the Clerk of the House and the Clerk of the Senate which shall be duly published in the Congressional Record, nor until six months after such intention has been declared.

"2. Provision by Congress for the thorough investigation by a special committee or commission of all endowed institutions both secular and religious, whose property income or holdings exceeds a moderate amount. The committee or commission should be given full power to compel the production of books and papers and the attendance and testimony of witnesses. It should be authorized and directed to investigate not only finances of such institutions but all their activities and affiliations.

"3. As the only effective means of counteracting the influence of the foundations, as long as they are permitted to exist, consists in the activities of governmental agencies along similar lines, the appropriations of the Federal government for education and social services should be correspondingly increased."

A supplemental report signed by John R. Commons, Florence J. Harriman, Harris Weinstock, S. Thurston Ballard, and Richard H. Aishton declared : "Considerable attention has been given by this commission to the largest foundations or endowments now in the hands of private trustees. Any proposed legislation on this subject should be preceded by a complete investigation of all foundations and endowments, else the law would have effects not contemplated by the legislation or Congress. Such an investigation would include all endowed charities, endowments of religious organizations, and universities and colleges. We are informed that such investigations have been made in England and France, resulting in legislation. The investigation should be complete, covering all aspects of the question and bringing out both the advantages and disadvantages of such foundations and endowments. The legislature could then act intelligently on the subject.

"We are convinced that many of these endowments in private hands have a beneficial effect on the work of the State and governmental institutions. Large private universities have set the example and stimulated the states to support and enlarge their state universities. Some of the investigations and reforms started by recent large foundations have already induced Congress and administrative departments to enter the same field and to extend it. In fact, almost everything the government now does was done at first through private initiative and it would be a misfortune if private endowments, unless plainly shown to have committed abuses, should be prohibited. Even their abuses can be rectified by the legislature through its control over charters, if reasonable ground can be shown. But it is better, for the most part, that they should go on at their own initiative in order that the people through the Government may see the value of their work and then take it up and extend it more widely than private foundations are able to do. It is largely for this reason that we recommend a 'Federal fund for social welfare' in order that the nation may compete with or displace private foundations in this vital matter.

"However, experience has abundantly shown that there

should be no alliance between these private foundations or endowments and the Government.   The State or Government should neither subsidize them nor be subsidized by them, nor cooperate with them.   Such cooperation has often led to public scandal.   Instead of subsidizing private charity the State should use money to displace it by better and more universal charity.   Instead of calling upon private foundations for help, the government should treat them as competitors.   No effort on the part of Government officials to secure financial assistance from them should be allowed." *

These reports were promptly forgotten by Congress and not even noticed by the general public.   The Rockefeller and Carnegie philanthropies claim to have taken these recommendations into consideration in the formulation of their policies. Yet since that time they have obtained a stronger grip on the universities than ever.   By providing professors with pensions, by being responsible for the raising of salaries, by furnishing the funds for research and educational expansion and experimentation, they place upon our whole educational system an overwhelming obligation.   Under such conditions only very stupid or courageous teachers go off the reservation so far as political and economic ideas are concerned.   The recommendations of Basil M. Manly may be more then twenty years old, but remember they were made before it was thoroughly realized how completely "beyond the law" the foundations are, once they are established.   It was before it was realized how they may be used by the extremely wealthy to avoid paying high income and inheritance taxes.   It was before they engaged in extensive stock market operations.   It was before they had built up a tremendous constituency of grateful recipients of their favors, of innumerable scholars, scientists, researchers, associations, and societies of every description, the most respectable and high-minded, which would serve as a bulwark and a protection against criticism or interference.   It was before the lawyers of

---

* A third minority report made no mention of foundations.

J. B. Duke discovered how entrenched privilege can fortify itself by means of a philanthropic perpetuity.

Since 1915 the number of foundations has multiplied enormously. It is undeterminable because the states do not keep a separate listing of corporations formed for charitable purposes. The librarian at Russell Sage worked for more than a year to bring up to date the descriptive list of foundations, just published. In 1937 Robert M. Lester of the Carnegie Corporation drew up a list of 97 less known or recently established foundations which have aggregate estimated resources of $250,000,-000. In that year the Hayden Foundation was established with $50,000,000 for boys and young men, for their education and "moral, mental, and physical well-being." The executors of the broker's will and trustees of the Foundation were Arthur J. Ronahagan, president of the Equitable Trust Company, Edgar A. Doubleday of Hayden, Stone and Company, Erle V. Daveler, vice president of the Utah Copper Company, and J. W. Hayden, Charles Hayden's brother. Following that came the announcement of the will of Andrew W. Mellon headlined by the *New York Times*, August 29, 1937 : "Mellon's Wealth Willed to Charity May Escape Taxes." An anonymous "spokesman" for the Mellon family said that there would be no federal inheritance taxes whatever and further, that the state taxes could only be 10%. The Bureau of Internal Revenue contended that the trustees of the A. W. Mellon Educational and Charitable Trust were members of the Mellon family and their lawyer, Donald D. Shepard. Except for $180,000 for employees, Andrew W. Mellon left the residue of his estate to this Trust, to be administered by the lawyer, his son Paul Mellon, his brother Richard K. Mellon, and his son in law, David K. E. Bruce. This Trust, it was revealed August 31, 1938, amounts to $37,000,000, chiefly in stock in Mellon companies.

"We don't know quite what can be done to meet the increasing use of such charitable trusts by men of wealth," said the *New York Evening Post*, "The law bars the establishment of perpetual trusts for the benefit of heirs. Need it allow the perpetual trust controlled by heirs and permitting the use of great lumps of capital unbroken by those heirs ?

"Why should not the Federal and State governments, our greatest current dispensers of charity, collect normal inheritance taxes in the case of such bequests ? Need we allow the dead hand to control forever so sizable a percentage of the national wealth as is now tied up in these private endowments ? We think that these are questions which must be answered at a very early day."

The Rockefeller and Carnegie philanthropies declare that they have made everything public. Only Congressional investigation would verify that. The Rockefeller group certainly tells the public only what they think it should know. The Davison Fund, established by John D. Jr in 1934, renders the public no account of its activities or tells the amount in the Fund. But even if they did, what of the countless other foundations about which we know nothing ? Only one quarter of the estimated number of foundations tell the public anything. What about the other three-quarters concerning which only a researcher armed with governmental authority could get the facts ?

Frederick P. Keppel, president of the Carnegie Corporation voices his fears in the 1937 report : "It would carry the writer too far afield, to reenter the discussion as to the proportion of American foundations which make no public record of their activities whatsoever — thereby failing to recognize their responsibility to the public as organizations enjoying exemption from taxation, a privilege shared with religious, educational, and charitable institutions. The instances in which it seems impossible to obtain pertinent information would indicate that this proportion is disquietingly large. The question is not whether the funds of these silent trusts are put to useful purposes — indeed, some of the so-called family foundations are to the writer's knowledge making their grants with intelligence and discretion — it is rather whether public confidence in the foundation as a social instrument, a confidence which is in no small degree based upon the policy of complete publicity adopted by the better known foundations, may not be endangered ; for as St Paul admonished the Corinthians . . . 'whether one member suffer, all the members suffer with it ; or one member be honoured, all the members rejoice with it.' "

In the search for new sources of income, new subjects for taxation, the city, state, and national governments will certainly give increasing attention to charitable and educational property, and, sooner or later, to the question of taxing the foundations.   It is not necessary to accept a Marxian view of history to be aware of recurring crises : economic, political, and financial, which endanger the perpetual existence of large endowments.   It is not necessary to be a New Dealer to take the view that such problems as the foundations are now attacking might be better carried on by the government itself, indeed, that in order to cope in any satisfactory manner with grave current problems, it is necessary to unite the energies and resources of the whole nation, private and governmental.   Some foundations take views approaching this and foresee their own extinction.   Raymond D. Fosdick suggested it in his 1938 "review," indicating that the General Education Board would wind up its affairs within eight years, announcing that the Rockefeller Foundation was cutting the strings which had hitherto been attached to its endowment gifts, and declaring : "How long the Rockefeller Foundation may continue depends upon the opportunities for expenditure which lie ahead."   In any case, it might be pointed out, that the Rockefeller Foundation has at least $150,000,000 still to expend, and the General Education Board $50,000,000 to disburse.

To get a complete picture of the role of corporate philanthropy in American life the work of many researchers must be fused.   Dr Lindeman in 1936 gave suggestions for further studies, such as a thorough examination of the investments of the foundations, the effects of the foundations on persons and organizations, a study of trusts as instruments for the redistribution of wealth. Studies should also be made under governmental or foundation auspices of the "unknown" foundations, a public analysis should be made of the foundations' rejections, a study open to public discussion should be made of how the foundations may be liquidated, how they may be transferred to a Federal charter, how a strict governmental and public control might be arranged. The relations of the foundations to the government and governmental agencies should be investigated, including the matter of "internships" sponsored by the Rockefeller Foundation and the "clinical service" offered by the agencies supported by the Spelman Fund. Much criticism has been made of WPA "boondoggling" but little has been said of the large number of useless or futile surveys paid for by the foundations. An investigation should also also be made of the surveys which were made yet were never published because the foundation did not approve of the conclusions. The ways and means by which the foundations influence public opinion, college teaching, social science research might be explored. Nearly everybody who might criticise foundations or their policies has received favors from them. The human nature that seeks foundation help, the reasons why that help is sought, the state of sycophancy, politics, wire-pulling, panhandling which is indulged in to get foundation support might be worth consideration. We should also know more about the international activities of the foundations and their possible relation to American business interests abroad. The control of foundations over other associations and societies, while often beneficial, is scarcely realized nor are the implications understood.

Considering what the foundations have obtained in favorable publicity, in security against hostile criticism, in control over education and public opinion, it is clear that vast as the Rockefeller benefactions, for example, have been, what they have gotten in return has more than justified the expenditure. They have made a good bargain and purchased their security very cheaply. Indeed, looking at the matter in that light, it is obvious what the function of the foundations is. When you have amassed or come into possession of a large fortune it is natural and logical to give a portion of it away to help to protect the remainder. Often that behavior is instinctive, traditional, unconscious on the part of the wealthy. But the result is the same : A scientific laboratory is endowed with securities in an oil company, an educational institution is endowed with securities in a steel corporation, a hospital is endowed with securities in a public utility. That is splendid. But if the government tries to break the corporate control of the United States held by the oil, steel, public utility interests, then the cry goes up that the government is wrecking our endowments. By these means privilege is entrenched, by these means corporate philanthropy plays its part in protecting the interests of corporate wealth.

There is no point in trying to pass a moral judgment on foundations. In answer to the question : "Are they good or bad ?" the reply must be that they do good in many fields ; that is their business. Nobody is seriously suggesting that they suddenly be abolished altogether. What we have to consider is their nature, the part they play in our economic system, and once that is recognized, then we may discuss the advisability of bringing them under greater public supervision and control. It is a problem for Congress, for millionaires thinking of establishing foundations, for the executives of philanthropic trusts, for the thousands dependent upon grants and endowments, for the millions influenced directly or indirectly by countless educational institutions and agencies. It is, in short, a question for public opinion to decide.

Note : The chief sources for this book have been the reports and publications of the foundations themselves and the *New York Times.* Other important sources are mentioned in the text or the foot-notes. For an extended bibliography on foundations the student may consult E. V. Hollis, *Philanthropic Foundations and Higher Education,* Columbia University Press, 1938.

INDEX